Robert Louis Stevenson and Nineteenth-Century French Literature

For Duncan, Frances and James

Robert Louis Stevenson and Nineteenth-Century French Literature

Literary Relations at the Fin de Siècle

Katherine Ashley

EDINBURGH
University Press

Edinburgh University Press is one of the leading university presses in the UK. We publish academic books and journals in our selected subject areas across the humanities and social sciences, combining cutting-edge scholarship with high editorial and production values to produce academic works of lasting importance. For more information visit our website: edinburghuniversitypress.com

© Katherine Ashley, 2022, 2024

Edinburgh University Press Ltd
The Tun – Holyrood Road
12(2f) Jackson's Entry
Edinburgh EH8 8PJ

First published in hardback by Edinburgh University Press 2022

Typeset in 11/13 Adobe Sabon by
IDSUK (DataConnection) Ltd,
CR0 4YY

A CIP record for this book is available from the British Library

ISBN 978 1 4744 9323 9 (hardback)
ISBN 978 1 4744 9324 6 (paperback)
ISBN 978 1 4744 9325 3 (webready PDF)
ISBN 978 1 4744 9326 0 (epub)

The right of Katherine Ashley to be identified as the author of this work has been asserted in accordance with the Copyright, Designs and Patents Act 1988, and the Copyright and Related Rights Regulations 2003 (SI No. 2498).

Contents

Acknowledgements	vi
Note on References	vii
Introduction: 'The Complete Gaul'	1
1. Stevenson as a Reader of French Literature	26
2. Stevenson as a Writer of French	66
3. French Translations and Translators of Stevenson	109
4. Stevenson in French Literary History	150
Postscript	186
Appendix A: Stevenson in Translation: Serials and Magazines	189
Appendix B: Stevenson in Translation: Books	191
Bibliography	193
Index	216

Acknowledgements

I first became aware of RLS's interest in French literature when I spotted Charles Sarolea's *Robert Louis Stevenson and France* on a shelf in the School of European Languages and Cultures at Edinburgh University. That was many moons ago. I have had Stevenson on the mind since then, but this book has only come together in the past few years. Thanks are due to the people and institutions who have made it possible. They include librarians and archivists at the Vaughan Memorial Library, the National Library of Scotland, the Writers' Museum, the Beinecke Library, the Musée Rodin and the Bibliothèque nationale de France. Thanks are also due to colleagues in Canada and the UK who listened and provided feedback as I presented parts of the work-in-progress at various conferences. Thank you to my research assistants, Kaitlynn Sheculski and Margaret Finlay, whose enthusiasm and industriousness were motivating. Stevenson was by all accounts a very genial man, and his congeniality has spread to those who study him. The Stevensonians I have contacted with questions big and small have been unfailingly generous with their time and knowledge. Richard Dury and Roger G. Swearingen, in particular, deserve to be named. Finally, to Paul, my first reader: thank you for your encouragement and your willingness to read – and reread – this book as it has come to fruition.

Parts of Chapters 3 and 4 appeared in modified form in Katherine Ashley, 'In Search of the New Novel: Translations of R.L. Stevenson in Nineteenth-Century France', *Nineteenth Century Studies*, 27 (2013 [publ. 2017]), 129–42. © The Pennsylvania State University Press, 2013. This article is reproduced by permission of The Pennsylvania State University Press.

The manuscript page that is reproduced on the cover is from General Collection, Beinecke Rare Book and Manuscript Library, Yale University.

Funding for this project was made possible by the Acadia University Research Fund.

Note on References

Unless otherwise noted, all references to Stevenson's correspondence are to the following edition:

The Letters of Robert Louis Stevenson, ed. by B.A. Booth and E. Mehew, 8 vols (New Haven/London: Yale University Press, 1994–5)

All references to Stevenson's novels and essays are to the following volumes of the Tusitala Edition, unless otherwise noted. First references to essays will include the title of the volume in which they can be found:

The Works of Robert Louis Stevenson, Tusitala Edition, 35 vols (London: Heinemann, 1923–4)

I. *New Arabian Nights*
II. *Treasure Island*
III. *The Dynamiter*
IV. *Prince Otto*
V. *Dr. Jekyll and Mr. Hyde; Fables & Other Stories and Fragments*
VI. *Kidnapped*
VII. *Catriona*
IX. *The Black Arrow*
XII. *The Wrecker*
XV. *St. Ives*
XVI. *Weir of Hermiston & Some Unfinished Stories*
XVII. *An Inland Voyage; Travels with a Donkey*
XVIII. *The Amateur Emigrant; The Old and New Pacific Capitals; The Silverado Squatters; The Silverado Diary (excerpts)*
XXV. *Virginibus Puerisque & Other Essays in Belles Lettres*
XXVI. *Ethical Studies; Edinburgh: Picturesque Notes*

XXVII. *Familiar Studies of Men & Books*
XXVIII. *Essays Literary and Critical*
XXIX. *Memories and Portraits & Other Fragments*
XXX. *Further Memories*

Introduction

'The Complete Gaul'

'I have been in France, sir,' says the captain, so that it was plain he meant more by the words than showed upon the face of them.[1]

I am Scotch; *que voulez-vous?*[2]

This book studies how Stevenson wrote about France, how he interpreted French literature, how he incorporated French into his writing, and how and why the earliest French critics translated, disseminated and interpreted his work. It does so in the context of the debates surrounding the development of the novel at the end of the nineteenth century. While Stevenson was sometimes dismissed as a writer of genre fiction, this study aims to show that he was held in high regard by the beacons of the intellectual establishment in France, who co-opted him in the mutiny against Naturalism and held up his novels as models of generic and stylistic innovation. It also shows how artistic debates taking place in France influenced the evolution of Stevenson's theory of art. Situating Stevenson and his work within the context of Franco-British literary relations opens up new ways of approaching his oeuvre, offers new insights into the transnational nature of nineteenth-century literature and allows us to think of him not only as a Scottish author, but as an English-language author writing in a French tradition. By approaching Stevenson and his fiction from this angle, this book hopes to add to our understanding of what Ian Duncan has referred to as the 'complex networks of affiliation that bind Scottish literature [. . .] to other literatures and cultures'[3]

---

[1] R.L. Stevenson, *Kidnapped*, p. 56.
[2] Letter to Alexander White, [Late December 1883], *Letters*, IV, p. 227.
[3] 'On the Study of Scottish Literature', *ScotLit*, 28 (2003), available at <http://www.gla.ac.uk/ScotLit/ASLS/Studying_Scottish_Literature.html>.

and in this way confirm Stevenson's own assertion that 'the mere extent of a man's travels has in it something consolatory. That he should have left friends or enemies in many different and distant quarters, gives a sort of earthly dignity to his existence.'[4] Figuratively, Stevenson met some of his first literary friends when reading French literature and he continued to visit these friends long after he left the country; the French artistic community in turn embraced Stevenson as a friend, lending dignity to his work when it was in the process of being diminished by English-language critics and writers of the Modernist period.

France, its people, its language and its literature were never far from Stevenson's life and art. Many of his formative years were spent in France, which he first visited in 1863, when he was thirteen years old. He returned to the country countless times before setting sail for the South Seas.[5] He had a lasting friendship with Jules Simoneau, a Frenchman who operated a restaurant frequented by Stevenson in Monterey,[6] and even when he was on the other side of the world, he planned at various points to return to Europe and make France his base during these visits. These early stays in France and these early encounters with French culture had a lasting influence on Stevenson's identity and his development as a writer. As the *Journal des débats* commented when extracts from his correspondence were published in French in 1902, during certain periods of his life, his existence was almost as French as it was Scottish.[7] By 1868, he had adopted the French spelling Louis in the place of Lewis, although with characteristic good humour he clarified that he did not want his name pronounced

---

[4] Letter to Charles Warren Stoddard, [December 1880], *Letters*, III, p. 138.
[5] As Graham Balfour notes, 'there was no year from 1874 to 1879 in which he did not pay one or more visits of several weeks' duration to [. . .] France'. *The Life of Robert Louis Stevenson*, 2 vols (London: Methuen, 1901), I, p. 128.
[6] See his letters to Jules Simoneau in June 1883 (*Letters*, IV, pp. 136–8) and September 1883 (*Letters*, IV, pp. 151–2). The first mention of Simoneau is in a letter to Sidney Colvin on 21 October 1879 (*Letters*, III, p. 19); in late October/early November 1879 he asked Henley to send Simoneau a volume of Eugène Labiche's plays (*Letters*, III, p. 21). See also Josephine Mildred Blanch, *The Story of a Friendship: Robert Louis Stevenson, Jules Simoneau; a California Reminiscence of Stevenson* (New York: Charles Scribner Sons, 1921).
[7] 'Il est presque aussi Français qu'Écossais par son existence.' 'Robert-Louis Stevenson d'après sa correspondance', *Journal des débats politiques et littéraires*, 24 November 1902, p. 3. The same phrasing is used in Georges Grappe, *R.L. Stevenson: l'homme et l'œuvre* (Paris: Sansot, 1904), p. 10, which suggests that Grappe was also the author of this article.

'Louee; to rime wi' pee'.⁸ This one small spelling change neatly encapsulates the dual Franco-Scottish aspects of his persona. Likewise, he was happy to assume the identity bequeathed to him by the locals of Le Monastier in 1878, letting himself be called 'M. Louis' rather than the unpronounceable Monsieur Stevenson ('M. Steams'), since, as he explained to his mother, Monsieur Louis 'somehow sounds homelike and friendly'.⁹ France itself was 'homelike and friendly' to Stevenson.

As is evident in essays like 'The Foreigner at Home' (1882) and letters such as the one he wrote to an Australian correspondent, Arthur Patchett Martin,¹⁰ Stevenson was in the habit of asserting his identity as a Scot. This did not preclude him from embracing his French alter ego, however: during a stay in Frankfurt in 1872, he took immense pleasure in being mistaken for a Frenchman and he was similarly flattered by compliments on his lack of accent when speaking French;¹¹ elsewhere he wittily (and with a punning flourish) refers to himself as 'the complete Gaul'.¹² Much of Stevenson's wit stems from his playfulness with language, and his correspondence teems with comical French calques and multilingual jokes.

Like many educated British men of the day, Stevenson kept up with current affairs in France: despite telling his friend, poet W.E. Henley, that he could never have the pleasure of reading *Treasure Island* because he was its author,¹³ he took out a subscription to *Le Temps* when it serialised the novel and kept the subscription up after serialisation ended.¹⁴ He also subscribed to *Le Figaro* for several years.¹⁵ His letters contain multiple references to political, social

---

⁸ Letter to Charles Baxter, [19 October 1883], *Letters*, IV, p. 185. See also Balfour, *The Life of Robert Louis Stevenson*, I, pp. 29–30, n. 1; Anderson Galleries, *Autograph Letters, Original Manuscripts, Books, Portraits, Curios from the Library of the Late Robert Louis Stevenson* (New York, 1914), p. 4.
⁹ Letter to his Mother, [c. 11 September 1878], *Letters*, II, p. 272. In *An Inland Voyage* (p. 118), he makes the fact that he has, to French ears, an 'unspellable name', work to his advantage.
¹⁰ [? October 1883], *Letters*, IV, p. 193.
¹¹ Letters to his Mother, 29 July 1872, *Letters*, I, p. 236 and [17 January 1874], *Letters*, I, p. 452.
¹² Letter to Sidney Colvin, [c. 5 February 1874], *Letters*, I, p. 477.
¹³ Letter to W.E. Henley, [? June 1884], *Letters*, IV, p. 307.
¹⁴ Letters to Alfred Nutt, 4 October 1884, *Letters*, V, p. 13 and 16 December [1884], *Letters*, V, p. 50.
¹⁵ He mentions it in a letter to Charles Scribner on [c. 22 November 1887] (*Letters*, VI, p. 66) and he is reading it in December 1893 (Letter to W.H. Triggs, 6 December 1893, *Letters*, VIII, p. 203).

and historical events in France, sometimes in passing, sometimes in more detail. For example, his comments on the *écoles laïques* that were created in 1880 and remain the foundation of public education in France show him sardonically raising an eyebrow at aspects of the new system that seemingly undermined its pretention to be a progressive tool of a free-thinking Republic:

> I met the other day one of the new lay schoolmasters of France; a pleasant, cultivated man, and for some time listened with wonder to his ravings. 'In short,' I said, 'you are like Louis Quatorze, you wish to drive out of France all who do not agree with you.' I thought he would protest; not he! – 'Oui, Monsieur,' was his answer. And that is the cause of liberty and free thought.[16]

Stevenson's engagement with contemporary French political life is also evident in texts like *An Inland Voyage* (1878), where, as Laurence Davies notes, 'in scene after scene, he recalls discussions and debates on the issues of the day and reveals, in passing, his knowledge of French politics and French ways of seeing the world'.[17] Further commentary makes its way in a disguised form into his fiction. This process has been traced by Robert P. Irvine, who sees in 'The Treasure of Franchard' (1883), for instance, a 'political allegory of the Third Republic' in which Stevenson shows that 'that which grounds the nation, and will save it in times of crisis, is more deep-rooted and instinctual than secular education, science, citizenship, or any of the other institutions of modernity'.[18] Stevenson presents French politics as a cautionary tale of the perils of the modern nation and, unlike others, seems to recognise that much of the instability was caused by the nature of the new political system rather than by any inherent tempestuousness on the part of the French.[19] As such, he rarely resorts to clichéd comparisons of France and Britain. His letters voice his concern that British Prime Minister William

---

[16] Letter to Jules Simoneau, [? October or November 1883], *Letters*, IV, p. 197.
[17] 'The Time of His Time: *Travels with a Donkey* and *An Inland Voyage*', in *European Stevenson*, ed. by Richard Ambrosini and Richard Dury (Newcastle upon Tyne: Cambridge Scholars Publishing, 2009), pp. 73–89 (p. 77).
[18] 'Stevenson in the Third Republic: Fiction and Liberalization', *Victorian Review*, 39.1 (2013), 125–40 (p. 138).
[19] See Christophe Campos, *The View of France from Arnold to Bloomsbury* (London: Oxford University Press, 1965), pp. 49–50.

Gladstone's illness might cause Britain to 'fall, like the French, into the impotence of four parties, any three of which can at a given moment, outvote the fourth'.[20] They contain multiple angry assessments of French President MacMahon, whom he describes as 'very bad, or very stupid, or else both'. Part of this is personal: he explains to Kinjiro Fujikura that he is angered by MacMahon's actions relating to the 1877 legislative election because he has 'very dear friends [in France], who may suffer inconvenience or even hurt'.[21]

Stevenson was an avid reader of French history, and his interest in the historical period of François Villon and Charles d'Orléans is well documented and need not be retrodden. He was also keen to understand the more recent history of France, imploring publisher Charles Scribner, for instance, to send him Hippolyte Taine's *Origins of Contemporary France* – 'I want (with a big W) Taine's French Revolution books – and if it is all the same to get them so, in the French not a translation.'[22] Upon reading the volume, he concludes that Taine's account is somewhat lacking in the subjective, human, emotional qualities that would have brought it to life (these are, of course, precisely the qualities that Stevenson brought to his essays):

> It is not absolutely fair, for Taine does not feel, with a warm heart, the touching side of those poor souls' illusions; he does not feel the infinite pathos of the Federations, poor pantomime and orgie, that (to its actors) seemed upon the very margin of heaven; nor the unspeakable, almost unthinkable tragedy, of such a poor, virtuous, wooden-headed lot as the methodistic Jacobins. But he tells, as no one else, the dreadful end of sentimental politics.[23]

Stevenson's letters also contain references to events that affect him on an emotional, rather than an intellectual, level. In 'Memoirs of an Islet' (1887) and in an 1894 letter to then editor of the *Cornhill Magazine*, James Payn, for example, he describes how he suffered during the Franco-Prussian War. He was nowhere near the battlefront or besieged Paris: 'when the tide of invasion swept over France',[24] he was hundreds of miles away on a tiny Hebridean island tending to

---

[20] Letter to his Parents, [c. 12 March 1884], *Letters*, IV, p. 248.
[21] Letter to Kinjiro Fujikura, [6 December 1877], *Letters*, II, p. 230.
[22] [c. 22 November 1887], *Letters*, VI, p. 66.
[23] Letter to Ida and Una Taylor, [c. 18 December 1887], *Letters*, VI, p. 84.
[24] 'Fontainebleau' (1884), in *Further Memories*, p. 113.

lighthouses. The war did, however, touch him emotionally. He writes that even though he

> was on Eilean Earraid, far enough from the sound of the loudest cannonade, I could *hear* the shots fired and I felt the pang in my breast of a man struck. It was sometimes so distressing, so instant, that I lay on the heather on the top of the island, with my face hid, kicking my heels from agony.[25]

Histrionics aside – he was only twenty years old when the war broke out – it is obvious that the young Stevenson felt connected to, implicated in, the events taking place in France. Like Loudon Dodd in *The Wrecker* (1892), who sits in the Luxembourg Gardens, conscious that it is 'a public place of history and fiction' (p. 34), in his head and his heart and his imagination Stevenson was very much existing in more than one place at a time.

Regardless of his genuine interest in French history and current affairs, Stevenson was a creative writer first and foremost, and it is his relationship with French literature – in particular, nineteenth-century French literature – that is at the heart of this study. As a young man, his experiences of ennui, depression, teenage angst and first love are all filtered through French literature. Like a textbook sufferer of Romantic *mal du siècle*, he confesses to attacks of 'morbid melancholy' and writes to his cousin Bob Stevenson that he is 'better now; but [. . .] in a state of intellectual prostration, fit for nothing but smoking, and reading Charles Baudelaire'.[26] He evokes the wandering, melancholic Romantic hero of Chateaubriand's 1802 novel, *René*, in a discussion of disillusion, and concludes that 'there is no door of escape from this ennui'.[27] Rather like René, who 'souffr[e] plus qu'un autre des

---

[25] Letter to James Payn, [11 August 1894], *Letters*, VIII, p. 347. See also 'Memoirs of an Islet', in *Memories and Portraits*: 'And all the while I was aware that this life of sea-bathing and sun-burning was for me but a holiday. In that year cannon were roaring for days together on French battlefields; and I would sit in my isle (I call it mine, after the use of lovers) and think upon the war, and the loudness of these far-away battles, and the pain of the men's wounds, and the weariness of their marching' (pp. 63–4).
[26] 29 March 1870, *Letters*, I, pp. 193–4. This was obviously something that could be caught: he confesses elsewhere, 'I do nothing but read George Sand and sit in the sun by the sea shore.' Letter to Elizabeth Crosby, 5 December 1873, *Letters*, I, p. 399.
[27] Letter to Elizabeth Crosby, July 1873, *Letters*, I, p. 277.

choses de la vie'[28] and who went to Scotland on an Ossianic pilgrimage before travelling to Canada and the United States in search of existential meaning, Stevenson turned to travel and the search for novelty, at least in his early years, as a means of escape from 'what has been mendaciously called "life"'.[29] Romance may have been Stevenson's early literary ideal, but unlike Chateaubriand, he was no *bona fide* Romantic. As he explained to his mother, 'You must take my nomadic habits as a part of me.'[30] For Stevenson the adventurer and explorer, travel was intimately connected to reading and writing. At times, he approached travel through reading, as when he turned to fiction when travelling to the United States, reading the adventure novels of Gustave Aimard so that they could 'teach [him] independence and philosophy' and so that he could 'learn something of the ways of New York'.[31] As Laurence Davies has shown, Stevenson also mediated his experiences of travel through writing: his first books are French travelogues in which movement through space prompts reflections on movement through time, as well as on the connections between the past and the present.[32]

Nowhere is this early tendency to mediate life through literature more apparent than in his letters, particularly to Frances Sitwell, his first – unrequited – love. These letters are so intimate as to be almost embarrassing to read, like peeking into someone's private diary when they are out of the room. Yet, they are fascinating in the way they abound in references to Stevenson's reading of European Romantics like Heine, Goethe and Théophile Gautier, as when he quotes Baudelaire's *L'Art romantique* in an otherwise excised letter to Sitwell.[33] The letters he wrote (to Sitwell and others) when he was 'ordered South' to France for medical reasons in 1874 teem with references to George Sand, who was very much in vogue, and Stevenson sees in Sand's protagonist elements of Fanny Sitwell's life: 'If you want to be unpleasantly moved,' he writes to her, 'read [*Mademoiselle Merquem*]; it is

---

[28] François-René de Chateaubriand, *Atala. René* [1802] (Paris: Garnier-Flammarion, 1964), p. 155. ('Suffers more than others from the stuff of life.')
[29] Letter to Elizabeth Crosby, July 1873, *Letters*, I, p. 277.
[30] [16 October 1874], *Letters*, II, p. 60.
[31] Letter to Sidney Colvin, [6 August 1879], *Letters*, III, p. 3.
[32] See 'The Time of His Time'.
[33] [12 October 1873], *Letters*, I, p. 338. He quotes verses from Pierre Dupont, a now little-read poet and songwriter. A chapter of *L'Art romantique* is dedicated to Dupont and reproduces his poems extensively.

in some ways so strangely like your story.'[34] Eventually, he begins – rather cringingly, it must be said – to call Sitwell 'Consuelo', seeing in her the heroine of Sand's 1842 novel of the same name:

> O Consuelo de mia alma, I wish you were here. I am so tired and played out this morning. My head is like lead, and my heart; but I have found the name for you at last – Consuelo. Consolation of my spirit. Consolation.[35]
>
> My own heart is reconciled to itself, that is perhaps the great thing and that no one can take away from me. How much this has been your doing, Consuelo, I can never tell you, for I can never explain it to myself; only, as I said before, you came to me as it were the point of day and I began to see clearly. Now, they cannot rob me of that, my peace of mind is not, I think, such as the world can take away; and they cannot take away from me your precious friendship.[36]

Stevenson got over his first love, but he did not get over his love of French literature, and he kept his friends and family abreast of his reading and book buying throughout his life. His excitement is palpable in an 1876 letter to his mother where he describes his 'wild hunt for books' in Paris – before asking for more money.[37] Molière, Montaigne, Alfred de Musset and Alexandre Dumas are just some of the 'eternal books that never weary' that can be found on the shelves of his ideal house.[38] Molière and Montaigne crop up time and again in his letters as 'men of genius', de Musset as a 'geniusett[e]',[39] and his letters allow us to reconstruct his nineteenth-century passions. He was a keen reader of contemporary French poetry, Romantic and Parnassian. He owned Jean Richepin's early collection *Les Caresses* (1877), and in 1875 he

---

[34] [1 December 1873], *Letters*, I, p. 385. Lesley Graham notes that Yves Stranger believes that *Travels with a Donkey* was inspired by Sand's 1860 novel *Le Marquis de Villemer*. Lesley Graham, 'I Have a Little Shadow: Travellers After Stevenson in the Cévennes', in *European Stevenson*, ed. by Ambrosini and Dury, pp. 91–107 (p. 99). Juliette Atkinson discusses Sand's enormous (and early) popularity in Britain in *French Novels and the Victorians* (Oxford: Oxford University Press, 2017), passim.
[35] [1 December 1873], *Letters*, I, p. 385.
[36] [11 December 1873], *Letters*, I, p. 404. In fairness, he claims elsewhere, 'I feel like a person in a novel of George Sand's.' Letter to Frances Sitwell, [? May 1875], *Letters*, II, p. 136.
[37] [20 September 1876], *Letters*, II, p. 191.
[38] 'The Ideal House' (XXV, p. 195) was unpublished until 1898. It is included in the *Virginibus Puerisque & Other Essays in Belles Lettres* volume of the Tusitala Edition.
[39] Letter to W.E. Henley, [Early May 1883], *Letters*, IV, p. 116.

'offered Appleton a series of papers on the modern French school – the Parnassians, I think they call them – de Banville, Coppée, [. . .] Soulary, Sully-Prudhomme'.[40] Contemporary French theatre also interested him: he saw Sarah Bernhardt perform, and read Gautier, Dumas fils and Labiche. Although Balzac was a favourite of his, he did not write about him at any length, nor did he write about Stendhal, despite the fact that he owned several of his books.[41] He told W.E. Henley that Balzac's *Le Cousin Pons* was 'a glory – a glory halleluia [sic]'[42] and suggested to an unidentified correspondent (perhaps Henley, with a view to the Prose Masters series he was planning to edit) that they read Balzac's lesser-known novel, *Béatrix* (1839) and his unfinished posthumously published novel, *Le Député d'Arcis* (1854). While it is unclear how French critic Augustin Filon would have known of Stevenson's predilection for Balzac, unless he had read *The Wrecker*, he nevertheless commented in 1895 that Stevenson 'connaissait Balzac à fond, y compris les œuvres de jeunesse que si peu d'entre nous ont pris la peine de lire'.[43] Stevenson held passionately to his opinions on French writers. Writing to Henley about George Saintsbury's *A Short History of French Literature* (1882), Stevenson lets loose against the opinions of his friend, the highly regarded critic:

> I hope Saintsbury is ashamed; I hate him. Dumas and de Musset are the two writers whom I like and respect most of the whole modern French crew; De Musset I put along with, *magno sed intervallo*, the radiant Montaigne and the immortal Poquelin [Molière]. Balzac could put Gautier and Merimée into his waistcoat pocket; and George Sand was worth either, I think, both of them. You can tell Saintsbury. Hugo is a Scoot; *j'en ai pardessus la tête, moi; qu'il s'en va se faire foutre ailleurs*; I know all his merits as well or better than George Saintsbury; but when he tells me his whole works are worth three of de Musset's comedies, it is like actual cautery. Is there then no credit for that which is shapely, luminous, softspoken, fondu, crystally pellucid – *va te faire foutre!*[44]

---

[40] Letter to Sidney Colvin, [14 January 1875], *Letters*, II, p. 107; EdRLS: Stevenson's Library Database, <http://bit.ly/RLSLibrary>.
[41] See EdRLS: Stevenson's Library Database.
[42] [? Mid-October 1883], *Letters*, IV, p. 184; 18 July 1886, *Letters*, V, p. 286.
[43] 'Balzac et les Anglais', *Journal des débats politiques et littéraires*, 27 August 1895, evening edn, pp. 1–2 (p. 1). ('Knew Balzac thoroughly, including the early works that so few of us have taken the time to read.')
[44] [November 1882], *Letters*, IV, p. 21.

France is also where Stevenson's life as a writer began to eventually take shape. His earliest publications, including his first professional essay, 'Ordered South' (1874), were written while he was in France, and his first two books, *An Inland Voyage* (1878) and *Travels with a Donkey* (1879), are accounts of his journeys across the country. Just as he was happy to be mistaken for a Frenchman or to use a Frenchified name, there is a continual crossing between Scotland and France in his writing: he wrote *An Inland Voyage*, a text about northern France, in Edinburgh, but *Edinburgh: Picturesque Notes* (1878) in Le Monastier. In the years following his 1873–4 sojourn in Menton, Stevenson also wrote stories set in France, including 'A Lodging for the Night' (1877) and other works later published in *New Arabian Nights* (1882). These early literary border crossings continued, and he wrote 'The Treasure of Franchard' in the Scottish Highlands.[45] Furthermore, although Andrew Lang's suggestion that there were similarities between *Strange Case of Dr. Jekyll and Mr. Hyde* (1886) and Théophile Gautier's story 'Le Chevalier double' (1840) seems tenuous at best,[46] traces of Stevenson's reading of French newspapers can be found in his fiction: Richard Dury, for example, has analysed evidence that *Strange Case of Dr. Jekyll and Mr. Hyde* was inspired by an unidentified article Stevenson read in a French scientific journal.[47] Stevenson's French reading seeps into his fiction in other ways, too: Alan Sandison has made the connection between Eugène Sue's Prince Rodolphe, Grand Duke of Gerolstein, in *Les Mystères de Paris*, and the setting of the often-overlooked novel *Prince Otto* (1885).[48] Likewise, it is hard not to associate Théophile Gautier, consummate artist of *la bohème*, with Theophilus Godall, the alias used by Florizel, Prince of Bohemia, in *The Dynamiter* (1884).

---

[45] Balfour, *The Life of Robert Louis Stevenson*, I, p. 201.
[46] Letter to Stevenson, 4 December [1885], in *Dear Stevenson: Letters from Andrew Lang to Robert Louis Stevenson with Five Letters from Stevenson to Lang*, ed. by Marysa Demoor (Leuven: Uitgeverij Peeters, 1990), p. 91. Letter to Andrew Lang, [Early December 1885], *Letters*, V, p. 158, n. 2. Gautier's short story is a pseudo-Northern European fable in which the main character must physically defeat his alter ago in order to marry the woman he loves. The only common point between the stories is the theme of duality.
[47] 'Crossing the Bounds of a Single Identity: *Dr. Jekyll and Mr. Hyde* and a Paper in a French Scientific Journal', in *Robert Louis Stevenson: Writer of Boundaries*, ed. by Richard Ambrosini and Richard Dury (Madison: University of Wisconsin Press, 2006), pp. 237–51.
[48] *Robert Louis Stevenson and the Appearance of Modernism* (London: Macmillan, 1996), p. 93.

In a letter to Sidney Colvin, Stevenson reflects that he 'was happy once: that was at Hyères',[49] where he lived with his wife Fanny Van de Grift Stevenson in 1883–4. This is not surprising, given how productive he was there: it was in Hyères that 'Fontainebleau' (1884) was written, it was in Hyères that *A Child's Garden of Verses* (1885), *Prince Otto*, *The Dynamiter* and *The Black Arrow* (1883/1888) were begun, and it was in Hyères that the proofs of *Treasure Island* (1883) were revised.[50] France continued to play a part in Stevenson's late works, written in Samoa: *Catriona* (1893) takes place at least partly in France, the protagonist of *St. Ives* (1897) is a Frenchman, and *The Wrecker* hearkens back to Stevenson's experiences in France in the 1870s. In *The Wrecker*, France is striving artist Loudon Dodd's *idée fixe*, the carrot to his stick, but the distance created by his retrospective first-person narration of past events means that Dodd's romantic notions are exposed as a pose that was all too familiar among British and American visitors to France. Clearly, Stevenson could separate fact from fiction as far as representations of France were concerned. The effect of passages like the following is to burst the bubble of romanticised, bohemian Paris and to expose it – however appealing – as a fantasy:

> Every man has his own romance; mine clustered exclusively about the practice of the arts, the life of Latin Quarter students, and the world of Paris as depicted by that grimy wizard, the author of the *Comédie Humaine*. I was not disappointed – I could not have been; for I did not see facts, I brought them with me ready-made. Z. Marcas lived next door to me in my ungainly, ill-smelling hotel of the Rue Racine; I dined at my villainous restaurant with Lousteau and with Rastignac: if a curricle nearly ran me down at a street-crossing, Maxime de Trailles would be the driver. I dined, I say, at a poor restaurant and lived in a poor hotel; and this was not from need, but sentiment. My father gave me a profuse allowance, and I might have lived (had I chosen) in the Quartier de l'Étoile and driven to my studies daily. Had I done so, the glamour must have fled: I should still have been but Loudon Dodd; whereas now I was a Latin Quarter student, Murger's successor, living in flesh and blood the life of one of those romances I had loved to read, to re-read, and to dream over, among the woods of Muskegon. (p. 30)[51]

---

[49] 20 March 1891, *Letters*, VII, p. 93.
[50] Letter to his Father, [25] August 1883, *Letters*, IV, p. 148.
[51] Campos notes that Henry James experienced something similar and wrote 'to his parents of his delight at having met characters after Balzac in provincial towns and villages'. *The View of France from Arnold to Bloomsbury*, p. 11.

Initially, at least, Dodd is presented as what Pierre Bourdieu might call a 'bohemian of the upper bourgeoisie'[52] – he is attempting to live in a Balzac novel. When Stevenson was in France, he was attempting to carve out a career as a professional author. *The Wrecker* is a novel about art, but it is also 'full of the need and the lust of money, so that there is scarce a page in which the dollars do not jingle' (p. 404). Stevenson was in tune with the new reality of the nineteenth-century literary marketplace, but there is nothing in him of the mercenary approach endorsed by the calculating, ambitious Jasper in George Gissing's *New Grub Street* (1891), who lectures his sisters on the nature of literary success in the late nineteenth century:

> Literature nowadays is a trade. Putting aside men of genius, who may succeed by mere cosmic force, your successful man of letters is your skilful tradesman. He thinks first and foremost of the markets; when one kind of goods begins to go off slackly, he is ready with something new and appetising. He knows perfectly all the possible sources of income. Whatever he has to sell he'll get payment for it from all sorts of various quarters; none of your unpractical selling for a lump sum to a middleman who will make six distinct profits.[53]

I suspect that Stevenson was not organised enough, or not financially ambitious enough, to pull off the type of wheeling and dealing Jasper describes. But as a consummate, though sometimes commercial, artist, Stevenson nonetheless wanted to be presented (or marketed) as French writers were, and when he was negotiating the publication of *The Amateur Emigrant* in 1879, he instructed Sidney Colvin that 'whatever is done about any book publication, two things remember: I must keep a royalty; and second, I must have all my books advertised, in the French manner, on the leaf opposite the title'.[54]

In his professional choices, Stevenson (like his character, Dodd) deviated from the course set out for him and refused to follow in the engineering footsteps of his family and become a 'lighthouse Stevenson'. How he interacted with France and French literature was different from many other writers of the Victorian period, as well.

---

[52] 'Le Marché des biens symboliques', *L'Année sociologique*, 22 (1971), 49–126 (pp. 75–6).
[53] Ed. by John Goode, Oxford World's Classics (Oxford: Oxford University Press, 1993), pp. 8–9.
[54] [Early December 1879], *Letters*, III, p. 29.

W.M. Thackeray, Matthew Arnold and George Moore all experienced France essentially through Paris. Thackeray lived in Paris from 1833 to 1836, and wrote extensively about it, but always with a view to English newspaper readers. Although Arnold visited the south of France (Sorèze and Toulouse), he did so for the specific purpose of researching his work 'Schools and Universities on the Continent'. Moore's *Confessions of a Young Man* (1888) deals with his experiences in Parisian literary circles in the 1870s. Walter Pater, meanwhile, visited provincial France with an eye to studying its churches and chateaux. Even the most superficial reading of Stevenson's travelogues attests to a difference in approach, and of all English-speaking authors, Henry James perhaps resembles Stevenson most closely in terms of French experience (James lived in Boulogne and Paris and published his travel notes in 1884 as *En Province*). This may have contributed to the development of their unlikely friendship.

In *Travels with a Donkey in the Cévennes* and *An Inland Voyage*, Stevenson records his wanderings across under-explored parts of France. Rather than document fashionable society or bohemian lives in places like Provence, Paris or the Alps, which he nonetheless knew well, his travelogues describe brief encounters with French peasants and bourgeois provincials in the rainy industrial north of the country, and the discoveries of a pseudo-Covenanting Camisard past in the Cévennes,[55] that lesser-visited region that is prosaically referred to as the 'Centre'. Naturally, this was appreciated in France. In a review of the French translation of *An Inland Voyage*, a critic from the *Grand Écho du Nord de la France* commented that 'Stevenson fut un véritable ami de notre pays.'[56] Edmond Jaloux, who took up a seat in the Académie française in 1936, qualifies Stevenson's French books as '[de] ravissants volumes' ('delightful volumes'), but paints a highly romanticised picture of the version of France that Stevenson describes, minimising any discussion of the political conflicts and debates that Stevenson alludes to in his texts. According to Robert P. Irvine, 'Stevenson's trek from Le Monastier to Florac can be seen as a journey away from the actual divisions of contemporary politics and toward the consoling perspective of a particular type of

---

[55] For more on Stevenson and the Camisards, see Roslyn Jolly, 'Stevenson and the European South', in *European Stevenson*, ed. by Ambrosini and Dury, pp. 19–36 (pp. 25–6).

[56] R.M., 'À la pagaie dans la région du Nord', *Grand Écho du Nord de la France*, 15 March 1900, p. 3. ('Stevenson was a true friend of our country.')

fiction.'⁵⁷ Jaloux, by contrast, falls squarely in the consolatory camp, describing Stevenson's France as:

> La France des petites villes et des villages, la France des petites gens et des artisans, gaie, courageuse, réservée, avec sa bonhomie, son sens du comique et sa délicatesse, celle que l'on voit enfin au portail des cathédrales, où, taillée dans la pierre, elle incarne une race qui, au fond, ne change pas. Cette France-là, c'est celle qui assure une durée à notre pays, constamment secoué par les crises de nerfs de Paris.⁵⁸

Prior to writing these travelogues, Stevenson had spent time in the Forest of Fontainebleau in 1875 and 1876, a period important for his personal life (he met his future wife there) and the development of his artistic theories. By Stevenson's own account, 'half the famous writers of modern France have had their word to say about Fontainebleau',⁵⁹ but Stevenson associated principally with American, Irish and British artists in Fontainebleau – all of them outsiders. This was picked up on by Albert Savine in his preface to the translation of *Kidnapped*, where he refers to Stevenson's 'séjour dans la forêt de Fontainebleau où s'était installée toute une colonie de peintres britanniques'.⁶⁰ This is not to say that Stevenson did not associate with the French; in fact, he sent a copy of *An Inland Voyage* to the (minor) painter Henry Lachèvre, who

---

⁵⁷ 'Stevenson in the Third Republic', p. 129.
⁵⁸ 'Un ami de la France', *Le Gaulois*, 25 April 1922, p. 1. ('The France of small towns and villages, the France of common folk and artisans, cheerful, courageous, reserved, with its bonhomie, its sense of humour and its gentleness, the France that can be seen on the portals of cathedrals, where, carved in stone, is embodied a race that, at heart, never changes. That is the France that provides constancy to our country, which is constantly rocked by the nervous breakdowns in Paris.') Jean Frollo concurred: 'ses récits de voyage fourmillent de traits du caractère français qui sont à citer à notre honneur'. 'Anglais et Français', *Le Petit Parisien*, 23 September 1902, p. 1. In a similar vein, *L'Intransigeant* claims that *An Inland Voyage* can help people remember what Noyon was like before the war: Le Wattman, 'On dit que', *L'Intransigeant*, 19 August 1916, p. 2.
⁵⁹ 'Forest Notes', in *Further Memories*, pp. 117–40 (p. 136), was first published in *Cornhill Magazine* in May 1876. George Moore also wrote a Barbizon story: 'Henrietta Marr' from *Celibate Lives* (1927) takes place there.
⁶⁰ 'Robert-Louis Stevenson, sa vie, son œuvre, 1850–1894: une étude', in Robert-Louis Stevenson, *Enlevé! Mémoire relatant les aventures de David Balfour en l'an 1751*, trans. by Albert Savine, Bibliothèque cosmopolite (Paris: Stock, 1905), pp. v–lxxii (p. xxv). ('Stay in the Forest of Fontainebleau where a veritable colony of British painters had set up.')

was one of Jules Dupré's students. Lachèvre participated in the *Salons de peinture et de sculpture* between 1865 and 1868 and had become friendly with Stevenson in Barbizon.[61]

Unlike his close friends, Henry James and Edmund Gosse, and unlike other British writers and artists who played a role in bringing French literature to Britain, like Matthew Arnold, Algernon Swinburne and Arthur Symons, Stevenson never frequented the coteries and salons of his French peers and never wrote for French reviews, and he did not personally know the prominent French writers of the time. By contrast, Arnold visited with Renan, Sainte-Beuve and Sand; Swinburne, despite not passing extended periods of time in France, knew Manet and Fantin-Latour and wrote to Victor Hugo and Mallarmé; Henry James knew Flaubert, Maupassant and Daudet. This did not harm Stevenson's reception in France, though; whereas James's novels were mostly translated into French in the mid-twentieth century, Stevenson's appeared in France as early as 1885.[62] Stevenson did know and correspond with Rodin, whom he met through his friend, poet W.E. Henley, and who had planned to do a bust of Stevenson,[63] and he did later correspond with Marcel Schwob when Schwob was himself an emerging writer; but generally, Stevenson kept a distance, remained an observer, the better, perhaps, to chart his own course. Throughout his life, he remained 'away from the little bubble of the literary life'[64] and displayed an exceptional independence of literary spirit. His withdrawal from the cultural centre(s) of Europe allowed him to develop a hybrid, transnational body of work; but, a consequence of his keeping a distance from literary centres is that Stevenson has been left out of many academic studies of Franco-British comparative literature at the end of the nineteenth century. This is the more surprising since a strong case can be made for considering Stevenson as not only a Scottish author, but as an author writing in a French and European tradition.

Stevenson's fascination with France is therefore more or less well documented, but the research that has been conducted on Stevenson

---

[61] Letter to Henry Lachèvre, [May 1878], *Letters*, II, p. 250.
[62] See Julie Wolkenstein, 'Henry James in France', in *A Companion to Henry James*, ed. by Greg W. Zacharias (Oxford: Blackwell, 2008), pp. 416–33 (p. 432).
[63] Letter to his Mother (joint letter with Fanny Stevenson), [February 1884], *Letters*, IV, p. 240, n. 1. According to the EdRLS: Stevenson's Library Database, Stevenson bought a copy of *New Arabian Nights* to give to Rodin in 1886. See the 'RLS Presentations' tab.
[64] Letter to Edmund Gosse, April 1891, *Letters*, VII, p. 106.

and French literature warrants updating because it rarely takes account of Stevenson's role in the evolution of French literary history and is seldom referred to in wider comparative literary studies. The first study of Stevenson written in French was published in 1904 by Georges Grappe, a journalist who also wrote biographies of Jules Claretie and Edgar Degas, among others. Grappe's short study, *R.L. Stevenson: l'homme et l'œuvre*, is an expanded version of an article published in the *Journal des débats* in 1902,[65] and while his approach is biographical, it gives a strong sense of French preoccupations at the turn of the century. In particular, Grappe uses the trope of the amateur emigrant to draw attention to the many genres in which Stevenson worked.[66]

A cluster of comparative studies appeared in the 1920s and 1930s, during the Modernist moment, which in itself is of literary-historical interest. The first English-language book to adopt a comparative perspective was Charles Sarolea's *Robert Louis Stevenson and France* (1924). Sarolea was part of the network of Franco-Scottish cultural figures of the Nineties and the early twentieth century. A professor of French at the University of Edinburgh, in 1895 he contributed an essay on 'La Littérature nouvelle en France' to the inaugural issue of Patrick Geddes and William Sharp's magazine, *The Evergreen: A Northern Seasonal*. His article decries the bankruptcy of pseudo-science and called for a renaissance of idealism in the novel.[67] For Sarolea, the French influence was present in Stevenson in 'the quality of his style, the structure of his novels and short stories and the philosophy of his Essays'.[68] While Sarolea's book is eminently readable because it began life as an address to the RLS Fellowship, it suffers, like many works of literary criticism of the time, from a lack of evidence, barring occasional references to Stevenson's letters. In 1930, Harriet Dorothea MacPherson published *R.L. Stevenson: A Study in French Influence*, which is more academic in approach. In 1936, the first full-length academic study in French, *La France dans l'œuvre de*

---

[65] 'Robert-Louis Stevenson d'après sa correspondance', p. 3.

[66] 'Il parcourut le monde et fut véritablement, suivant sa pittoresque expression, un perpétuel *émigrant-amateur*. C'est là le dessin même de sa carrière.' *R.L. Stevenson: l'homme et l'œuvre*, p. 22. ('He travelled the world and truly was, to use his own colourful expression, a perpetual amateur emigrant.')

[67] Spring (1895), pp. 92–7. *Evergreen Digital Edition*, ed. by Lorraine Janzen Kooistra, 2016–18. *Yellow Nineties 2.0*, Ryerson University Centre for Digital Humanities, 2019, available at <https://1890s.ca/egv1_sarolea_nouvelle/>.

[68] *Robert Louis Stevenson and France* (Edinburgh: Robert Louis Stevenson Fellowship, 1924), p. 53. The book also contains an essay on twelve points that Stevenson has in common with Montaigne.

R.L. Stevenson, by Cecil MacLean, was published in France. Most recently, Louis Stott published *Robert Louis Stevenson & France* in 1994. While Stott's book is not an academic study, it does usefully condense and summarise some of the highlights of Stevenson's relationship with France.

These books and biographies provide us with ample information, but they do not go far enough in their analysis of the whys and wherefores of Stevenson's French literary tastes, and it is my belief that more can be made of the French connection from the perspective of the comparative literary history of the late nineteenth and early twentieth centuries, a period of transition from realism to Modernism. Like David Balfour and the Captain, quoted in the epigraph to this Introduction, we know that Stevenson has 'been in France', but we need to read between the lines. In recent years, there has been concerted effort to reassert the fundamental importance of Stevenson's role in European literature and reframe his work within a European context. There have also been strides made in situating Stevenson within a transatlantic and global context.[69] A love of Stevenson's novels and essays is what prompted me to explore his relationship with and his place within nineteenth-century French literature, but the present study is in essence a work of literary history, a continuation of the research already begun by scholars like Richard Ambrosini and Richard Dury in collections like *European Stevenson* and *Robert Louis Stevenson: Writer of Boundaries*.

The first two chapters of this study deal with Stevenson as a reader of French literature and a writer of French; the last two chapters deal with French translations of Stevenson and interpretations of his work. The point of departure for my analysis of the French Stevenson is an exploration of his early essays on French literature. These essays on Late Medievalists François Villon and Charles d'Orléans, and nineteenth-century figures Pierre-Jean de Béranger, Victor Hugo, Jules Verne and Alexandre Dumas, call for generic innovation, present the novel as a transnational genre of modernity, and situate Stevenson within French literary history. They also emphasise the tension between the romance tradition and the dominant realist strain of writing in the second half of the nineteenth century. Stevenson's better-known essays from the 1880s – 'A Gossip

---

[69] See, for example, Glenda Norquay's *Robert Louis Stevenson, Literary Networks and Transatlantic Publishing in the 1890s: The Author Incorporated* (London: Anthem Press, 2020).

on Romance' (1882), 'A Note on Realism' (1883) and 'A Humble Remonstrance' (1884) – broaden the scope of the ideas presented in the French essays and engage more fully with an idea that he expresses succinctly in a letter to his cousin Bob: 'Realism, I regard, as a mere question of method.'[70] Although they were published in English periodicals and written for an English-speaking audience, I argue that these essays can be interpreted as responses to debates taking place in France about Naturalism. As such, they not only help us to situate Stevenson's art within a French literary tradition, they help illustrate the close connections between British and French theories of the novel at the fin de siècle.

Stevenson was not writing in a void – Henry James first published *French Poets and Novelists* in 1878 and George Saintsbury published *A Short History of French Literature* in 1882 – but Stevenson's perspective on French literature has not been given the attention it deserves precisely because he does not fit (and does not fit himself) into a Victorian or French realist tradition. He also never published a volume collecting his French writings. Although this is unfortunate in terms of recognition of his role in Franco-British literary history, it confirms his transnational approach to literature insofar as he treats all literatures as equal. Taking Stevenson's ideas on French literature more seriously, considering them as a body of work, presents new avenues for understanding the evolution of the novel at the end of the nineteenth century, amid the competing pressures of attracting a mass readership and fulfilling artistic ambitions. While Stevenson did not write any further essays on French literature or the theory of the novel after these essays were published in the 1870s and 1880s, he continued to keep up with new developments in French letters by reading popular authors and authors associated with Decadence and the psychological novel.

Chapter 2 moves away from a discussion of the history and theory of the novel *per se* to examine how Stevenson's French reading fits with his infamous 'sedulous aping' of his favourite authors. While Stevenson was an avid reader of Eugène Sue, Dumas père, Fortuné du Boisgobey and Xavier de Montépin, he acknowledged that style was not necessarily their forte. Conversely, while he criticised authors like Flaubert and Gautier for their storytelling deficiencies, he was perfectly able to appreciate their stylistic achievements. Essentially, Stevenson was someone for whom the pleasure of the

---

[70] [? 30 September 1883], *Letters*, IV, p. 169.

text was linked to both storytelling and aesthetics, and not necessarily at the same time. Insofar as this is the case, he shows himself an adept reader for both form and content. This in turn contributed to the development of his own style. Stevenson was known in both Britain and France as a stylist. By virtue of its complex layering, its musicality and its emphasis on perception, Stevenson's style never lets readers forget the artistic vision that shapes his texts. In fact, for many British reviewers, Stevenson's emphasis on style belied a French influence on his writing. As 'On Some Technical Elements of Style in Literature' (1885) illustrates, Stevenson's thinking on matters stylistic has much in common with Flaubert and Baudelaire, and his early experimentation with Baudelairian *poèmes en prose* continued to bear fruit long after Stevenson wrote them in 1875.

French plays another role in Stevenson's development as an author, as well. If Stevenson was accused of being too much of a stylist, it is perhaps because in places he seems to be writing in French using English words – and vice versa. In his comic poems and in countless letters, he engages in continual code-switching, transforming linguistic contact into a literary spectacle. This is a source of much humour born of calques, word play and linguistic absurdities, which are further signs of the stylistic self-awareness that is ever-present in his writing. This stylistic awareness can also be seen in the discussions about the French language, *patois* and linguistic difference that he has while in France, as well as the uses to which he puts French in his fiction and letters. In the novel of the same name, St. Ives, who is nothing if not a consummate performer of English and French identities, confesses, 'I was often called to play the part of an interpreter' (p. 1). Language is a performance to be acted out here. For Stevenson, drawing attention to language contact is a means not only of perfecting his style, but of challenging the foundations of the realist novel. In his books, the use of French highlights the subjective nature of language by bringing different perspectives to bear on the same people and events.

In Chapters 3 and 4, I turn my attention to Stevenson's reception in France, looking first at how his books reached the French market, then at how French critics interpreted his works and why they were thought to be important to the evolution of French literature. The third chapter focuses on 'les nombreuses traductions de Stevenson' ('the numerous translations of Stevenson')[71] that were published

---

[71] Jean Longnon, 'Aventures et aventuriers d'outre-mer', *Le Gaulois*, 24 September 1921, p. 3.

during the Third Republic (for the most part), while the fourth deals with French perceptions of his work, as evidenced in articles written by both literary professionals and casual reviewers.

Criticism on Stevenson has been marked by a series of reversals in the English-speaking world, and as Graham Good noted in the 1980s,

> the whole process of Stevenson's canonization and decanonization, though itself an interesting study in literary sociology, is something of an obstacle to reaching an understanding of Stevenson's place in his own time, in the literary context of the 1870s and 1880s.[72]

Although there has been no decanonisation of Stevenson in the French-speaking world, there is still no better way to reconstruct the debates of the time or Stevenson's place in the literary context of the Third Republic than to go straight to historical documents of the period. Stevenson was extensively translated and published in France, beginning in the 1880s, and the 1893 edition of the *Dictionnaire universel des contemporains*, a sort of French *Who's Who*, contains an entry on him.[73] As Stanislas Rzewuski, nephew of Balzac's wife Mme Hanska, and a critic in his own right, pointed out a few years after Stevenson's death, 'Stevenson était assez connu et assez populaire, même en France, où les célébrités étrangères ne parviennent que difficilement à obtenir la plus élémentaire justice.'[74] In June 1894, a few months before he died, the *Journal des débats* referred to Stevenson (along with Kipling) as 'un des plus brillants représentatifs de la littérature actuelle en Angleterre'.[75] Despite his assertion to Marcel Schwob that he 'might write with the pen of angels or of heroes, and no Frenchman be the least the wiser',[76] Stevenson was unquestionably one of the most well-known English-language authors in France during the Third Republic. Unfortunately, his premature death meant that he would never see what his reputation in France would become.

---

[72] 'Rereading Robert Louis Stevenson', *The Dalhousie Review*, 62.1 (1982), 44–59 (p. 45).
[73] *Dictionnaire universel des contemporains*, ed. by G. Vapereau, 6th edn (Paris: Hachette, 1893), p. 1470.
[74] 'Le Dernier roman de Stevenson', *Le Gaulois*, 30 August 1897, p. 2. ('Stevenson was fairly well known and fairly popular, even in France, where foreign celebrities only manage with difficulty to be given their most basic due.')
[75] 'Au jour le jour', *Journal des débats politiques et littéraires*, 5 June 1894, p. 1. ('One of the most brilliant representatives of contemporary literature in England.')
[76] 19 August 1890, *Letters*, VI, p. 401.

In Chapter 3, I offer an overview of translations of Stevenson's work into French during the Third Republic, presenting information on both serialisation and bound books. The chapter analyses where and when his work was published and presents the literary-historical circumstances as to why some books were translated before others and marketed in different ways. That *Treasure Island* was serialised is well known, but serialisation and publication of Stevenson's stories in periodicals was perhaps more widespread than thought, with tales like 'The Merry Men' (1882), 'The Bottle Imp' (1891), 'Markheim' (1885) and others appearing in the French press. In this chapter, I also look at the people and publishers who first translated Stevenson into French, including authors and journalists both known and unknown to him, publishers targeting a general readership, and others targeting artistic connoisseurs and internationalists. By situating the French translations of Stevenson within the French literary field and by analysing which publishers were bringing out his books, it becomes immediately apparent that the translations served different purposes according to where they were published. Stevenson was published in both mass market and highbrow editions, a situation that risked creating confusion in terms of how to interpret his works and how to categorise him as a writer. The chapter concludes with a discussion of some of the perceived difficulties and problems with translations of Stevenson into French. Commentators at the time rarely went beyond vague references to the 'elegance' of translations, but some, particularly Thérèse Bentzon, Teodor de Wyzewa and Marcel Schwob, were prepared to engage with notions of cultural difference, and with the implications of different translational strategies on Stevenson's diffusion and reception in France.

The French fascination with Stevenson was in full swing by the turn of the twentieth century. In England, as Ambrosini and Dury explain, 'from the 1920s Stevenson was relegated to the status of second-rate writer'.[77] By contrast, by the 1920s, lectures on RLS were being delivered across the French empire, from Lille to Tunis.[78] There is little doubt that he would have been discussed at

---

[77] 'Introduction', in *Robert Louis Stevenson: Writer of Boundaries*, ed. by Ambrosini and Dury, pp. xiii–xxviii (p. xv).
[78] By way of example, in 1927, Pierre Humbourg gave a lecture on 'Les écrivains de la mer' in Tunis, advertised in Lucien Peyrin, 'Courrier littéraire', *L'Homme libre*, 25 November 1927, p. 2. M. Delattre's public talk at the Université de Lille, 'Un dilettante de l'aventure: Robert-Louis Stevenson', was advertised in 'Cours et conférences', *Grand Écho du Nord de la France*, 7 January 1931, p. 4.

the Entretiens de Pontigny on the novel in the summer of 1912,[79] especially since these events were organised by Paul Desjardins, who had close connections to Patrick Geddes, founder of the Franco-Scottish Society, organiser of summer cultural meetings, and promoter of the Scottish Romance revival.[80] A lot of the public interest in Stevenson was tied to adventure, travel, exploration and exoticism, as is obvious in the title of the talk 'Robert-Louis Stevenson: la vie aventureuse du célèbre écrivain anglais', delivered at the prize-giving ceremony at the prestigious Parisian Lycée Henri IV in July 1914.[81] French adaptations of and allusions to his work had already started by the turn of the twentieth century: André Flotron's novella *Le Docteur Jancourt*, 'imité de R.L. Stevenson', was serialised in *Le Temps* in 1897;[82] Léon Daudet's 1907 novel, *Le Partage de l'enfant*, contains a passage about *Treasure Island*; in 1908, André Mouëzy-Éon adapted 'The Suicide Club' as a play for the Grand-Guignol, with the title *Les Nuits du Hampton-Club*;[83] in 1915, composer Reynaldo Hahn set five poems from *A Child's Garden of Verses* to music, with translations by Maurice Léna;[84] to

---

[79] On the Entretiens, see David Steel, 'Alain-Fournier's *Le Grand Meaulnes*, the *Nouvelle Revue Française* and the English Adventure Novel', in *Franco-British Cultural Cultural Exchanges, 1880–1940: Channel Packets*, ed. by Andrew Radford and Victoria Reid (London: Palgrave Macmillan, 2012), pp. 116–30 (p. 118).

[80] See Michael Shaw, *The Fin-de-Siècle Scottish Revival: Romance, Decadence and Celtic Identity* (Edinburgh: Edinburgh University Press, 2020), p. 90, and Siân Reynolds, *Paris-Edinburgh: Cultural Connections in the Belle-Époque* (Farnham: Ashgate, 2007), pp. 89–90. The Franco-Scottish Society was founded in 1895.

[81] One century on, there is something melancholy about the thought of the assembled youth listening to tales of Stevenson's adventures and dreaming of their own, on the eve of the outbreak of World War I. Like Alain-Fournier, whose *Le Grand Meaulnes* (1913) bears the mark of Stevenson, their adventure would be too short. This was not Stevenson's only appearance in schools: he made it on to the Agrégation in 1958, when a passage from *Silverado Squatters* was proposed as a translation 'sujet destiné aux femmes' ('geared towards women'). 'The Sea Fogs', *Langues modernes: bulletin mensuel de la société des professeurs de langues vivantes de l'enseignement public*, 7 (1958), 15–16.

[82] *Le Temps*, 26 June–8 July 1897.

[83] See the review of the premiere: Charles Martel, 'Les Premières', *L'Aurore: littéraire, artistique, sociale*, 23 February 1908, p. 2. In 1912, a theatrical adaptation of *Treasure Island* was in the works at the Théâtre du Châtelet: 'M. Granval [...] vient d'obtenir des héritiers du grand romancier anglais Stevenson le droit de tirer une pièce du célèbre roman: *L'Île au trésor*.' Serge Basset, 'Courrier des théâtres', *Le Figaro*, 8 June 1912, p. 5.

[84] *Five little songs. Cinq petites chansons. Poems selected from 'A Child's Garden of Verses'* (Paris: Heugel, 1916), available at <https://catalogue.bnf.fr/ark:/12148/cb430370811>.

say nothing of Proust's famous reference to Stevenson in the final volume of *À la recherche du temps perdu*. The interest in Stevenson extended beyond his fiction: there was reporting on Stevenson and Samoan politics, on the possibility of him becoming King of Samoa,[85] on the crumbling of the Stevenson statue following the 1906 San Francisco earthquake; in addition, there was at least one article published in a major French newspaper on the death of Fanny Van de Grift Stevenson.[86]

Chapter 4 looks specifically at Stevenson's reception in France. Furthering the discussion of Stevenson's mass market and highbrow French publishing history, it analyses articles and essays of the time to ascertain how his works were interpreted. The chapter shows that French critics were largely unconcerned with internal debates in the Anglo-Scottish literary field and focused almost exclusively on the contributions that Stevenson could make to French literature. French critics associated Stevenson with other European authors, but they seldom analysed his own essays on French literature in order to see how he positioned himself in relation to French literary history. They were interested in Stevenson's fiction because 'il n'avait aucun souci d'école'[87] – he was not concerned with literary schools and movements. This could only have been attractive in an environment where there were literary schools for every proclivity, as evidenced in Anatole Baju's 1892 *état des lieux* of French literature, whose title reflects the cultural and artistic chaos of the time: *L'Anarchie littéraire: les différentes écoles: les décadents, les symbolistes, les romans, les intrumentistes, les magiques, les magnifiques, les anarchistes, les socialistes, etc.* The instability of the fin-de-siècle literary scene is equally obvious in Jules Huret's *Enquête sur l'évolution littéraire* (1891), in which interviews with authors are classified according to literary affiliations: Psychologists, Magi, Symbolists and Decadents, Naturalists, Neo-Realists, Parnassians, Independents, and Theorists and Philosophers – Stevenson owned a copy of this book.[88]

---

[85] 'Romancier en passe de devenir roi', *Le XIXe siècle*, 27 April 1892, p. 2.
[86] 'Échos du matin', *Le Matin*, 30 May 1892, p. 3; 'Curieuses prophéties', *Le Petit Parisien*, 26 April 1906, p. 2; Alice Kuhn, 'La Compagne d'un grand écrivain', *Journal des débats politiques et littéraires*, 1 March 1914, p. 6.
[87] Grappe, *R.L. Stevenson: l'homme et l'œuvre*, p. 30.
[88] EdRLS: Stevenson's Library Database. Similar fragmentation of the literary field was seen in Britain. J.M. Barrie satirises it in 'Brought Back from Elysium' (1890), in which Dickens, Fielding, Scott, Smollett and Thackeray are brought back from the dead to converse with a Realist, a Romancist, a Stylist, an Elsmerian and an American Novelist.

Because Stevenson rejected realism and Naturalism – because he rejected all affiliation – many French critics considered him to be a model of generic innovation who could influence the course of French literature. Stevenson merged popular storytelling prowess with a style worthy of the finest wordsmith; as a result, he was a reference in the rebellion against Naturalism and, later Decadence and Symbolism. One of the things that makes *le cas* Stevenson so interesting is that he did not have the extensive personal ties to French literary circles that many of his contemporaries did. Stevenson was not, as it were, 'linked in'. He was an outsider by virtue of geography, but also through a choice not to be circumscribed by the values and norms of the London and Paris literary centres. Despite this – or maybe because of this – he drew the attention of the literati in France, who were more and more turning to foreign models for inspiration. This was consequential for Stevenson, because the implicit belief in the fin de siècle that the French novel set standards of style and sophistication meant that his reception in France could have knock-on effects for his reputation elsewhere. In this sense, integrating Stevenson into a French tradition based on his artistic merit (rather than simply his popular success) helped consolidate his wider artistic significance to a European literary tradition.

Studying Stevenson in relation to French literary history further exposes his status as a hybrid author, an author who is both within and without, pulled in many directions. He was a Scot raised in Edinburgh who later lived in France, England, the United States and Samoa. He was a writer of boys' tales, historical romances, shilling shockers, essays, travel narratives, poetry and political tracts. He wrote in English, in Scots, occasionally in French and Samoan. His literary and geographical interests pulled him away from the London literary centre, and his French literary tendencies help account for the absence from his oeuvre of a 'long, large, multi-plotted, socially and psychologically realist novel that purported to represent the whole of national society'.[89] His internationalism can contribute to our understanding of the novel as an international form. At the same time, it can contribute to our understanding of national literary traditions beyond those of England and France: while English (or British) literary history was being written in such a way as to exclude Stevenson, his

---

[89] Ian Duncan, 'Stevenson and Fiction', in *The Edinburgh Companion to Robert Louis Stevenson*, ed. by Penny Fielding (Edinburgh: Edinburgh University Press, 2010), pp. 11–26 (p. 11).

internationalism and relationship with French literature are also significant in the context of the Scottish romance revival, which sought to revitalise Scotland's literary and cultural ties with Europe. As Michael Shaw explains, 'witnesses of cultural developments in 1890s Scotland detected a palpable desire to challenge the centralisation of culture and intellectualism to London and a conviction to reassert Scotland's distinctive cultural presence internationally'.[90] Although he was not in Scotland in the 1890s, Stevenson was without doubt Scotland's most well-known writer during the fin de siècle.

Stevenson is a Scottish author whose place in the British literary canon is ambiguous, but he is also an English-language author who positioned at least some of his writing within a French literary tradition and who was subsequently adopted by this tradition. Studying Stevenson from a comparative perspective helps illuminate some of the specific ways that French literature was received in Britain, and also how France was appropriating foreign books into its own literary history. It is a way of exploring the transnational nature of the arts during the late nineteenth century, something that is sometimes obscured by the national literary histories that were in the process of being codified. It helps account for Stevenson's exclusion from the British canon for parts of the twentieth century,[91] and for the fact that he does not even figure as a footnote in one of the first detailed studies of Franco-British literary relations at the end of the nineteenth century, Enid Starkie's *From Gautier to Eliot: The Influence of France on English Literature, 1851–1939*, a book that posits that the two things that French literature gave to English literature from the advent of the Second Empire to World War I were gritty subject matter and art for art's sake. Stevenson does not fit this neat framework, so he is excluded where many of his contemporaries, his friends – Edmund Gosse, Henry James, Andrew Lang, George Meredith, George Saintsbury, among others – are mentioned. It is my hope that this book will go some way towards rectifying this situation.

---

[90] *The Fin-de-Siècle Scottish Revival*, p. 3.
[91] See Richard Dury, 'Robert Louis Stevenson's Critical Reception', *The Robert Louis Stevenson Archive*, for a detailed overview of the reaction against Stevenson from the Modernist period onwards, available at <http://www.robert-louis-stevenson.org/richard-dury-archive/critrec.htm>.

Chapter 1

Stevenson as a Reader of French Literature

> I am now the only person who knows anything about writing stories; *attendez voir*.[1]

Such was the presence of French fiction in nineteenth-century Britain that there is hardly a British author who did not, at some point, write about French literature. The French novel featured extensively in debates on the morality and the corrupting power of literature. It also came to represent high art and scandal as opposed to the middle-class mediocrity of the books available through the system of circulating libraries.[2] Reviews and essays on French literature regularly appeared in journals and magazines like the *Athenaeum* and the *Fortnightly Review*. From the beginning of the century to the end, whether it be in terms of the *roman feuilleton*, the great romantics like Victor Hugo and George Sand, stylists like Gautier, Baudelaire, Flaubert and the Goncourts, or the Naturalism and Decadence of the 1880s and 1890s, French literature was a phenomenon to be reckoned with in Victorian Britain. While some authors, like Henry James, collected their writings on French literature in volumes, others – the majority – shared their ideas in reviews, columns and books alongside articles and chapters about English literature. Running through these debates were attempts both overt and covert to clearly delineate

---

[1] Letter to W.E. Henley, [Late July 1883], *Letters*, IV, p. 146.
[2] Josephine Guy notes that 'by the 1890s, France [. . .] serve[d] two quite contradictory purposes in British culture': it was a 'haven of artistic sophistication' and a 'site of iniquity'. 'Introduction', in *The Edinburgh Companion to Fin-de-Siècle Literature, Culture and the Arts*, ed. by Josephine Guy (Edinburgh: Edinburgh University Press, 2018), pp. 1–22 (pp. 1–2).

the distinct national literary characteristics of the French and British novel. The present chapter will explore how Stevenson fits in to this dynamic. It will begin by examining Stevenson's essays on French literature in relation to the development of the novel across national and generic boundaries. At the same time, it will demonstrate how Stevenson positions himself within this literary evolution. It will then turn to Stevenson's better-known essays on realism from the 1880s, so as to show how they function as responses to debates on realism and Naturalism in France. Finally, it will study Stevenson's reading of popular and non-canonical nineteenth-century French writers, as well as emerging figures in French literature who were attempting to renew the novel. In so doing, it will highlight how this reading relates to Stevenson's interest in generic innovation that merges plot-centric storytelling with stylistic sophistication.

Stevenson's French Essays

In the 1887 essay 'A College Magazine', Stevenson memorably described the process by which he learned to write by evoking his emulation of writers whose style he admired:

> Whenever I read a book or a passage that particularly pleased me, in which a thing was said or an effect rendered with propriety, in which there was either some conspicuous force or some happy distinction in the style, I must sit down at once and set myself to ape that quality. I was unsuccessful, and I knew it; and tried again, and was again unsuccessful and always unsuccessful; but at least in these vain bouts, I got some practice in rhythm, in harmony, in construction and the co-ordination of parts. I have thus played the sedulous ape to Hazlitt, to Lamb, to Wordsworth, to Sir Thomas Browne, to Defoe, to Hawthorne, to Montaigne, to Baudelaire and to Obermann.[3]

In the 1870s, the twenty-something Stevenson accompanied this writing practice with sustained reflections on the theory of the novel, and his essays on French literature are a key component of his apprenticeship as a writer. Stevenson read widely in French – there were 'well over one hundred [French] volumes'[4] in his Vailima collection – and

---

[3] In *Memories and Portraits & Other Fragments*, pp. 28–36 (p. 29).
[4] Neil Macara Brown, 'The French Collection: RLS's Vailima Library', *Scottish Book Collector*, 5.9 (1997), 22–5 (p. 22).

his first commissioned article on French literature was 'Victor Hugo's Romances', which he began writing for *Cornhill Magazine* while on an extended stay in Menton in 1874. *Cornhill* was 'the most prestigious literary monthly of the age',[5] and its editor, Leslie Stephen, had initially asked Sidney Colvin to write the article. Being unable, Colvin put forward Stevenson's name, and the article he produced was well received; in fact, since it was unsigned, a critic for the *Spectator* thought Leslie Stephen had written it himself.[6] Other essays dealing with French topics followed on the heels of 'Victor Hugo's Romances'. They include 'Béranger' for the *Encyclopedia Britannica* (1875); 'Jules Verne's Stories' (1876) for *The Academy*; the largely biographical 'Charles of Orléans' (1876), and 'François Villon, Student, Poet, and House-Breaker' (1877), both for *Cornhill*. The one French study that falls outside this general timeframe is 'A Gossip on a Novel of Dumas's', which did not appear until *Memories and Portraits* was published in 1887, the same year that Stevenson described himself as a 'sedulous ape' – perhaps unsurprisingly, the focus of this later essay is slightly different.

This flurry of essays in the 1870s undoubtedly stems from Stevenson's desire to support himself through writing so that he would not have to be financially dependent on his family – 'money', he states in a letter to W.E. Henley, 'is a means to art'.[7] The essays from the 1870s constitute an important part of his first public engagement with literature. They also prefigure the later, better-known essays in which he develops his theory of the novel more fully, namely 'A Gossip on Romance', written immediately after he finished writing *Treasure Island* (1883); 'A Note on Realism' (1883); and 'A Humble Remonstrance' (1884), his response to Henry James's 'The Art of Fiction'. Written before his career as a novelist was established in the mid-1880s, the French essays from the 1870s are important for many reasons, including for the way they establish the credibility of works that break new generic ground. As Graham Good has pointed out,

> if there is a common factor among the foreign writers that [Stevenson] read enthusiastically and wrote critical essays on, it is that most of them were in some way outside, or opposed to, the primarily secular, urban social perspective of the Victorian novel.[8]

---

[5] Duncan, 'Stevenson and Fiction', p. 14.
[6] Letter to H.B. Baildon, [? October 1874], *Letters*, II, p. 59.
[7] [c. 8 October 1884], *Letters*, V, p. 13.
[8] 'Rereading Robert Louis Stevenson', pp. 47–8.

Through their focus on literary-historical evolution and innovation across national boundaries, these early essays show how Stevenson was attempting to situate himself within nineteenth-century literature even while discussing other authors. Unusually, compared with other authors who acted as cultural mediators between France and Britain – say, Algernon Charles Swinburne or Walter Pater – Stevenson's focus is not primarily on formal, stylistic qualities or aestheticism, but on genre, in particular the perceived tension between romance and realism. This is the more remarkable given his own stylistic prowess.

What emerges from the 1870s French essays is a conception of literature based not on national literary histories, but on a generic tradition. This went decidedly against the grain of nineteenth-century critical tendencies in both France and Britain. Stevenson was not the first to do so. In introducing Baudelaire to England as the exemplar of the modern, for example, Swinburne had set the stage for a view of literary tradition that went beyond notions of 'national genius'.[9] While undeniably interested in Baudelaire, as we shall see in Chapter 2, Stevenson's conception of what was 'modern' and innovative included works written well before the nineteenth century. His French essays are underpinned by a belief in what Stevenson calls a 'principle of growth', and while discussing the past, they invoke the future. He states, for instance, that Late Medieval poet Villon 'was the one great writer of his age and country, and initiated modern literature for France'. Because of this, Stevenson believed that Villon should be measured by 'living duration of influence, not on a comparison with obscure forerunners, but with great and famous successors'. This approach has the benefit of 'insta[lling] this ragged and disreputable figure in a far higher niche in glory's temple than was ever dreamed of by the critic'.[10] A similar emphasis on successors is found in 'Victor Hugo's Romances', which is a study of five of Hugo's longer novels: *Notre-Dame de Paris* (1831), *Les Misérables* (1862), *Les Travailleurs de la mer* (1866), *L'Homme qui rit* (1869) and *Quatrevingt-treize* (1874). The essay opens with the statement that

> men who are in any way typical of a stage of progress may be compared more justly to the hand upon the dial of a clock, which continues to advance as it indicates, than to the stationary milestone which

---

[9] Patricia Clements, *Baudelaire and the English Tradition* (Princeton: Princeton University Press, 1986), pp. 9 and 14.
[10] 'François Villon, Student, Poet, and House-Breaker', in *Familiar Studies of Men & Books*, pp. 118–45 (pp. 140–1). Hereafter FV.

is only the measure of what is past. The movement is not arrested. That significant something by which the work of such a man differs from that of his predecessors, goes on disengaging itself and becoming more and more articulate.[11]

The 'significant something' also retains Stevenson's attention in his essay on Jules Verne. Several of Verne's novels, including *From the Earth to the Moon*, *Twenty Thousand Leagues Under the Sea* and *A Floating City*, were published in English translation in 1876,[12] thus prompting the review in *The Academy*. Stevenson correctly perceives a 'new vein of story-telling' in Verne and describes him as being 'one step beyond his generation, one step outside the habitable world', and his heroes as being 'in advance of contemporary science'.[13] Hugo and Verne are rarely placed side by side. Hugo's romances are structurally complex multi-volume novels dealing with the distant and the recent past, and only one of the texts Stevenson discusses in his essay on Hugo was serialised (*Les Travailleurs de la mer*). Verne, on the other hand, wrote plot-driven works of science-fiction and adventure for the most part designed for serialisation. Despite these differences, they both drew praise from Stevenson because they were beyond their genre in both time and space. They wrote about new places and things (Gothic Paris, the moon, underwater worlds, and so on) and in so doing widened the scope of the novel. This is abundantly clear in Verne's case, but Stevenson also draws attention to the breadth of Hugo's romances, underlining the way in which each of them deals with a different type of conflict:

> Superstition and social exigency having been thus dealt with in the first two members of the series [*Notre-Dame de Paris* and *Les Misérables*], it remained for *Les Travailleurs de la mer* to show, man hand to hand with the elements, the last form of external force that is brought against him. (VH, pp. 13–14)

Stevenson's essays on poets and songwriters similarly emphasise innovation: Villon broke 'with an *éclat de voix* out of his tongue-tied century' and chansonnier Pierre-Jean de Béranger is described as 'a figure of importance in literary history' because of the role

---

[11] In *Familiar Studies of Men & Books*, pp. 1–23 (p. 1). Hereafter VH.
[12] Stevenson owned this translation. See EdRLS: Stevenson's Library Database.
[13] 'Jules Verne's Stories', in *Essays Literary and Critical*, pp. 190–3 (p. 190).

he played in cultivating the hitherto 'minor form' of the song.[14] As Stevenson evocatively explains, '[Béranger's] was a sort of conservative reform preceding the violent revolution of Victor Hugo and his army of uncompromising romantics' (B, p. 177). These men of letters are simultaneously in and out of step with their contemporaries, representatives of their era, 'stationary milestones' in any future literary history by virtue of their past innovations, but also harbingers of what is to come: there is a clear forward movement. In this, at least, Stevenson is aligned with Hugo, who, in the infamous preface to *Hernani* (1830), wrote that 'en révolution, tout mouvement fait avancer'[15] – in times of revolution, all movement is movement forward. Consequently, Stevenson can say of Villon that 'beside that of his contemporaries, his writing, so full of colour, so eloquent, so picturesque, stands out in an almost miraculous isolation'. Villon is a so-called 'stationary milestone', but he also made possible the writing of his successors: 'out of him flows much of Rabelais; and through Rabelais, directly and indirectly, a deep, permanent, and growing inspiration' (FV, pp. 140–1).

When we consider these essays not so much in terms of what they say about French literature – which we will come back to – but what they say about Stevenson, and how they fit into his oeuvre, the focus on literary-historical evolution and influence begs the question of 'after'. Stevenson tells us what comes after Villon and Charles d'Orléans: according to him, the answer is Rabelais. But he cannot predict where the novel will go after novelists like Hugo, Dumas and Verne, because Dumas had only recently died (in 1870), and Hugo and Verne were both still alive when Stevenson wrote his essays. From the vantage point of the twenty-first century, however, the answer to the 'after' question presents itself naturally: the 'hand upon the dial of the clock' will continue to advance, and after Hugo, Dumas and company, there will be Stevenson. As Alan Sandison has pointed out, Stevenson's 'remarks on Hugo could very well be applied to himself'.[16] In this respect, the French essays come to reflect the development of Stevenson's own theory and practice of art. The idiosyncratic, personal nature of his approach is obvious when compared with the essays of

---

[14] 'Preface, by Way of Criticism', in *Familiar Studies of Men & Books*, pp. xi–xxiii (p. xx); 'Béranger', in *Essays Literary and Critical*, pp. 172–7 (p. 176) (hereafter B).
[15] *Hernani*, in *Théâtre. I*, ed. by J.-J. Thierry and Josette Mélèze, Bibliothèque de la Pléiade (Paris: Gallimard, 1963), p. 1148.
[16] *Robert Louis Stevenson and the Appearance of Modernism*, p. 5.

George Saintsbury, Arthur Symons and Henry James. For example, apart from a few essays on historical figures like Madame de Sabran and the Ampères, James's *French Poets and Novelists* (1878) is a compendium of established romantic and realist writers like de Musset, Gautier, Baudelaire, Balzac, Sand, Flaubert, Turgenev and Merimée, and his essays do not deal with popular or adventure fiction, nor do they situate James within French literary history.

Stevenson is often cited as a cosmopolitan man of letters because of his geographic and generic wandering, but he was nonetheless acutely attuned to distinctive national cultures. For confirmation, we have only to turn to his private letters, essays like 'The Foreigner at Home' (1882) or 'Ordered South' (1874), or his anti-colonial writings on Samoa. In 1873, he wrote to his mother saying,

> I cannot get over my astonishment – indeed it increases every day, at the hopeless gulph that there is between England and Scotland, and English and Scotch. Nothing is the same; and I feel as strange and outlandish here, as I do in France or Germany.[17]

Similar sentiments are expressed in 'The Foreigner at Home', where he states, 'A Scotsman may tramp the better part of Europe and the United States and never again receive so vivid an impression of foreign travel and strange lands and manners as on his first excursion into England.'[18] What makes the border crossings in Stevenson's essays on French authors particularly interesting is the focus on generic innovations that are not necessarily bound to national literary canons. As Richard Ambrosini has argued, 'in his first literary essay, "Victor Hugo's Romances", he [. . .] advocated a transnational romance-form whose genealogy would include Scott, Hugo, Dumas and Nathaniel Hawthorne'.[19] Despite his acute sensitivity to national differences, therefore, when it comes to fiction, Stevenson is not interested in the English (or British) Novel or the French

---

[17] [29] July 1873, *Letters*, I, p. 283.
[18] In *Memories and Portraits & Other Fragments*, pp. 1–11 (p. 4).
[19] 'The Miracle: Robert Louis Stevenson in the History of European Literature', in *European Stevenson*, ed. by Ambrosini and Dury, pp. 127–45 (p. 135). Ambrosini has already detected this in relation to the essay on Victor Hugo, where Stevenson 'sets Hugo, Sir Walter Scott, and Nathaniel Hawthorne within an evolutionary line culminating in himself – or at least his theories'. 'The Four Boundary-Crossings of R.L. Stevenson, Novelist and Anthropologist', in *Robert Louis Stevenson: Writer of Boundaries*, ed. by Ambrosini and Dury, pp. 23–35 (p. 26).

Novel, *per se*. He is interested in the Novel and with the art of storytelling, and with an older literary tradition that predates the formation of nation-based literary canons and the emergence of the realist novel as a genre. This not only highlights how the nineteenth-century novel was developing across national boundaries and was an inherently hybrid genre, but also somewhat paradoxically links him to the Scottish romance revival of the fin de siècle.

In order to contextualise his studies and, ultimately, write about his personal literary evolution, Stevenson writes comparative, rather than national, literary history. Villon is compared to Béranger, Burns and Byron, for instance. Likewise, Béranger 'by [his] socialism [. . .] becomes truly modern, and touches hands with Burns' (B, p. 177).[20] The comparisons work the other way, too: in the essay on Burns he compares the Ayrshire Bard to Théophile Gautier.[21] A more sustained example of this literary-historical border crossing is contained in 'Victor Hugo's Romances', where Stevenson presents Fielding, Scott and Hugo as existing on a continuum that accounts for the evolution of literature as much as it does the evolution of society. 'The fact is', he writes,

> that the English novel was looking one way and seeking one set of effects in the hands of Fielding; and in the hands of Scott it was looking eagerly in all ways and searching for all the effects that by any possibility it could utilise. The difference between these two men marks a great enfranchisement. With Scott the Romantic movement, the movement of an extended curiosity and an enfranchised imagination, has begun. (p. 2)

The choice of words here is telling: 'enfranchisement' points to a liberation of the imagination (the novel is crossing into new thematic and subject-matter territory), but also to a democratisation of literature, a widening of audience that accompanies its expanded imaginative borders (there are new reading publics). As Hugo himself

---

[20] Matthew Arnold also appreciated Béranger. According to Arthur Clough, 'Matt is full of Parisianisms [. . .] he enters the room with a chanson of Béranger's on his lips.' Quoted in Campos, *The View of France from Arnold to Bloomsbury*, pp. 17–18.

[21] This occurs in other essays, as well: in 'A Gossip on Romance', first published in 1882 in *Longman's Magazine*, Stevenson states that at the 'end of *Esmond*', 'the great and wily English borrower [Thackeray] has here borrowed from the great, unblushing French thief [Dumas]'. In *Memories and Portraits & Other Fragments*, pp. 119–31 (p. 124). Hereafter GR.

demands, 'à peuple nouveau, art nouveau'[22] – for each new people, there must be a new art form, a new literature. The notion of enfranchisement also figures in the essay on Béranger, where Stevenson notes that Béranger distanced himself from his 'influential friends' and determined to 'sing for the people' (p. 176), thereby adapting his art to his environment. In terms of nineteenth-century literature, the genre that came to dominate was the Novel (with a capital 'N'), because it 'aspired to represent an entire national society which was also its reading public'.[23] This is as true of France as it is of Britain, even if it is manifested differently in the two countries.

The evolution that Stevenson maps out in his French essays is, however, concerned with a different trajectory, and it is significant that although he had strong opinions on them, he did not write any essays explicitly on the great French realists (e.g. Balzac, Flaubert, the Goncourts, Zola). The novelists he did write about are associated in one way or another with romance. When Stevenson writes that Hugo's romances are 'descended by ordinary generation from the Waverley Novels' (VH, pp. 6–7), it is a simple statement of fact: Hugo wrote *Notre-Dame de Paris* after his publisher, for financial reasons, suggested he write a novel à la Walter Scott; when Stevenson states that 'it is in [Hugo's romances] chiefly that we shall find the revolutionary tradition of Scott carried farther [. . .]' (VH, p. 7), he is drawing attention to the broadening scope of the novel. *Notre-Dame de Paris*'s romance lineage is evident; in *Les Misérables*, Hugo adapts romance to a story that takes place in the nineteenth century and has a distinct socio-political bent.

As this discussion shows, Stevenson's writings on French literary history are tied to his development as an author whose generic preferences did not coincide with those of his time, which, as far as the novel was concerned, was above all the age of realism. He argues that

> when we come to Hugo we see that the deviation, which seemed slight enough and not very serious between Scott and Fielding, is indeed such a great gulf in thought and sentiment as only successive generations can pass over: and it is but natural that one of the chief advances that Hugo has made upon Scott is an advance in self-consciousness. (VH, pp. 6–7)

---

[22] *Hernani*, p. 1148.
[23] Duncan, 'Stevenson and Fiction', p. 11.

The 'advance in self-consciousness' consists of a deliberate attempt to widen the scope of the romance to include elements capable of accommodating the dominant realist mode – and subject matter – of much nineteenth-century literature. It also relates to character delineation and increased psychological complexity. Hugo's 'great stride' is that 'no longer content with expressing more or less abstract relations of man to man, he has set before himself the task of realising, in the language of romance, much of the involution of our complicated lives' (VH, p. 8). Stevenson is using 'the language of romance' as shorthand for Hugo's mode of writing, how he sets out the events of his novels, and how he does so in relation to 'our complicated lives' – the 'our' is important, for it includes Stevenson and his readers and in so doing anchors existential questions about 'complicated lives' in nineteenth-century realities. This is romance in the process of being updated for the nineteenth century, romance in which the importance of chivalry and courtly love is falling by the wayside, but the indispensable focus on plot, adventure and intrigue is retained. Indeed, as Corinne Saunders explains,

> Romance is often self-conscious, reflecting some degree of choice against realism, and demonstrating over the course of literary history the enduring power and relevance – social, intellectual, emotional – of a mode of writing underpinned by the imaginative use of the symbolic and the fantastic, by idealism, and by universal motifs such as quest and adventure.[24]

This is precisely the direction in which Stevenson himself would develop as a novelist.

The 'advance in self-consciousness' also relates to an awareness of genre and the function of the novel. The essay on Victor Hugo is structured around a distinction between what Stevenson calls Hugo's 'two deliberate designs: one artistic, the other consciously ethical and intellectual'. According to Stevenson, Hugo took the 'artistic design' of the romance and applied it to the contemporary world so as to present ethical reflections relevant to nineteenth-century society. Stevenson perceives this dual function in each of Hugo's romances, yet is careful to distinguish between the ethical function of Hugo's romances, on the one hand, and novels whose primary function is

---

[24] 'Introduction', in *A Companion to Romance: From Classical to Contemporary*, ed. by Corinne Saunders (Oxford: Blackwell, 2004), pp. 1–9 (p. 4).

to provide didactic moral commentary, on the other. For example, the great historical novel *Notre-Dame de Paris* deals with decidedly modern themes in its denunciation of 'the external fatality that hangs over men in the form of foolish and inflexible superstition' (p. 9). Yet, notwithstanding the denunciations that Hugo's romances contain, they

> are not to be confused with 'the novel with a purpose' as familiar to the English reader: this is generally the model of incompetence; as we see the moral clumsily forced into every hole and corner, or thrown over it like a carpet over a railing. Now the moral significance, with Hugo, is of the essence of the romance; it is the organizing principle. (pp. 20–1)

What Stevenson appreciates is that the so-called moral significance of Hugo's romances is not pre-ordained by an external force, but is, rather, tied to the artistic conception of the work of art itself. Thus, the 'moral lesson' of *Les Misérables* is 'worked out in masterly coincidence with the artistic effect' (p. 12). Stevenson is not advocating the upholding of a predetermined moral standard; indeed, as the author of such morally ambiguous stories as *Treasure Island*, *Strange Case of Dr. Jekyll and Mr. Hyde* (1886) and *The Master of Ballantrae* (1889) reminds us in 'A Gossip on a Novel of Dumas's', 'there is no quite good book without a good morality; but the world is wide, and so are morals'.[25] This tension between art and ethics is one of the central conundrums of Stevenson's writing. His preoccupation with morality sets him apart from many a realist writer in both France and Britain, who perceived their purpose to be the observation and recording of a fixed external reality, devoid of any authorial or narratorial judgement or commentary.

In the 'Preface, by Way of Criticism' that introduces *Familiar Studies of Men and Books* (1882), the volume in which the essays on Hugo, Villon and Charles d'Orléans were collected alongside essays on Burns, Pepys, Whitman, Thoreau, John Knox and Yoshida-Torajiro, Stevenson confesses, 'these were all men whom, for one reason or another, I loved; or when I did not love the men, my love was the greater to their books' (p. xxii). These men are, to borrow Liz Farr's term, Stevenson's 'surrogate literary family', chosen to

---

[25] In *Memories and Portraits & Other Fragments*, pp. 110–18 (p. 115).

'promote his own literary interests and aesthetic agenda'.[26] Love is rarely unconditional, however. His praise for these authors is tempered by criticism that is revealing in terms of what Farr defines as the relationship between 'art (aesthetic production) and life (social conformity)' in biographical writing.[27] It is also revealing in terms of the negotiation between realism and romance, where Stevenson consistently comes out in favour of the subjective, anti-realist qualities of romance. Although Stevenson contends that Hugo 'occupies a high place among those few' who can express themselves in the language of romance and 'bend it to any practical need' (VH, p. 20), he also accuses Hugo of the sin of improbability, which was a recurring complaint that Stevenson levelled against authors who upset the balance between realism and romance. In a fit of youthful pique, he accuses Chateaubriand of being 'clever to the last degree, but [...] such a – liar, that I cannot away with him. He is more antipathetic to me than anyone else in the world.'[28] Similar accusations are made against other writers who stray from the realm of the possible. Stevenson is at times incredulous at the plot of *Les Misérables*, expresses his 'disbelief' in the 'existence' of the character Gavroche, and condemns a scene in *Quatrevingt-treize* by stating, 'I have tried it over in every way, and cannot conceive any disposition that would make the scene possible as narrated' (VH, pp. 13, 20). He also suggests that *Notre-Dame de Paris* approaches 'melodramatic coarseness' in places; indeed, according to Stevenson, Hugo's 'avidity after effect' at times makes him 'verge dangerously on the province of the penny novelist' (VH, pp. 13, 11). Yet, there is understanding and an acknowledgement that occasional errors of truthfulness are perhaps inevitable when in 'each of these books one after another, there has been some departure from the traditional canons of romance' (VH, p. 18). The challenge therefore is to renew the romance without sacrificing realism at the temple of the popular taste for excess.

Stevenson's critique of Verne, whom he refers to as a 'practical man' who tells 'extravagant stories', is in the opposite direction. He calls Verne's characters 'marionettes', claims that 'of human nature it is certain [Verne] knows nothing', and suspects that 'the science throughout [the novels] is very flimsy'. Nonetheless, he maintains

---

[26] 'Stevenson and the (Un)familiar: The Aesthetic of Late-Nineteenth-Century Biography', in *Robert Louis Stevenson: Writer of Boundaries*, ed. by Ambrosini and Dury, pp. 36–47 (p. 41).
[27] 'Stevenson and the (Un)familiar', p. 44.
[28] Letter to Frances Sitwell, [10 November 1873], *Letters*, I, p. 360.

that Verne's tales, while 'not true, [. . .] do not seem to fall altogether under the heading of impossible'. The focus on details that are not necessarily 'trustworthy' is still 'mighty reassuring to unscientific readers' (pp. 190–1). He concludes his short review of Verne by emphasising the importance of storytelling:

> I fell upon the second volume [of *The Fur Country*; *Le Pays des fourrures*] and read it with such pleasure that I lost no time in procuring and reading the first. It would be difficult to pay a higher compliment to a book without any pretension to style, human nature, or philosophy, which offers no interest but the legitimate interest of the fable, and hinges for a great while on an elaborate mystery. (p. 193)

The critical importance of these French essays in articulating Stevenson's aesthetic is underscored by the one essay that falls outside the timeframe of the others, 'A Gossip on a Novel of Dumas's', which Stevenson thought was 'one of the best of all my papers'.[29] Rather than concentrating on Dumas's place in French literary history, or even discussing his place in the history of the novel or the romance in general, the 'Gossip' begins by situating *Le Vicomte de Bragelonne* within Stevenson's habits as a reader. It traces the evolution of his appreciation of the novel from first reading as a boy in 1866 (which he also discusses at length in a letter to his cousin Bob),[30] to the time of writing the essay in the spring of 1887. Its place in Stevenson's reading history is of interest precisely because by the time Stevenson wrote it, he was himself known as an author of fiction: *Treasure Island*, *Prince Otto*, *New Arabian Nights*, *The Dynamiter*, *Strange Case of Dr. Jekyll and Mr. Hyde* and *Kidnapped* were all published between 1882 and 1886. Julia Reid has argued that in the 1880s, Stevenson emphasised 'the inherited and racial nature of imaginative processes'.[31] This is obvious in the essay on Dumas in the way his past reading informs his present writing and becomes a part of his hereditary inheritance. Furthermore, as Glenda Norquay elegantly illustrates, the 'Gossip' flips the role of reader and writer and charts Stevenson's transition from a critic to an author of fiction.[32] Here

---

[29] Letter to W.E. Henley, [c. 2 January 1888], *Letters*, VI, p. 97.
[30] 26 November [1866], *Letters*, I, pp. 112–13.
[31] 'Stevenson, Romance, and Evolutionary Psychology', in *Robert Louis Stevenson: Writer of Boundaries*, ed. by Ambrosini and Dury, pp. 215–27 (p. 224).
[32] *Robert Louis Stevenson and Theories of Reading* (Manchester: Manchester University Press, 2007). See chapter 6, 'Textual Haunting: Stevenson and Dumas' (pp. 144–69).

is how he describes his fifth reading of *Bragelonne*, his 'favourite novel'. (The fact that he read it five times is no small feat, as the *Vicomte de Bragelonne* is the third instalment in the d'Artagnan trilogy, after *Les Trois Mousquetaires* and *Vingt ans après*, and itself consists of three parts: *The Vicomte de Bragelonne, Louise de la Vallière* and *The Man in the Iron Mask*).

> Perhaps I have a sense of ownership, being so well known in these six volumes. Perhaps I think that d'Artagnan delights to have me read of him, and Louis Quatorze is gratified, and Fouquet throws me a look, and Aramis, although he knows I do not love him, yet plays me with his best graces, as to an old patron of the show. Perhaps, if I am not careful, something may befall me like what befell George IV, about the battle of Waterloo, and I may come to fancy the *Vicomte* one of the first, and Heaven knows the best, of my own works. (p. 112)

Stevenson is a 'patron', a spectator, but also a supporter who lends his patronage – something he can now do because of his own position within the literary world: by this point he was an established novelist. This explains the delight, the gratification, the knowing looks, and the good graces of the characters who are observing him. Dumas's novel itself is now a part of Stevenson, one of his own works – it is but a small etymological step from patron to pater. Although Stevenson never presents himself directly as a French author, Norquay makes a convincing case that 'in his joy of reading Stevenson had indeed been transformed into the reader as the "writer's ghost"'.[33] Notice, also, the change in terminology, and how the terminology in the Dumas essay aligns with late-nineteenth-century tastes and the growing dominance of the novel. Stevenson talks of Hugo's 'romances' and uses this first essay to formulate ideas related to the apparent conflict between realism and romance. He talks of Verne's 'stories', drawing attention to the centrality of storytelling and recalling his early comment to Bob that their projected (but never written) joint works, inspired by Swinburne's *Atalanta in Calydon*, would be 'more exciting, more *plotty* and I hope better'.[34] Finally, in his last essay on a French author, he talks of Dumas's 'novel', even though of the three, Dumas is the one whose historical novels most closely resemble romances.

Over the course of these essays, Stevenson writes his way into French literary history: he focuses on authors (novelists, poets, songwriters)

---

[33] *Robert Louis Stevenson and Theories of Reading*, p. 152.
[34] Letter to Bob Stevenson, [? March 1868], *Letters*, I, p. 123.

whose writing, while being adapted to the circumstances of their time, broke new generic ground. He uses French authors as springboards for articulating his own approach to prose fiction, implicitly challengingly official narratives of national literary history and connecting himself to a broader literary tradition. He argues that the influence of these French authors on future generations is just as important as their innovations vis-à-vis previous generations and ends up positioning himself as the author of a French novel. French authors are 'stationary milestones' in his personal evolution as an author, but in the end he himself is 'the hand upon the dial of the clock'. The next section will show how Stevenson's interventions in British discussions of the art of fiction function as commentaries on contemporary French literature, thereby underscoring the internationalism of the novel in the fin de siècle.

Stevenson, Realism and Naturalism

The aesthetic theory that Stevenson teases out in his early essays on French authors is more thoroughly developed in 'A Gossip on Romance', 'A Note on Realism' and 'A Humble Remonstrance', which were written when he was starting to garner attention as a novelist. Of the three essays, 'A Note on Realism' engages most fully with French literature – most of its examples are French. In fact, 'A Note on Realism' can be read as a response to developments in French realism during the 1870s and 1880s.[35] As such, it reveals the similarities between British debates over romance and realism and French debates over Naturalism, while highlighting the interconnected nature of discussions of the theory of the novel in the late nineteenth century. In many ways, 'A Note on Realism' recycles the language used in 'Victor Hugo's Romances', but whereas the discussion of Hugo in 1874 hinges on the opposition between the artistic and ethical functions of fiction, in 'A Note on Realism', the debate is framed around the concepts of realism and the ideal, which brings us back to the very definition of romance. Stevenson asserts that

> all representative art, which can be said to live, is both realistic and ideal; and the realism about which we quarrel is a matter purely of

---

[35] Stevenson describes 'A Note on Realism' as 'a dreadful rag' and says 'space is to blame; I could not really deal with the subject readably under double the amount'. Letter to W.E. Henley, [Early September 1883], *Letters*, IV, p. 153.

externals. It is no especial cultus of nature and veracity, but a mere whim of veering fashion, that has made us turn our back upon the larger, more various, and more romantic art of yore.[36]

What Stevenson proposes is a redirection of the literature of his age. Realism, in his view, is a matter of technique, not a genre in and of itself. In this he sets himself against the theories favoured by contemporary French authors, who, as Henry James claims in 'The Art of Fiction', 'have brought the theory of fiction to remarkable completeness'.[37] Stevenson explains:

> This question of realism, let it then be clearly understood, regards not in the least degree the fundamental truth, but only the technical method, of a work of art. Be as ideal or as abstract as you please, you will be none the less veracious. (NR, p. 71)

He expresses the same opinion in a letter to A. Trevor Haddon, not long before 'A Note on Realism' was published in *Magazine of Art* in November 1883: 'Beware of realism; it is the devil: it is one of the means of art, and now they make it an end!'[38]

Stevenson read a wide variety of contemporary French novelists, poets and intellectuals, but he uses Émile Zola as the example to illustrate his argument, seeming to lament the fact that Zola expended his 'unquestionable force' on 'technical successes' (NR, p. 70). That Zola is the contemporary French author of whom Stevenson is most critical stands to reason given Zola's dominance of the French literary field at the end of the nineteenth century: not only was Zola the very public leader of a literary movement, his sheer output as a novelist, playwright and journalist was remarkable. His books were, for example, regularly reviewed in the *Athenaeum*, either anonymously or by Arthur Symons or George Saintsbury. On the evidence of Stevenson's correspondence, we can conclude that he read, at the very least, *Thérèse Raquin* (1867), *Pot-Bouille* (1883), *L'Œuvre* (1886), *La Bête humaine* (1890) – 'perhaps the most excruciatingly silly book that I ever read to an end'[39] – and *La Débâcle* (1892). In addition, Neil Macara Brown confirms that Stevenson owned *Le Docteur Pascal* (1893), the final novel in the

---

[36] In *Essays Literary and Critical*, pp. 69–75 (p. 70). Hereafter NR.
[37] *Longman's Magazine*, 4.23, 1 September 1884, pp. 502–21 (p. 513).
[38] 5 July 1883, *Letters*, IV, p. 141.
[39] Letter to Edmund Gosse, 10 June 1893, *Letters*, VIII, p. 104.

twenty-volume Rougon-Macquart series, and also read the sixteenth novel, *Le Rêve* (1888).[40]

L'Œuvre, Zola's künstlerroman and fictional account of his friendship with Paul Cézanne, was serialised in 1885–6 in *Gil Blas* and published by Charpentier in 1886. Stevenson, who was in Bournemouth in 1886, was obviously keeping abreast of developments in France. In April he recommended the novel to both W.E. Henley and to his friend, the American painter, Will H. Low, whom he had first met at the artist colony in Fontainebleau in 1875.[41] Fittingly, for Stevenson the appeal of the novel is fuelled by nostalgia: 'Get Zola's *L' Œuvre*! It is dreary, but – it *is* Youth and Art. No: it is dam fine [. . .] The first four or five chapters are like being young again in Paris; they woke me like a trumpet.'[42] *La Débâcle*, Zola's novel about the Franco-Prussian War, elicited qualified praise from Stevenson, possibly because, as someone who had spent extended periods of time in France and, to a lesser extent, Germany, he took an interest in the political upheaval caused by the war. He confessed to Edmund Gosse that he had read Zola's account of 'the fall of Sedan with rapturous admiration', and told Sidney Colvin in October 1892:

> I am now well on with the third part of *La Débâcle*. The two first I liked much; the second completely knocking me; so far as it has gone, this third part appears the ramblings of a dull man who had forgotten what he has to say – he reminds me of an M.P. But Sedan was really great, and I will pick no holes. The batteries under fire, the red-cross folk, the cavalry charge – perhaps, above all, Major Bouroche and the operations, all beyond discussion; and every word about the Emperor splendid.[43]

These assessments temper Stevenson's petulant condemnation of a decade earlier: 'For Zola, I have no toleration.'[44] Naturalism was condemned and critiqued by British authors from across the social and literary spectrum for both artistic and ethical reasons.[45] W.E. Henley told

---

[40] 'The French Collection', p. 2.
[41] Letter to W.E. Henley, [Mid-April 1886] and [Late April/early May 1886], *Letters*, V, pp. 243 and 248; Letter to Will H. Low, [Mid-April 1886], *Letters*, V, p. 244.
[42] Letter to W.E. Henley, [Mid-April 1886], *Letters*, V, p. 243.
[43] Letter to Edmund Gosse, 17 July 1893, *Letters*, VIII, p. 135; Letter to Sidney Colvin, [date unknown] 1892, *Letters*, VII, p. 384.
[44] Letter to Alexander Ireland, [Late March 1882], *Letters*, III, p. 302.
[45] See Kirsten MacLeod, *Fictions of British Decadence: High Art, Popular Writing, and the Fin de Siècle* (New York: Palgrave Macmillan, 2006), p. 59.

Henry James, for instance, 'I hate the whole movement. It's aesthetic syphilis.'[46] Like many of his contemporaries, Stevenson was critical of the 'steady current of what I may be allowed to call the rancid' (NR, p. 70) that was thought to be a staple of Zola's writing. Yet, this allegedly baser aspect of Zolian Naturalism plays a relatively minor part in Stevenson's critique of Zola and there is nothing overly prudish or puritanical in his observations. Certainly, Stevenson did not figure among the ranks of anti-Zola critics and journalists who, supportive of and supported by the National Vigilance Association, sought on the grounds of immorality to prevent Zola's novels from circulating in Britain.[47] While Stevenson was critical of Zola, his opinion of Zola was not, despite what some critics have intimated, uniformly negative.[48] On this note, it is worth pointing out that in the introduction to a collection of Zola's short stories in English translation, Edmund Gosse, Stevenson's close friend, compared Zola's essays to Stevenson's, writing that the former's 'semi-autobiographical essays called "Aux champs," little studies of past impression, [are] touched with a charm which is almost kindred to that of Mr. Robert Louis Stevenson's memories'.[49] Stevenson appreciated Gosse's essay. This suggests that he could appreciate different versions of Zola and appreciate Zola's talent, if not his artistic theories.

'Loathing for Naturalism', as Joseph Bristow calls it, is not the same thing as a loathing for Naturalist novels.[50] Stevenson's reflections in 'A

---

[46] Letter to Henry James, 12 March 1882, *The Selected Letters of W.E. Henley*, ed. by Damian Atkinson (London: Routledge, 2016), p. 106.

[47] Zola's London publisher, Vizetelly, was put on trial in 1888 and again in 1889. Both times he was found guilty. For more on the trial, see Enid Starkie, *From Gautier to Eliot: The Influence of France on English Literature, 1851–1939* (London: Hutchinson/Scholarly Press, 1971), pp. 79–80, and Katherine Mullin, 'Pernicious Literature: Vigilance in the Age of Zola (1886–1899)', in *Prudes on the Prowl: Fiction and Obscenity in England, 1850 to the Present Day*, ed. by David Bradshaw and Rachel Potter (Oxford: Oxford University Press, 2013), pp. 30–51 (pp. 38–40). Stevenson's work was subject to disapproval on moral grounds, too. 'The Treasure of Franchard' was refused by *Cornhill* because it was not fit for British 'proprieties'. Letter to James Payn, 21 December 1882, *Letters*, IV, p. 39, n. 1. A *Chicago Tribune* review of *New Arabian Nights* called it a 'monstrosity of a book' that 'out-Zola's Zola ... travesty on the dignity of literary work, and an insult to the purity of literary ethics'. Letter to his Father, 15 June 1883, *Letters*, IV, p. 131, n. 2.

[48] See, for example, Cecil MacLean, *La France dans l'œuvre de R.L. Stevenson* (Paris: Jouve, 1936), p. 144.

[49] Émile Zola, *The Attack on the Mill and Other Sketches of War* (London: Heinemann, 1892), p. 31.

[50] *Empire Boys: Adventures in a Man's World* (Abingdon: Routledge, 2016), p. 120.

Note on Realism' predate and do not entirely fit the parameters of the 'immoral literature' culture wars that raged in Britain between 1885 and 1894 following the creation of the National Vigilance Association. The closest Stevenson comes to entering the ranks of the shocked and appalled is in his letter to the editor of *The Times* in early September 1886: 'M. Zola is a man of a personal and forceful talent, approaching genius, but of diseased ideals; a lover of the ignoble, dwelling complacently in foulness, and to my sense touched with erotic madness.'[51] Even if Stevenson is concerned with morality and aesthetics, 'A Note on Realism' is not an intervention fuelled by sexual prudery, nor is it a salvo fired in the what-constitutes-acceptable-reading-for-women-and-other-impressionable-people debate; it is, rather, an intervention on the development and evolution of the novel as a genre at the end of the nineteenth century. Taken together with some of the praise that Stevenson expresses for Zola, it can be argued that his comments on realism in the 1883 essay are a response to Naturalist theories of the novel, rather than to any particular Naturalist novels. In fact, it is my contention that 'A Note on Realism' should be read as a response – whether direct or indirect (I tend to think it direct) – to the theory of the novel that Zola formulated in the series of critical works that he published in the 1870s and early 1880s. Many of these were published in *Le Messager d'Europe* (*Vestnik Europy*) and then reprinted in French newspapers. Zola's essay on Flaubert, for instance, was published in the *Figaro* (11 July 1880), a newspaper that was readily available in Britain and that Stevenson is known to have read – he even subscribed to the *Figaro*'s weekly literary supplement when he lived in Samoa.[52]

Zola published four major critical works between 1880 and 1882 – *Le Roman expérimental*, *Les Romanciers naturalistes*, *Documents littéraires* and *Une campagne* – but the essays that deal most closely with the subject matter of 'A Note on Realism' were first printed in the newspaper, *Le Voltaire*. 'Le Sens du réel' (20 August 1878) outlines the importance of documentation, as opposed to imagination, in the creative process; 'L'Expression personnelle' (27 August 1878) brings the author's personal manner of seeing and sense of style to bear on the creative process outlined in 'Le Sens du réel'; 'La Formule critique appliquée au roman' (27 May 1879) builds on the work of Hippolyte Taine and Charles Augustin Sainte-Beuve (two men whose work Stevenson admired), and likens the role of the novelist to that

---

[51] *Letters*, V, p. 311.
[52] Letter to Charles Scribner, [10 October 1887], *Letters*, VI, p. 27.

of the critic or historian; finally, 'De la description' (8 June 1880) argues that description must always be a means of showing how environment determines characters' behaviour.⁵³ These ideas were gaining currency at precisely the time that Stevenson was spending long periods in France and on the Continent, for the purpose of both travel and health. In August 1878, when the first of these essays were published, Stevenson was in Paris for the Exposition Universelle, acting as Fleeming Jenkin's secretary. He wintered in Davos, Switzerland, in both 1880 and 1881, and he spent the winter of 1882 in France. Much of 1883 was spent in Hyères.

The premise of 'A Note on Realism' is that the 'great change of the past century has been effected by the admission of detail' (p. 69). This is something with which Zola would agree, for the entire process of creation outlined in 'Le Sens du réel' is based on the role of documentation in the writing of realist texts. Stevenson, however, contends that 'for some time [detail] signified and expressed a more ample contemplation of the conditions of man's life; but it has recently (at least in France) fallen into a merely technical and decorative stage' (NR, p. 69) – in other words, it is a matter of externals. The relationship between detail, description and realism is something that Stevenson had already addressed in 'Victor Hugo's Romances', where he claims that while readers may forget specifics, they do retain impressions:

> We forget all that enumeration of palaces and churches and convents which occupies so many pages of admirable description [in *Notre-Dame de Paris*], and the thoughtless reader might be inclined to conclude from this, that they were pages thrown away; but this is not so: we forget, indeed, the details, as we forget or do not see the different layers of paint on a completed picture; but the thing desired has been accomplished, and we carry away with us a sense of the 'Gothic profile' of the city [. . .]. (p. 9)

These details and descriptions serve the story, they are not themselves the story. And, if readers do not notice the details, it is because the details are more than 'merely technical', more than merely 'decorative'.

---

⁵³ See Henri Mitterrand's introduction to the collection, 'Zola théoricien et critique du roman', in Émile Zola, *Du roman: sur Stendhal, Flaubert et les Goncourt*, ed. by Henri Mitterrand (Brussels: Éditions Complexe, 1999), pp. 7–29 (p. 12).

'A Gossip on Romance', published a year before 'A Note on Realism', contains similar comments:

> we may forget the words, although they are beautiful; we may forget the author's comment, although perhaps it was ingenious and true; but these epoch-making scenes, which put the last mark of truth upon a story and fill up, at one blow, our capacity for sympathetic pleasure, we so adopt into the very bosom of our mind that neither time nor tide can efface or weaken the impression. (p. 123)

Stevenson objects to the tendency in contemporary literature, in particular Naturalist literature, to subordinate story to detail, such that the details, the facts, or what the Naturalists would call 'documents humains', no longer create impressions but instead create a reality effect. The danger lies in pushing this reality effect too far, such that it becomes a fetishisation of detail for its own sake. As Arthur Symons notes of Zola, 'he cannot leave well alone; he cannot omit'.[54] Stevenson is adamant that 'the tendency of the extreme detail, when followed as a principle, [can] degenerate into mere *feux-de-joie* of literary trickery' (NR, p. 70). This comment draws attention to the relationship between Naturalism and Decadence that was affecting the French novel. This relationship was already perceptible at the time, with columnists like Paul Perret of *La Liberté* calling Zolism a 'religion bien décadente'.[55] The evolution from Naturalism to Decadence is most obviously associated with changes in subject matter – think of the difference between Huysmans's novel of prostitution, *Marthe: histoire d'une fille*, and *À Rebours*, the aesthete's (and Dorian Gray's) bible. Where Stevenson's reading of French literature is especially prescient, though, is in its identification of the 'literary trickery' of 'extreme detail' as a factor contributing to the degeneration and 'odd suicide of one branch of realists' (NR, p. 70).

For Zola, 'tous les efforts de l'écrivain tendent à cacher l'imagination sous le réel'.[56] For this reason, he rejects the word 'roman' because it no longer adequately describes what the Naturalists are doing. In

---

[54] *Studies in Two Literatures* (London: Leonard Smithers, 1897), p. 208.
[55] 'Revue littéraire et historique', *La Liberté*, 5 August 1897, p. 1. ('A very decadent religion.')
[56] 'Le Sens du réel', in *Du roman: sur Stendhal, Flaubert et les Goncourt*, ed. by Mitterrand, pp. 33–42 (p. 34). ('All of the novelist's effort is spent hiding imagination behind the real.')

Zola's estimation, the term 'roman' is too closely tied to the notion of romance and invention ('affabulation'):

> Il est fâcheux d'abord que nous n'ayons pu changer ce mot 'roman', qui ne signifie plus rien, appliqué à nos œuvres naturalistes. Ce mot entraîne une idée de conte, d'affabulation, de fantaisie, qui jure singulièrement avec les procès-verbaux que nous dressons.[57]

From Stevenson's perspective, authors should never 'sacrifice the beauty and significance of the whole to local dexterity, or, in the insane pursuit of completion, to immolate [...] readers under facts' (NR, p. 74). Such a strategy serves no purpose other than to draw attention to the facts and details themselves, rather than to story or character, incident or ideal. Whereas Stevenson is trying to retain the 'romance' elements of the 'roman', Zola is pushing them farther away; whereas 'Le Sens du réel' opens by citing Dumas, Hugo, Sand and Eugène Sue as negative examples because they rely on imagination, Stevenson cites these same authors as positive examples precisely because they are powerful storytellers.

It is no surprise, then, that Stevenson warns against falling 'into the error of the French naturalists, [who] consider any fact as welcome to admission if it be on the ground of brilliant handiwork' (NR, p. 74). This admonition is clarified in Stevenson's letter to the editor of *The Times* in September 1886, in defence of his friend, sculptor Auguste Rodin. In the letter, Stevenson explains how acute attention to detail does not improve or render Zola's writing more truthful:

> M. Zola presents us with a picture, to no detail of which can we take grounded exception. It is only on the whole that it is false. We find therein nothing lovable or worthy; no trace of the pious gladnesses, innocent loves, ennobling friendships, and not infrequent heroisms by which we live surrounded; nothing of the high mind and pure aims in which we find our consolation. Hence we call his work realistic in the evil sense, meaning that it is dead to the ideal, and speaks only to the sense.[58]

---

[57] 'La Formule critique appliquée au roman', in *Du roman: sur Stendhal, Flaubert et les Goncourt*, ed. by Mitterrand, pp. 51–8 (p. 56). ('It's unfortunate that we haven't been able to replace the word "roman", which no longer means anything when applied to our Naturalist works. The word suggests the notion of fairy tales, invention, or fantasy, which is at singular odds with the reports that we're compiling.')
[58] [Early September 1886], *Letters*, V, p. 312.

In other words, so-called realist texts lack veracity in anything other than details taken in isolation. To claim otherwise is to make a fetish of facts. In light of this, it is not difficult to see in Stevenson's appreciation of Hugo, for instance, a foreshadowing of his later contention that 'breathing as we do the intellectual atmosphere of our age, [we] are more apt to err upon the side of realism than to sin in quest of the ideal' (NR, p. 74). The ideal is, of course, central to romance. If we conceive of realism and romance as being extremes on the spectrum of fiction, to say that Zola's work is dead to the ideal is tantamount to saying it is dead to romance.[59] Thus, in rejecting the romance, Zola lurches to the other extreme: realism. Stevenson, on the other hand, is looking to reconcile these opposites. He objects to the tendency in contemporary literature, in particular Naturalist literature, to subordinate storytelling and idealism to realist detail. Instead, Stevenson envisages deviating from the established course and finding a way to write realist romances in which mimetic detail and nineteenth-century realities could be 'pious', 'ennobling', 'pure' and 'high'. In this, he was writing very much against the grain of Naturalism but very much within a fin-de-siècle context where realism – and the purpose of the novel – was open to reassessment. By the end of the century, this reassessment was well under way. For example, Sarolea, writing in 1895, summarises the direction in which French literature ought to evolve as reflecting 'la banqueroute de la philosophie pseudo-scientifique. La banqueroute du naturalisme. La renaissance de l'idéalisme.'[60]

Given that in Stevenson's view realism is a technique that can be adapted to any number of stories, genres, forms, it follows that in his view great writers reveal themselves not in their adherence to a prescribed genre or technique, but through their ability to adapt their style to their story. This is precisely what Stevenson had already lauded in Hugo, who, in his opinion, 'stands so far above all his contemporaries,

---

[59] Recent work has analysed the connection between Idealism and Naturalism and shown that Zola was not, in fact, dead to Idealism, especially in his post-Rougon-Macquart books. Toril Moi writes that 'Idealists [...] objected to realism that did not subscribe to idealist aesthetics. This kind of realism came increasingly to be called "naturalism", and in the 1880s, the question at the heart of the culture wars unleashed by naturalism was precisely whether anti-idealist realism [...] could be art.' Toril Moi, *Henrik Ibsen and the Birth of Modernism: Art, Theatre, Philosophy* (Oxford: Oxford University Press, 2006), p. 67.

[60] 'La Littérature nouvelle en France', p. 92. ('The bankruptcy of pseudo-scientific philosophy. The bankruptcy of Naturalism. The renaissance of idealism.')

and so incomparably excels them in richness, breadth, variety, and moral earnestness' (VH, p. 23). Hugo's adaptability resulted in flawed novels, but it also meant that there is an intimate and necessary, yet always changing, connection between *forme* and *fond*, style and matter, in his work. By way of illustration, consider how Stevenson enumerates the faults with Hugo's *L'Homme qui rit*, but in the end concludes that 'when we judge it deliberately, it will be seen that, here again, the story is admirably adapted to the moral. The constructive ingenuity exhibited throughout is almost morbid' (VH, p. 16). Much the same thing could be said of Stevenson's novels.

This same ideal is described in 'A Gossip on Romance' and 'A Humble Remonstrance'. In 'A Gossip on Romance', Stevenson argues for the inseparability of the constitutive elements of art:

> In the highest achievements of the art of words, the dramatic and the pictorial, the moral and the romantic interest, rise and fall together by a common and organic law. Situation is animated with passion, passion clothed upon with situation. Neither exists for itself, but each inheres indissolubly with the other. (p. 125)

'A Humble Remonstrance', on the other hand, emphasises variety of compositional method. Stevenson asserts that with each new subject

> the true artist will vary his method and change the point of attack. That which was in one case an excellence, will become a defect in another; what was the making of one book, will in the next be impertinent or dull.[61]

Zola would not deny that there is a connection between *forme* and *fond*. It is more that in his theory of the novel the connection is pre-established. The creative process described in 'Le Sens du réel' is nothing less than a formula, even allowing that there is always a disconnect between theory and practice:

> Un de nos romanciers naturalistes veut écrire un roman sur le monde des théâtres. Il part de cette idée générale, sans avoir encore un fait ni un personnage. Son premier soin sera de rassembler dans des notes tout ce qu'il peut savoir sur ce monde qu'il veut peindre. Il a connu

---

[61] In *Memories and Portraits & Other Fragments*, pp. 132–43 (p. 137). Hereafter HR. First published in *Longman's Magazine* in 1884.

tel acteur, il a assisté à telle scène. Voilà déjà des documents, les meilleurs, ceux qui ont mûri en lui. Puis, il se mettra en campagne, il fera causer les hommes les mieux renseignés sur la matière, il collectionnera les mots, les histoires, les portraits. Ce n'est pas tout: il ira ensuite aux documents écrits, lisant tout ce qui peut lui être utile. Enfin, il visitera les lieux, vivra quelques jours dans un théâtre pour en connaître les moindres recoins, passera ses soirées dans une loge d'actrice, s'imprégnera le plus possible de l'air ambiant. Et, une fois les documents complétés, son roman, comme je l'ai dit, s'établira de lui-même. Le romancier n'aura qu'à distribuer logiquement les faits. De tout ce qu'il aura entendu se dégagera le bout de drame, l'histoire dont il a besoin pour dresser la carcasse de ses chapitres. [. . .] Faire mouvoir des personnages réels dans un milieu réel, donner au lecteur un lambeau de la vie humaine, tout le roman naturaliste est là.[62]

In this model of the creative process, documents, facts and details reveal the story, and the author's imagination plays a relatively minor

---

[62] pp. 35–6. ('Suppose one of our Naturalist novelists wants to write a novel on the world of the theatre. He sets off from this general idea, without having any facts or characters. His first care is to gather notes of all that he can find out about the world he wishes to depict. He knows such and such an actor, he has watched such and such a play. This is already some documentation, the best kind, for it has ripened within him. Then he will set to work, he will talk to the men who are best informed on the subject, he will collect their expressions, their stories, their portraits. That's not all: next he will turn to written documents, reading everything that could prove useful to him. Finally, he visits the locales, will live for a few days at the theatre to know its deepest recesses, will spend a few evenings in the dressing room of an actress, will steep himself as much as possible in the ambiance. And, once this documentation is complete, his novel, as I have said, will write itself. The novelist need only distribute the facts logically. From all that he has learned, the plot, the story that he needs to shape the framework for his chapters, will emerge. Making realistic characters move in a realistic milieu, giving the reader a scrap of human life: that is the essence of the Naturalist novel.') Compare this with Baudelaire writing in *Salon de 1859*: 'Men who are clever at analysis and sufficiently quick at summing up, can be devoid of imagination. [. . .] It is Imagination that first taught man the moral meaning of colour, of contour, of sound and of scent. [. . .] As it has created the world (so much can be said, I think, even in a religious sense), it is proper that it should govern it. What would be said of a warrior without imagination? that he might make an excellent soldier, but that if he is put in command of an army, he will make no conquests. The case could be compared to that of a poet or a novelist, who took away command of his faculties from the imagination to give it, for example, to his knowledge of language or to his observation of facts.' Translation from *Art in Theory, 1815–1900: An Anthology of Changing Ideas*, ed. by Charles Harrison and Paul Wood with Jason Gaiger (Oxford: Blackwell, 1998), pp. 490–1.

role. For this reason, Arthur Symons refers to Zola's method of writing as a 'filling-up of his outlines'.[63]

A corollary of this belief that documentation is the source of plot is that Naturalist fiction focuses on the contemporary world and on what can be observed. This might explain Stevenson's comment that 'the historical novel is forgotten' (NR, p. 70). This is not to say that Stevenson rejects modernity – far from it; it means that he has an appreciation for older literary traditions and perceives different avenues for adapting them to the nineteenth century. His advice to the 'young writer' is pertinent: 'in this age of the particular, let him [the young writer] remember the ages of the abstract, the great books of the past, the brave men that lived before Shakespeare and before Balzac' (HR, p. 142). To all appearances, then, there is little common ground between Stevenson's conception of literature and Zola's. Yet, none of this takes away from the fact that Stevenson admired and enjoyed Zola's writing when it dealt with 'cavalry charge[s]' and 'batteries under fire' – memorable incidents and adventures – or when it dealt with artists debating their theories of art, as in *L'Œuvre*.

Zola bears the brunt of Stevenson's criticism, but it is obvious that Stevenson was up to date with the French novels published during his lifetime, and that he must have read a fair number of Naturalist texts. Moreover, given that he read at least seven of Zola's novels, there is no reason to suppose that he did not also read others. In addition, while other French authors are mentioned in his essays and letters, there is no definitive way of knowing what books he was exposed to through subscription libraries like Visconti's in Nice or the London Library and Rolandi's in England, through friends and conversations at clubs like The Athenaeum and The Savile, or what he may have read in serials. For example, while he mocks Alphonse Daudet's 'babbling about audible colours and visible sounds' – a clear reference to so-called *écriture artiste* – there is no indication where precisely Stevenson read Daudet 'babbling' on the subject (NR, p. 70). We do know, though, that he regarded Daudet's *Les Rois en exil* highly.[64]

---

[63] *Studies in Two Literatures*, p. 204.
[64] Letter to Alexander Ireland, [Late March 1882], *Letters*, III, p. 302. Stevenson owned four of Daudet's books: *Fromont jeune et Risler aîné* (1874), *Le Nabab* (1877), *Les Rois en exil* (1878) and *Tartarin sur les Alpes* (1885). See EdRLS: Stevenson's Library Database. Margaret Oliphant was also appreciative of Daudet. See her article 'A Few French Novels', which contains a lengthy discussion of Daudet's *Numa Rumestan*. *Blackwood's Edinburgh Magazine*, 130.794 (December 1881), pp. 703–23.

Stevenson was clearly acquainted with Guy de Maupassant's works, too. *Bel-Ami* is mentioned in passing in Stevenson's published correspondence, as is *La Maison Tellier*, which Stevenson describes as 'almost a chief of works. [. . .] Very very funny and well seen.'[65] He also recommended Henry James's 1888 *Fortnightly Review* article on Maupassant to Richard Watson Gilder.[66] Given that Stevenson read Zola's *La Débâcle*, it is highly likely that he would have read *Les Soirées de Médan*, the collection of six short stories about the Franco-Prussian War published in 1880 by Zola, Maupassant, Joris-Karl Huysmans, Henry Céard, Léon Hennique and Paul Alexis, especially since the book was touted at the time as a sort of Naturalist manifesto and spawned many articles in the French press. Edmund Gosse refers to the collection as

> a manifesto by the Naturalists, the most definite and the most defiant which had up to that time been made. It consisted of six short stories, several of which were of remarkable excellence, and all of which awakened an amount of discussion almost unprecedented.[67]

Les Soirées de Médan presents no aesthetic theory, as such, but instead groups these Naturalist tales together, along with a brief preface advertising the authors' common stance. One of the stories, Maupassant's 'Boule de Suif', is to this day considered a tour de force of short fiction; at the time, Gosse called it 'a veritable masterpiece in a new vein' and Henry James deemed it a 'triumph'.[68]

The Maupassant case is pertinent for several reasons, not least of which is Maupassant's predilection for the short form. While Maupassant did write six novels, he is principally known for his short stories. This will not have gone unnoticed by Stevenson, a master of the shorter form, who not only bemoaned Flaubert's 'longueurs', but by his own admission looked 'upon every three-volume novel with a sort of veneration'.[69] As his participation in *Les Soirées de Médan* attests, Maupassant was associated with the Naturalist movement,

---

[65] Letter to George Saintsbury, [February 1891], *Letters*, VII, p. 84; Letter to W.E. Henley, [? June 1884], *Letters*, IV, p. 308. See also EdRLS: Stevenson's Library Database.
[66] [c. 31 March 1888], *Letters*, VI, p. 142.
[67] *French Profiles* (New York: Dodd, Mead and Company, 1905), p. 142.
[68] *French Profiles*, p. 142; *Partial Portraits* (London: Macmillan, 1888), p. 267.
[69] From 'My First Book: *Treasure Island*' (*Treasure Island*, p. xxiv), first published in *The Idler* and *McClure's Magazine* in 1894.

and 'his vision of the world' was, according to Henry James, 'for the most part a vision of ugliness'.[70] Like Stevenson's, however, it was also a vision that admitted the uncanny, and many of his stories, like the famous 'Le Horla', contain supernatural elements. Maupassant's conception of 'the real' was therefore more generous than Zola's. Stevenson himself remarked in an interview that Maupassant is 'suppos[ed] to be the realist of the realists' but has 'gone into the supernatural up to his ears, and does it very well if it comes to that'.[71]

In the preface to the novel *Pierre et Jean* (1888) – which, it appears, prompted Henry James to write his *Fortnightly Review* article – Maupassant diverges from a strictly Zolian vision and elaborates a theory of the novel that is more in line with Stevenson's, inasmuch as it defends the fiction of observation while insisting on individual expression as an absolute. This leads Maupassant to be critical of terms like 'realism' and 'naturalism' and to state that 'les Réalistes de talent devraient s'appeler plutôt des Illusionnistes'.[72] Crucially, he states that 'le vrai peut quelquefois n'être pas vraisemblable' (in other words, what is real is not always plausible), and that 'objectivity' is a 'vilain mot' ('an awful word').[73] There seems little doubt that Maupassant would concur with Stevenson's advice to 'be as ideal or as abstract as you please, you will be none the less veracious' (NR, p. 71).[74] As Stevenson wrote to Charles Warren Stoddard in 1886 about his own tale, *Prince Otto* (1885), 'every story can be made *true* in its own key; any story can be made *false* by the choice of a wrong key of detail and style'.[75] Concerns about the nature of realism were shared on both sides of the Channel, even if the precise terms of the debate varied.

---

[70] *Partial Portraits*, p. 252.
[71] 'Idealism and Realism in Literature. A Talk with Robert Louis Stevenson', *Argus*, 13 September 1890, cited in entry Guy de Maupassant, 'Other Evidence of Ownership', EdRLS: Stevenson's Library Database.
[72] 'Realists of talent should really call themselves Illusionists.'
[73] *Pierre et Jean* (Paris: P. Ollendorff, 1888), pp. xv and xx.
[74] It is interesting to compare Arthur Symons's description of Maupassant with the observations that critics like Schwob and Wyzewa made about Stevenson, which we will come back to in the final chapter. Symons's remarks about the importance of incident to Maupassant could almost be said about Stevenson, were it not for Stevenson's equal interest in character: 'He wanted to tell stories just for the pleasure of telling them; he wanted to concern himself with his story simply as a story; incidents interested him, not ideas nor even characters, and he wanted every incident to be immediately effective.' *Boule de Suif and Other Stories, The Works of Guy de Maupassant*, ed. by Arthur Symons (New York: Bigelow, Smith & Co., 1909), I, p. xii.
[75] 13 February 1886, *Letters*, V, p. 203.

Reading for Pleasure

Stevenson did not write any further essays specifically on French authors or the theory of the novel after his own career as a novelist was established in the mid-1880s. This does not mean that he was no longer curious about contemporary French fiction. In common with many of his contemporaries, he had already rejected the allegedly dainty, provincial plots of the English novel, as is evident in his observation that

> English people of the present day are apt, I know not why, to look somewhat down on incident, and reserve their admiration for the clink of teaspoons and the accents of the curate. It is thought clever to write a novel with no story at all, or at least with a very dull one. (GR, p. 124)

Towards the end of the century, the French novels that were promoted as counter-models to the English novel were associated primarily with Naturalism and Decadence. Stevenson also discards this proposed alternative, as he believed that Naturalism was both devoid of any idealism and in terms of technique confused a literary means with a literary end. In so doing, it had lost sight of the pleasures of the imagination and the pleasures of reading. Thus, while George Moore was busily defending Zola and Naturalism in England in the early 1880s, and Oscar Wilde was bringing an accessible French-style Decadence to English-speaking readers via Dorian Gray and his yellow book in the 1890s, Stevenson's way out of 'the realism problem', his means of reconciling romance and realism, was, in part, to continue to explore the possibilities offered by fiction that defied genre and pointed to new directions for the novel.

Throughout his life, Stevenson devoured French books that deviated from accepted standards of good writing and quality literature and were consequently scorned by both the French and British intellectual classes. This bothered some critics. Sarolea, for example, opines that Stevenson's 'reading is omnivorous and promiscuous, it is uncritical and desultory'.[76] Stevenson was an avid reader of Ponson du Terrail, to whom we owe Rocambole and the rocambolesque; he

---

[76] *Robert Louis Stevenson and France*, p. 37.

and Henley considered translating Gaboriau's *Le Crime d'Orcival*;[77] he consumed the stories of Eugène Sue, described by George Eliot as 'noxious' in their portrayal of 'idealized proletaires';[78] he read Dumas père, Xavier de Montépin, Jules Verne – writers of page-turning genre fiction and popular serial novels. He tells W.E. Henley about Frédéric Soulié's *La Lionne*, describing it as 'another flawed jewel of energy and Drunken Genius',[79] and in 1894 he requested the recently published *Le Roi de la ligue*, Paul Mahalin's pastiche sequel to Dumas's *La Reine Margot*.[80] While in a slump, he wrote to Sidney Colvin in 1891, explaining: 'Thursday, I was better but still out of ability to do aught but read awful trash. This is the time one misses civilization; I wished to send out for some police novels: Montépin would have about suited my frozen brain.'[81] This statement reverses expectations: it does not equate civilisation with access to high culture, but with access to the popular, with bestsellers and commercial literature. Stevenson, the man of culture, longs for civilisation because civilisation is where he can find 'awful trash' to read. This serves to confirm Andrew Lang's statement that 'there was nothing of the "cultured person" about' Stevenson – he was democratic in his reading. As such, Stevenson would no doubt have agreed with Lang's contention that 'what is good, what is permanent, may be found in fiction of every *genre*' and that 'there is still room for romance, and love of romance, in civilized human nature'.[82]

The triolets that Stevenson wrote about Montépin in 1883 foreshadow this opposition by humorously contrasting the pleasures of the mind and the heart, the intellect and the emotions:

---

[77] W.E. Henley letter to Charles Baxter, 25 August 1877, *The Selected Letters of W.E. Henley*, ed. by Atkinson, p. 41. *Le Crime d'Orcival* was published in *London* magazine from 22 September 1877 to 1 June 1878. Henley edited *London*, but there is no evidence that Stevenson was involved in the translation.

[78] 'The Natural History of German Life', in *Essays of George Eliot*, ed. by Thomas Pinney (New York: Columbia University Press, 1963; London: Routledge and Kegan Paul, 1963), pp. 266–99 (p. 272).

[79] [? 1 February 1883], *Letters*, IV, p. 65. He owned four books by Soulié. See EdRLS: Stevenson's Library Database.

[80] Letter to Edward L. Burlingame, 29 January 1894, *Letters*, VIII, p. 237.

[81] 18 April [1891], *Letters*, VII, pp. 98–9. Elsewhere, Stevenson says that he 'forgot [Zola's *La Bête humaine*] as I would forget a Montépin'. Letter to Edmund Gosse, 10 June 1893, *Letters*, VIII, p. 104.

[82] 'Recollections of Robert Louis Stevenson', *The North American Review*, 160.459 (1895), 185–94 (p. 188); 'Realism and Romance', *Contemporary Review*, 52 (1887), 683–93 (pp. 685 and 692).

> Si je l'aime, ce Montépin,
> J'aime de cœur mais pas de tête!
> J'en atteste le roi Pépin
> Si je l'aime, ce Montépin!
> Son meilleur roman, le Sapin,
> Je n'y crois pas, mais je l'achête [sic]!
> Si je l'aime, ce Montépin,
> J'aime de cœur mais pas de tête.

This playful triolet is surprisingly complex. The AB rhyme declares that 'If I love that Montépin / It's with my heart and not my head!'; Stevenson plays on the meaning of 'si' in the fourth line, where it is closer to 'Yes, I love that Montépin!' 'Sapin' and 'Pépin' are likely an in-joke referring to Montépin's 1880 novel, *Le Fiacre no. 13*. 'Sapin' ('pine tree') was slang for 'fiacre' ('stagecoach'). There were several historical 'Roi Pépins', but Stevenson is playing on words: 'pépin' also means 'seed', which was slang for being pregnant ('avoir avalé un pépin'). In Montépin's *Le Fiacre no. 13*, a baby is left on a stagecoach. The triolet proclaims that this was Montépin's best story, but in line 6, Stevenson confesses, 'I don't believe it, but I buy it!'

In Stevenson's third triolet about Montépin, he addresses Montépin's style. According to the poem, it's always the same old song in Montépin's novels ('Il n'y a que de la rengaine') and their style is full of clichés ('En fait de style, des clichés!'). In lines 5–6, Stevenson states that 'we all make fun of them / but we prefer them to Taine!' The AB rhyme uses the popular word 'liché, which is derived from 'lécher' (to lick), and here means something to the effect that Montépin's 'books were easy to digest' or 'were gobbled up' by readers:

> Ses romans sont pas mal lichés.
> Il n'y a que de la rengaine!
> En fait de style, des clichés!
> Ses romans sont pas mal lichés,
> Nous nous en sommes tous fichés
> Mais nous les préférons à Taine!
> Ses romans sont pas mal lichés.
> Il n'y a que de la rengaine![83]

Stevenson's stylistic sure-footedness and playful allusion to Montépin's *Le Fiacre no. 13* stand in stark contrast to the poems' observations

---

[83] Letter to W.E. Henley, [c. 11 January 1883], *Letters*, IV, p. 50.

on Montépin's lack of refinement. Stevenson writes in French using a French poetic form, and he plays with the form to comic effect while simultaneously commenting on the pleasures of reading unsophisticated literature. Reading Montépin is a fundamentally pleasurable, not necessarily intellectual, pursuit, but it is nonetheless a pursuit that contributed to Stevenson's writing.

Stevenson's taste for du Boisgobey is similar and shows how popular fiction was an escape for him. Following the death of Stevenson's father, Lloyd Osbourne wrote to a family friend saying that Stevenson 'has sworn off every kind of care, responsibility or decency and will do nothing but read the novels of du Boisgobey'.[84] Stevenson did so even though in 1884 he had already complained that the allure of du Boisgobey was waning:

Even le bon Fortuné has faded and gone out. Once I could sing

Je me loue d'être né –
 Je l'affirme et je le signe.
O que je suis Fortuné
 –Je le suis de ligne en ligne.

But now the light is sinking: he is dull.[85]

Good stories have a salutary effect, regardless of their stylistic shortcomings. As Stevenson explains to John Meiklejohn in 1880, 'when I suffer in mind, stories are my refuge; I take them like opium'.[86] Would style on its own produce the same effect? Sometimes; sometimes not. Style notwithstanding, Stevenson actively disliked Flaubert's unfinished *Bouvard et Pécuchet*, which he called 'a most loathsome work'.[87] Thus, despite the effort he put in to achieving his own style, Stevenson largely rejected the notion that style was sufficient to carry a novel. As Harriet Dorothea MacPherson observes

---

[84] *Letters*, V, p. 431, n. 1.
[85] Letter to W.E. Henley, [? June 1884], *Letters*, IV, pp. 307–8. It is really no surprise that du Boisgobey's appeal was waning by this point. There are seven books by du Boisgobey in the EdRLS: Stevenson's Library Database: *Les Collets noirs* (1874), *La Peau d'un autre* (1877), *L'Équipage du diable* (1881), *La Revanche de Fernande* (1882), *Le Crime de l'omnibus* (1882), *Pignon maudit* (1882) and *Margot la Balafrée* (1884).
[86] 1 February 1880, *Letters*, III, p. 61.
[87] Letter to W.E. Henley, [Late April 1881], *Letters*, III, p. 174.

about Stevenson's assessment of Flaubert, Stevenson 'reveled in the beauty of Flaubert's phrasing, but here and there we find a suggestion that R.L.S. rather wearied of the lack of freedom of thought behind the form'.[88] In his reading of these popular novels, Stevenson considers style independently from matter in a way that confirms Kate Flint's assertion that among middle-class nineteenth-century readers, 'increasingly, a distinction developed between intellectually, psychologically and aesthetically demanding fiction, and that which primarily served the needs of escapism and relaxation'.[89] Stevenson appreciated both types of fiction and strove to merge them in his own writing. Indeed, this reading of French detective fiction and sensation novels for sheer pleasure is part of Stevenson's literary apprenticeship, for we know from Lang's recollections that the two men 'once plotted a Boisgobey story together'.[90] In addition, as noted at the beginning of this chapter, Stevenson readily admitted that Jules Verne was without style, but he could not stop himself from reading his books. Stevenson read Montépin, du Boisgobey and Verne for intrigue and incident, and even though he himself is a renowned stylist, in his attempt to merge aesthetics and reading pleasure Stevenson rejects both English novels with 'very dull' plots and Flaubert's ideal of a 'book about nothing'.

Stevenson's writings on French literary history and his tastes in French literature are tied to his development as an author whose generic preferences did not coincide with those of his time, which, as far as the 'serious' novel was concerned, was above all the age of realism and Naturalism. He confessed to Will H. Low, for example, that he wanted to 'get free of this prison yard of the abominably ugly, where I take my daily exercise with my contemporaries'.[91] When it comes to so-called quality non-Naturalist literature, as opposed to popular fiction, Stevenson had a taste for novelists who are little read today – at least by the wider English-speaking reading public, despite their importance to French literature and literary

---

[88] *R.L. Stevenson: A Study in French Influence* (New York: Institute for French Studies, 1930), p. 37.
[89] 'The Victorian Novel and its Readers', in *The Cambridge Companion to the Victorian Novel*, ed. by Deirdre David (Cambridge: Cambridge University Press, 2001), pp. 17–36 (p. 20).
[90] 'Recollections of Robert Louis Stevenson', p. 189. Details about the projected novel *Where is Rose?* are outlined in Lang's letters to Stevenson in 1882. See Letters 14–22, in *Dear Stevenson*, ed. by Demoor, pp. 48–60.
[91] 2 January 1886, *Letters*, V, p. 163.

history. These include Villiers de l'Isle-Adam (*Contes cruels*, 1883) and Anatole France, whose *Le Crime de Sylvestre Bonnard* and *La Rotisserie de la reine Pédauque* Stevenson ordered in 1894, and of whom he became 'a faithful adorer'.[92] He also had a decided taste for Jules Barbey d'Aurevilly and Paul Bourget, two authors who are notable for their complicated, nuanced conservative Catholicism, which is proof of Stevenson's own open-minded (or small 'c' catholic) tastes.[93] Stevenson praised Barbey d'Aurevilly, an esoteric, independent, Catholic dandy, and dedicated *Across the Plains* (1892) to Bourget.

Religious differences notwithstanding, it is not hard to see certain similarities between Barbey d'Aurevilly and Stevenson insofar as Barbey was, in terms of his impact, a central figure in the artistic circles of the day, but was always also marginal, belonging to (or perhaps accepted by) no group, subscribing to no literary manifesto. Huysmans's des Esseintes describes Barbey as a pariah who 'appartenait plus, à tous les points de vue, à la littérature séculière qu'à cette autre chez laquelle il revendiquait une place qu'on lui déniait'.[94] Barbey wrote books that through their blend of romance, supernaturalism and decadence defied generic categorisation and worked against the dominant realist strain in French literature. Towards the end of his life, while he was writing *Catriona* (1893), Stevenson went on something of a Barbey d'Aurevilly binge: he ordered *Le Chevalier des Touches* (1864) and the short story collection *Les Diaboliques* (1874) from Edward Burlingame in March 1892, and then asked Charles Scribner in July of that same year to send him *Un prêtre marié* (1865), *L'Amour impossible* (1841) and *Ce qui ne meurt pas* (1884).[95] Stevenson was revisiting Barbey, however. In 1884, he had written to Colvin, asking if he had 'ever read [. . .] the incredible Barbey d'Aurevilly?' Stevenson

---

[92] Letter to Charles Baxter, 18 June [1894], *Letters*, VIII, p. 308; Letter to Henry James, 7 July 1894, *Letters*, VIII, p. 314.
[93] Graham Good also mentions 'Stevenson's catholicity of taste in reading'. 'Rereading Robert Louis Stevenson', p. 49.
[94] *À Rebours*, ed. by Pierre Waldner (Paris: Garnier-Flammarion, 1978), p. 192. ('Belonged more, from every point of view, to secular literature than to the other in which he was for claiming a place that was denied him.' Translation from *Against the Grain* (New York: Dover Publications, 1969), p. 151.)
[95] Letter to Edward L. Burlingame, [30 March 1892], *Letters*, VII, p. 257; Letter to Charles Scribner, [14 July 1892], *Letters*, VII, p. 334.

calls Barbey 'a Psychological Poe', elaborating on the reasons for his taste for *Ce qui ne meurt pas*:

> I own with pleasure I prefer him with all his folly, rot, sentiment and mixed metaphors, to the whole of the modern school in France. It makes me laugh, when it's nonsense; and when he gets an effect (though it's still nonsense and mere Poëry – not poesy) it wakens me. *Ce qui ne meurt pas* nearly killed me with laughing, and left me – well, it left me very nearly admiring the old ass. At least, it's the kind of thing, one feels one couldn't do.[96]

In another letter to Colvin, this time in 1893, Stevenson expresses a preference for Barbey's 'Norman stories'.[97] One such story is *Le Chevalier des Touches*, a tale whose narration emphasises storytelling in much the same way as works like *New Arabian Nights* (1882) and *More New Arabian Nights* (1885): the narrator relates how six characters – of whom he is one – are gathered in a room listening to another character, a woman who had fought as a man, tell a story about her involvement in an episode of anti-Republican, pro-Royalist Chouannerie to save the Chevalier des Touches from hanging. It features the mysterious, slightly off-kilter countess of Lathallan, a noblewoman who is descended from a Scottish clan, but who has become detached from reality following the events being recounted, during which her fiancé was killed. Each character adds to the tale, which is being recounted because of an apparent sighting of the Chevalier, but it is initially unclear whether it was the Chevalier himself – gone mad – who was seen, or a revenant. Importantly, in this letter to Colvin Stevenson's discussion of *Le Chevalier des Touches*, *L'Ensorcelée* (1854) and 'Le Rideau cramoisi' from *Les Diaboliques* is immediately followed by musings on his own contributions to literature:

> I wonder exceedingly if I have done anything at all good; and who can tell me? And why I should wish to know? In so little a while, I, and the English language, and the bones of my descendants will have ceased to be a memory! And yet – and yet – one would like to leave an image for a few years upon men's minds – for fun.[98]

---

[96] 9 March 1884, *Letters*, IV, pp. 246–7.
[97] 6 June 1893, *Letters*, VIII, p. 91.
[98] 6 June 1893, *Letters*, VIII, p. 92.

'For fun': the pleasure of reading is still foremost in his mind, even when he is reading more refined (but flawed) fiction. Stevenson's reading of Barbey, a genre-defying yet literary author, prompts questioning of his own talent. Who is qualified to judge Stevenson's books? Readers, surely, for they love a good yarn? Or is it authors, those who can appreciate craftsmanship? And why does Stevenson want to know what others make of his books, anyway? The answer is that he is concerned with his place in literary history, with being a 'hand upon the dial of a clock'.

Stevenson's introduction to Bourget's work came thanks to Henry James, who sent him Bourget's *Sensations d'Italie*, with which he was quickly smitten. Once again, the pleasure of reading is foremost in his mind: 'I have gone crazy over Bourget's *Sensations d'Italie*; hence the enclosed dedication, a mere cry of gratitude for the best fun I've had over a new book this ever so!'[99] The *Across the Plains* dedication stands out among Stevenson's works, since most of his other books are dedicated to family members or friends, rather than authors whom he had never met. Stevenson, with humour and perhaps a bit of false modesty, seems aware of possible awkwardness:

> I wonder if this exquisite fellow, all made of fiddlestrings and intelligence, could bear any of my bald prose. If you think he could, ask Colvin to send him a copy of these last essays of mine, when they appear; and tell le Bourget they go to him from a South Sea Island as literal *hommage*: I have read no new book for years that gave me the same literary thrill as his *Sensations d'Italie*. If (as I imagine) my cut-and-dry literature would be death to him, and worse than death – journalism – be silent on the point. For I have a great curiosity to know him, and if he doesn't know my work, I shall have the better chance of making his acquaintance.[100]

On reading *Sensations d'Italie*, Stevenson 'beg[s] for Bourget's *Essais de Psychologie Contemporaine, Nouveaux Essais* do, and *Études et Portraits*: four volumes of Bourget'.[101] He also owned Bourget's short story collection, *Un scrupule* (1893).[102] Bourget was a theorist of decadence whom Max Nordau qualified with customary bombast, but erroneously, as the 'repulsive theorist of the most abandoned

---

[99] Letter to Sidney Colvin, [8 December 1891], *Letters*, VII, p. 205.
[100] Letter to Henry James, 7 December [1891], *Letters*, VII, p. 211.
[101] Letter to Edward L. Burlingame, [? 8 December] 1891, *Letters*, VII, p. 197.
[102] EdRLS: Stevenson's Library Database.

anti-social ego-mania'.[103] This opinion likely stems from similar attitudes to those that saw Bourget cited in the Vizetelly trials. Bourget's essays charmed Stevenson. Just as Stevenson kept up with French literature, Bourget spent time in England fraternising with authors like Walter Pater and Henry James and using his interest in British culture as a means of elaborating his theories of decadent cosmopolitanism.[104] What is more, Bourget's breakthrough novel, *Le Disciple* (1889) deals with precisely the moral and ethical responsibilities incumbent upon 'masters' who espouse Positivist determinism and who advocate for cold observation of phenomena, without providing their 'disciples' with a moral framework for interpreting them. Bourget addresses the preface of *Le Disciple* to a generic young man of 1889 and calls on his generation to chart a new morality that moves beyond cynical Positivism and nihilistic fin-de-siècle epicurean intellectualism. One of the titular disciple's philosophical treatises is titled *Contribution à la multiplication du Moi*, which would not have gone unnoticed by Stevenson, whose *Strange Case of Dr. Jekyll and Mr. Hyde* dealt with the subject of multiple identities, and who also as early as 1873 declared 'my whole game is morality now'.[105] Indeed, in a letter to J.M. Barrie, Stevenson refers to Bourget as André, the name of his stand-in character in *Le Disciple*, Count André de Jussat, and the name of the protagonist of his early novel *André Cornélis* (1887).[106]

Although the 1870 and 1880 essays represent Stevenson's most sustained public engagement with French literature and show his preoccupation with finding his place in literary history and developing an aesthetic theory that merges romance and realism, he continued to read widely and request contemporary books that were pushing beyond the bounds of Naturalism. For instance, in 1893 he requested a copy of Rachilde's *L'Animale* (1893), which foreshadows another literary crossing.[107] Rachilde defied all norms, presented herself as a man, and was famous for the novel *Monsieur Vénus* (1884). This gender crossing would surely have been of interest to Stevenson, the

---

[103] *Degeneration* [*Entartung*, 1892] (Lincoln/London: University of Nebraska Press, 1993), p. 279.
[104] See Juliet Simpson, 'Bourget's Oxford Aesthetes: Towards Decadent Cosmopolitanism', *Comparative Critical Studies*, 10.2 (2013), 183–97.
[105] Letter to Charles Baxter, 4 December [1873], *Letters*, I, p. 395.
[106] [? Late March 1894], *Letters*, VIII, p. 258. According to Dury, 'in Bourget, Stevenson would have found ideas that were close to his own about the moral nature of the artist'. 'Stevenson and Bourget: An Enigma', EdRLS blog, 3 May 2020, available at <https://edrls.wordpress.com/2020/05/03/stevenson-and-bourget-an-enigma/>.
[107] Letter to Edward L. Burlingame, 16 October 1893, *Letters*, VIII, p. 176.

creator of characters like Viscount Anne in *St. Ives* (1897), Colonel Geraldine in *The Suicide Club* (1878), or even Joanna/Jack Sedley in *The Black Arrow* (1883/1888). What is more, Rachilde was married to Alfred Vallette, the director of *Mercure de France*, which would later publish several articles on Stevenson, serialise 'The Isle of Voices' (1893), and publish the translation of *The Black Arrow*. Who knows how the Stevenson–Rachilde–Vallette literary relationship could have developed, and whether it might have altered Stevenson's publication history in France.

Stevenson also requested a copy of Joris-Karl Huysmans's *Là-bas* (1891) soon after it was reviewed in the *Figaro*.[108] The *Figaro* review was written by Maurice de Fleury, a psychiatrist and literary critic who later entered the Académie française. He describes Huysmans as someone trying to shake off the Naturalist mantle and move into a more refined literature: 'Bien des jeunes le considèrent le maître de la littérature raffinée, supra-naturaliste, dont ils souhaitent l'avènement.'[109] Moving beyond Naturalist materialism is a core concern of *Là-bas*, which opens *in medias res* during a conversation between the main character, Durtal, and his friend, des Hermies, on the (de)merits of Naturalism:

> Vouloir se confiner dans les buanderies de la chair, rejeter le supra-sensible, dénier le rêve, ne pas même comprendre que la curiosité de l'art commence là où les sens cessent de servir! Tu lèves les épaules, mais voyons, qu'a-t-il donc vu, ton naturalisme, dans tous ces décourageants mystères qui nous entourent? Rien. –Quand il s'est agi d'expliquer une passion quelconque, quand il a fallu sonder une plaie, déterger même le plus bénin des bobos de l'âme, il a tout mis sur le compte des appétits et des instincts. Rut et coup de folie, ce sont là ses seules diathèses. En somme, il n'a fouillé que des dessous de nombril et banalement divagué dès qu'il s'approchait des aines; c'est un herniaire de sentiments, un bandagiste d'âme et voilà tout! Puis, vois-tu, Durtal, il n'est pas qu'inexpert et obtus, il est fétide, car il a prôné cette vie moderne atroce, vanté l'américanisme nouveau des mœurs, abouti à l'éloge de la force brutale, à l'apothéose du coffre-fort. Par un prodige d'humilité, il a révéré le goût nauséeux

---

[108] Letter to Edward L. Burlingame, [Early November 1891], *Letters*, VII, p. 189.
[109] 'Le Satanisme à la Salpêtrière', *Le Figaro*, 24 April 1891, p. 1. ('Many young people consider him the master of refined, supra-Naturalist literature, whose advent they are awaiting.') *Là-bas* was serialised in *L'Écho de Paris* starting on 16 February 1891.

des foules, et, par cela même, il a répudié le style, rejeté toute pensée altière, tout élan vers le surnaturel et l'au-delà. Il a si bien représenté les idées bourgeoises qu'il semble, ma parole, issu de l'accouplement de Lisa, la charcutière du *Ventre de Paris*, et de Homais![110]

In response to his friend's rant, Durtal offers a half-hearted defence of Naturalism, based primarily on the fact that it had proved useful in ridding French literature of the residual trappings of Romanticism. Privately, he remains baffled by the appropriate novelistic path forward, perplexed about how the novel will evolve:

Durtal ne voyait pas, en dehors du naturalisme, un roman qui fût possible, à moins d'en revenir aux explosibles fariboles des romantiques, aux œuvres lanugineuses des Cherbuliez et des Feuillet, ou bien encore aux lacrymales historiettes des Theuriet et des Sand![111]

In Huysmans's case, the rejection of Naturalism took the form of *Làbas* itself, which is the story of an author who is writing a book on the fifteenth-century murderer, Gilles de Rais. There is no reason to believe that Stevenson shared des Hermies's ideas on the 'Americanisation of manners' or the 'nauseous taste of the masses', but Stevenson

---

[110] *Là-bas* (Paris: Tresse & Stock, 1891), pp. 2–3. ('To willingly confine oneself to the wash-houses of the flesh, to reject the suprasensible, to deny the ideal, not even to realise that the mystery of art begins right there, where the senses cease to be of any use. You shrug your shoulders, but come, what has your Naturalism revealed to us about all those disheartening mysteries that surround us? Nothing. When it has to explain a passion of any kind, when it has to probe some trauma, to treat even the most innocuous of the soul's cuts and bruises, it puts everything down to the account of physical appetites and instincts. [. . .] And then you see Durtal, it's not just inept and dull, it's rotten. It's extolled our awful modern way of life, vaunted the current Americanisation of our manners, and ended up eulogising brute force in its deification of the cash-register. By a miracle of humility it has exalted the nauseous taste of the masses, and, as a result, repudiated style and rejected every high-minded thought, every yearning towards the transcendental and the world beyond. It has represented the ideals of the bourgeoisie so well, I swear it seems to be the product of a coupling between Lisa, the pork-butcher in *Le Ventre de Paris*, and Monsieur Homais . . .'. Translation from *Là-bas*, trans. by Brendan King (Sawtry: Dedalus, 2001), pp. 17–18.)
[111] *Là-bas*, pp. 5–6. ('Durtal couldn't see what form the novel could possibly take outside of Naturalism, unless it was to return to the inflated nonsense of the Romantics, the adolescent productions of Cherbuliez and of Feuillet, or to the tear-jerking tales of Theuriet and George Sand.' *Là-bas*, trans. by King, p. 20.)

did share Durtal's confusion and desire to explore avenues for updating the novel.

Sarolea finds fault in the 'strange course of French literature which Stevenson went through',[112] but Stevenson's course makes sense when considered as a means of finding a balance between realism and romance, between storytelling and aestheticism, between nineteenth-century-based conceptions of national literature and older literary traditions. While presenting his own aesthetic beliefs and situating himself within the history of the novel, Stevenson critiques both French literature's misunderstanding of the principle of realism and its drift towards decadence. His French essays and his essays on the novel are important documents in the history of literary relations between Britain and France in the nineteenth century, and Stevenson should be positioned beside the likes of Arnold, Symons, James and Saintsbury in analyses of the development of the novel across Franco-British literary borders. Stevenson's engagement with French literature explores alternatives to the type of literary Naturalism that was taking hold in late-nineteenth-century France and that was spreading to Britain via authors like George Moore and translators and publishers like the Vizetellys. Time and again we see Stevenson appreciating an author's storytelling qualities while remaining perfectly aware of stylistic and other shortcomings, trying to balance readability with artistry. As the next chapter will show, Stevenson was not solely interested in matters of genre as far as French literature was concerned: he also studied matters of form and style. What ultimately emerges is a picture of an author attempting to blend realist romance with a style worthy of French Aestheticism. For this very reason, he would be embraced by French critics at the turn of the century.

---

[112] *Robert Louis Stevenson and France*, p. 37.

Chapter 2

Stevenson as a Writer of French

(*que diable!* let us have style, anyway)[1]

There is something, or there seems to be something, in the very air of France that communicates the love of style. Precision, clarity, the cleanly and crafty employment of material, a grace in the handling, apart from any value in the thought, seem to be acquired by the mere residence; or if not acquired, become at least the more appreciated. The air of Paris is alive with this technical inspiration.[2]

We have already examined some of the ways in which Stevenson responded to debates in French literature as he attempted not only to situate himself within literary history, but to develop his ideas about genre at a time when the novel was rapidly evolving and new movements were emerging. This chapter looks at Stevenson as a writer of French and explores how he plays with French in his correspondence, how he incorporates French and discussions of language difference into his fiction and non-fiction, how he imitated French style at the beginning of his writing career, and how this early apprenticeship impacted his future writing. In so doing, it aims to study the creative process whereby French and French literature contributed to Stevenson's writing voice and to the disruption of the textual stability of realism in favour of aesthetic variation and stylistic self-awareness. As R.L. Abrahamson reminds us, 'there were all those times as a sedulous ape, when books were not companions, or therapy, or research, but textbooks on style'.[3] Ultimately, I hope to demonstrate that for Stevenson, language contact and transnational literary cross-pollination are means not only

---

[1] Letter to Edmund Gosse, [23 January 1880], *Letters*, III, p. 53.
[2] 'Fontainebleau', p. 103.
[3] 'Living in a Book: RLS as an Engaged Reader', in *Robert Louis Stevenson: Writer of Boundaries*, ed. by Ambrosini and Dury, pp. 13–22 (p. 15).

of perfecting his style, in all its playful, exuberant, striking experimentation, but of challenging the domination of the realist novel by opening it up to the possibilities of stylistically self-aware romance where multiple voices can coexist.

Stevenson's life as a writer of French began at an early age: he first used schoolboy French to comic effect in correspondence to his parents when he was thirteen years old.[4] Thereafter, he frequently turned to French in letters that display considerable linguistic virtuosity, as well as a marked predilection for transforming life into art. Many of these early, linguistically playful letters were written while Stevenson was in Britain, meaning that his use of French was not contingent upon being in France. Later, in the South Seas, French remained a part of Stevenson's daily life. Belle Strong, his step-daughter and amanuensis, recorded in her journal that on the day Stevenson died she 'heard him and Austin on the verandah by his study making a great noise over their French lesson, learning a little French dialogue to recite at Christmas'.[5]

Stevenson's friends noticed his propensity for French and how naturally it came to him. In his memoirs, Will H. Low recalls how, during a conversation about Balzac in Paris, Stevenson, 'hardly conscious of it', slipped into French, 'his sense of the proper word and the fit phrase leading him into this excursion into a foreign language'.[6] In a letter to Charles Baxter, Stevenson humorously uses the vocabulary of addiction to describe French as a secret pleasure to be suppressed:

> *Pouah! enfin, c'est assez, n'est-ce pas?* I don't know that I am very fit to write and I have a hideous tendency to relapse into bad French which I mean to resist and to keep on the Queen's Highway and Queen's English if I can.[7]

To the benefit of his future readers, keeping on the Queen's English was not really on Stevenson's agenda. His interest in language for its own sake and his desire to experiment with form meant that his private writing and his public texts were often exuberantly multilingual and multiliterary.

---

[4] 12 November 1863, *Letters*, I, p. 98.
[5] *Letters*, VIII, p. 401.
[6] *A Chronicle of Friendships: 1873–1900* (New York: Charles Scribner's Sons, 1908), p. 59.
[7] 28 April 1872, *Letters*, I, p. 228.

Unlike his father, Thomas Stevenson, who learned French under Victor de Fivas, the author of several books including *New Grammar of French Grammars*, Stevenson's knowledge of French was acquired mainly through conversation in France, especially in Menton during the winter of 1873–4.[8] By January 1874, he told his mother: 'I speak little else but French now; so you may fancy there is not as much grammar comes from between my teeth in the twenty-four hours as would cover a sixpenny piece. I am more fluent however.'[9] Indeed, by Lloyd Osbourne's account, Stevenson spoke 'French as fluently as his own language'.[10] Graham Balfour reports that Stevenson's 'French master at Mentone on his second visit gave him no regular lessons, but merely talked to him in French'. This immersion no doubt appealed to Stevenson, whose talent as a conversationalist has been repeatedly noted, and the comments he makes in his letters suggest that he was happy to learn holistically and accept occasional grammatical doubts. Balfour claims that 'in every language that he ever learned, the rules of its grammar remained unknown to him, however correctly he might use its idioms'.[11] This does not mean that Stevenson's French was ungrammatical; it means that he had little classroom knowledge of French. What self-doubt exists, however, is offset by self-deprecation, as when Stevenson explains that speaking French 'is not exactly an advantage as far as personal brilliancy is concerned'.[12]

Stevenson downplayed his own grasp of French grammar, but there is a sense that he revelled in the freedom to experiment with language and, by extension, with literature. Whatever self-perceived deficiencies Stevenson's French may have contained in terms of grammatical accuracy, they are more than made up for by his obvious, joyful idiomatic ease; the very fact that he plays with French testifies to this. Above all, Stevenson gives the impression of having had fun with French. From very early on, he made the most of the performative, theatrical aspects of language play, and it is telling that the first use of French in his correspondence appears in a stage direction in a mock dialogue sent to his parents, in which the French refers to laughter: 'Mr Hunter (en riant). Collie be quiet or I'll lick you.'[13] The

---

[8] Letter to James Dick, [? Late July 1887], *Letters*, V, p. 434, n. 1.
[9] [17 January 1874], *Letters*, I, p. 450.
[10] 'Stevenson at Thirty-Four', in *Prince Otto*, pp. vii–xi (p. viii).
[11] *The Life of Robert Louis Stevenson*, I, pp. 55 and 61.
[12] Letter to his Mother, 11 January 1874, *Letters*, I, p. 431.
[13] [September or October 1863], *Letters*, I, p. 96.

same technique is used in another letter, this time from Wick, where Stevenson describes a visit with friends in terms of dramatis personae who include 'père Russel', 'mère Russel', 'fille Russel' and the detail that '*c'est la mère qui parle*'.[14] Stories are being recounted in these private letters, and in both examples, French is used as a playful authorial comment to frame the action. These are early examples of Stevenson's typical switches in perspective and point of view.

Playing with French

The way that language is used in private letters is necessarily different from and freer than the way it is used in poems or essays or novels. Nevertheless, examining Stevenson's letters provides a fuller understanding of how his writing voice was fertilised by French, and it also provides insight into stylistic features of his published works. His letters offer examples of how Stevenson turned life into literature through language play that works against realist representation. More formal aspects of Stevenson's style will be dealt with in subsequent sections; for the moment, I would like to focus on the playful side of Stevenson's French voice, things like his phonetic spellings, his calques, and his use of French idiom and slang. The difference is one of spontaneity versus control: while some of his published works and unpublished prose poems contain deliberate, controlled attempts to adopt French literary style and experiment with artistic form, his letters are personal and spontaneous eruptions of language and raise different interpretative issues. The spontaneity and playfulness of the letters is particularly revealing because, as Annette R. Federico observes, in terms of his novels 'Stevenson was a studious formalist, but almost nothing he wrote seemed labored.'[15] This begs the question how spontaneity and a documented interest in literary form and style coincide.

In letters to French-speaking anglophone friends of the same age, Stevenson frequently used phonetic spellings, often to mock English tourists who spoke French using English phonology. The woeful French pronunciation he records is a source of intentional humour – as it is in some of his novels, too – but it also relates to

---

[14] Letter to his Mother, [19 September 1868], *Letters*, I, p. 156.
[15] *Thus I Lived with Words: Robert Louis Stevenson and the Writer's Life* (Iowa City: University of Iowa Press, 2017), p. 45.

his experimentation with style more generally insofar as it foregrounds sound and texture. Most of the instances of phonetic spellings are found in letters to close friends – Will H. Low, W.E. Henley, Charles Baxter – and they bear witness to a distinct interest in the sound systems that make up a language. He addresses a letter written from his home, La Solitude, in Hyères, 'La Solitood, Highairs–the Palm-trees / Var-a-non-Var. Frrrrance', drawing attention to English, French and Scottish rhoticity.[16] In a letter from San Francisco, he asks about the payment for 'The Pavilion on the Links' (1880) from *Cornhill Magazine*: 'Combiang pour le Pavillium? J'ai deseer connayter ce petty detail pour several reasons' (*Combien pour le Pavillon? Je désire connaître ce détail pour several reasons* [How much for the Pavilion? I want to know this detail for several reasons]).[17] A letter to his cousin Bob Stevenson, with whom he had previously spent time in France, contains all manner of creative phonetic renderings meant to comically reproduce a conversation with his wife Fanny ('Oo ay Margaret?' [*Où est Margaret?*]), but also recollections of Will H. Low ('Jooay voo ose eshek? Say le sool playseer doo mond' [*Jouez-vous aux échecs? C'est le seul plaisir du monde*]). The letter ends with a tour de force of comic transliteration:

> Jaycree tray faseelmong le Frongsay kong je me met com voo voyay la trongsleeterassheong ay shows faceel a poo de shows pray; ay oon person de kelkangtelle-shongs devray faseelmong parlay avek poo d'aksong appry dooz lessong. Poorkwaw ne pa l'ongsaynyay d'appry la maytood Stevenson?[18]

> (J'écris très facilement le français quand je m'y mets. Comme vous voyez la translittération est chose facile à peu de choses près; et une personne de quelque intelligence devrait facilement parler avec peu d'accent après douze leçons. Pourquoi ne pas l'enseigner d'après la méthode Stevenson?)

> (I can easily write in French when I put my mind to it. As you can see, transliteration is fairly easy, and a person of some limited intelligence should easily be able to speak French with little accent after twelve lessons. Why not teach French using the Stevenson method?)

---

[16] Letter to W.E. Henley, [Late May 1883], *Letters*, IV, p. 128.
[17] Letter to W.E. Henley, 23 January 1880, *Letters*, III, p. 50.
[18] Letter to Bob Stevenson and Family, 31 December [1883], *Letters*, IV, p. 229.

The opposition – or incongruity – between how the words should sound according to English and French sound/letter correspondence and how they do sound emphasises the orality of language. This playful momentary assumption of a persona with barbarous French pronunciation is acceptable for a personal letter or the conversation between good friends that it imitates. It is rarely going to be acceptable in fiction, however. In fiction, this kind of incongruity could be a potential barrier to comprehension: there is pleasure to be had in the deciphering, but making language a game can mean that understanding is deferred for those who are not in on the joke. Here, though, the mockery establishes a bond with Bob, who is Stevenson's equal: it mocks the pretence that a language can be learned 'appry dooz lessong'. It also demonstrates that Stevenson is favouring spoken language over grammar-based written language. This type of writing draws attention to surfaces – to spelling, to accent – such that language-as-play and pleasure becomes part of the message being conveyed. Drawing attention to accent highlights spoken language and interaction.

Stevenson's letters and early published works are also peppered with calques and borrowings that function on the level of semantics rather than phonetics. Calques are usually unconscious signs of unintended linguistic interference between two distinct languages; as such, they are perceived as something to be avoided because they suggest a lack of linguistic mastery. For Stevenson, however, Gallicisms and Franglais are both an intentional source of incongruous humour and evidence of his wit and stylistic self-awareness: there is satisfaction to be gained from transgressing linguistic laws and pleasure to be derived from occupying the space between English and French. Stevenson 'cotoyai'd' (mixed with) Englishmen in Earraid (Scotland), 'natated' (swam) in Belgium, and 'was *accablé* with fatigue' in France.[19] Sometimes he draws attention to these foreign words through underlining; sometimes they are assimilated wholesale into English with no attempt to mark them as different. The countless examples range from comic interjections ('my eye' [*mon œil*]) and lighthearted disagreements ('you do not abound in my sense' [*abonder dans mon sens*/agree with me]),[20] to discussions of

---

[19] Letters to his Parents, 5 August 1870, *Letters*, I, p. 199; Letter to his Mother, 25 [July] 1872, *Letters*, I, p. 232; Letter to his Mother, [25] January 1874, *Letters*, I, p. 463.
[20] Letter to W.E. Henley, [17 or 18 July 1883], *Letters*, IV, p. 143; Letter to W.E. Henley, [Early December 1882], *Letters*, IV, p. 33.

his health. Stevenson states: 'I begin to ingrease' (*s'engraisser*/to gain weight) and 'I linger over and degust my convalescence like a favourite wine' (*déguster*/savour).[21] The calques even touch proper names: Stevenson transforms French author and journalist Maxime du Camp into 'Maximus de la field'. He explains that his own abandoned novel-in-progress, *A Vendetta in the West*, 'contain[s] an illegitimate father for piece of resistance'.[22]

One of the most sparkling letters was sent to his cousin Bob, from Montpellier in 1882. In it, two French nouns become English verbs, which, if nothing else, highlights Stevenson's taste for action:

> This [letter] should have gone long ago but stuck, it is the work of a good many successive and unsuccessful *élans*. This is largely owing to *Silence et Repos*: Spat blood now for three days consistent – silence and repose: *very* tedious. I get works from the cabinet of lecture, spit blood, silence and repo (I repo, thou repost, he repose). I can silence better than I can repo. Both are fatally tedious.[23]

Here, the phonetic spelling of 'repo' leads Stevenson to imagine the French 'repos' ('rest') as an Anglo-Latin verb. The first-person declension 'repo' transforms into English and arrives at 'repose'. In all these examples of mixed language use, Stevenson is creating humorous texts. But rather than analysing the humour (in terms of the theories of incongruity, superiority and relief), what is most striking here is the interactional nature of the texts, the way Stevenson invites the reader to play. This aspect of human interaction was a dominant element of the human condition for Stevenson and has been explored by Matthew Kaiser, who outlines how Stevenson engages with 'the bewildering experience of modernity: the quintessentially Victorian sensation of a world in play'. Kaiser shows that through his aesthetic of play, Stevenson confronts, on the one hand, 'a world in flux: an inconstant condition, perpetual variation and unrest', and, on the other, 'a world that throws itself headlong *into* play, where it constructs a parallel universe, which displaces that world'.[24] Although

---

[21] Letter to Sidney Colvin, [Early October 1879], *Letters*, III, p. 15; Letter to A. Trevor Haddon, [23 or 24 April 1884], *Letters*, IV, p. 276.
[22] Letter to W.E. Henley, [Late July 1883], *Letters*, IV, p. 145; Letter to Sidney Colvin, 21 October [1879], *Letters*, III, p. 19.
[23] [1 October 1882], *Letters*, IV, p. 3.
[24] 'Mapping Stevenson's Rhetorics of Play', *Journal of Stevenson Studies*, 6 (2009), 5–22 (p. 6).

Kaiser discusses Stevenson's theories of play, it is not difficult to see these theories reflected in Stevenson's writings. The constant variation of play, for example, is apparent in Stevenson's letters, where he throws himself headlong into interlinguistic and intertextual play, constructing a world where language itself is subject to variation and flux. His letters contain and create a world where languages are in palimpsest, and in which the acoustics and lexicon of one language are written over another.

Beyond transliteration and semantic calques, there are many places where Stevenson incorporates French wholesale into his private writing, either in isolated words or in complete sentences or texts. 'I like, I love, I live upon, the *imprévu* in movements',[25] he writes to Sidney Colvin, and the same thing can be said about his enjoyment of language contact: he appreciates the *imprévu* – the variety and unpredictability – that arises from the meeting of languages. Yet, Stevenson's correspondence with his French friends is relatively tame and controlled, as evidenced in letters to Jules Simoneau, Auguste Rodin and others. There are, however, numerous examples of word play in French in his letters, as in the little ditty that constitutes the final flourish of his 'silence et repos' letter:

> Des sinapismes, gorge et dos,
> Et gardez Silence et Repos!
> J'étais triste comme un pot
> Qui avait perdu sa potte.[26]

The first two lines repeat doctor's orders ('poultices on throat and back', 'rest and quiet'); the last two lines are a play on the word 'pot', and the acoustics of the masculine/feminine *pot/potte* change. Towards the end of the nineteenth century, 'pote' took on its current meaning 'friend', so by inference Stevenson could be saying 'I was as sad as someone who had lost their female friend' or simply 'as sad as a masculine without a feminine'.

But what evidence do we have of Stevenson's ability to write French? Two of the most interesting examples of lengthy passages of French appear in letters Stevenson sent to W.E. Henley and Charles Baxter.

---

[25] [? 4 June 1874], *Letters*, II, p. 18
[26] Letter to Bob Stevenson, [1 October 1882], *Letters*, IV, p. 4. See also the poem in a letter to W.E. Henley, late July 1883, p. 146, which is likely a play on a French proverb: 'c'est l'eau qui nous fait boire'.

We have seen the change in voice and point of view before, but in these two letters the linguistic playfulness occurs in the context of what can only be called parody, an instance of stylistic imitation where Stevenson adopts other voices as his own. The letters draw on multiple voices and registers and seemingly refer to other texts and historical moments. Yet what comedy there is relates to Stevenson's use of language in a fluidly changing way – in other words, in these private letters he is using the source texts as springboards to experiment with style. As such, they illustrate how he transformed life into literature and how everything was susceptible to literary treatment.

B.A. Booth and E. Mehew refer to Stevenson's language in his December 1882 letter to Baxter as 'racy slangy French'.[27] Stevenson may have encountered similar language when he rubbed shoulders with art students in France in the 1870s, but the popular French here more likely reflects his reading of Naturalist novels. Stevenson had read Zola's *Pot-Bouille* the month before sending this letter, for instance.[28] Here, though, the slang and familiar syntax point to *L'Assommoir* (1877) as a model, since *L'Assommoir* was (in)famous for its incorporation of working-class street language. The use of the word 'assommant' in Stevenson's letter is a clue as to its source.[29] The focus on food also recalls *L'Assommoir*, because one of the novel's memorable characters, Mes-Bottes, is known for his insatiable appetite. In this letter to Baxter, Stevenson is trying his hand at mimicking a French literary rendering of popular speech. The passage, which switches from a third-person description of the character 'Thomson' to a first-person account by 'Thomson', is all the more interesting because Thomson represents Stevenson himself. Stevenson and Baxter adopted the interchangeable personae of Thomson and Johnstone when they were students in Edinburgh and they maintained this 'extraordinary epistolary performance' for years.[30] In this letter, Stevenson uses a dual persona to act out two different roles: he speaks through the character of Thomson but speaks with the voice of a Parisian proletarian. That is, he imitates someone imitating someone else. This is a personal letter, but it is Stevenson at a linguistic remove, speaking in fictionalised French:

---

[27] [? December 1882], *Letters*, IV, p. 37, n. 2.
[28] Letter to John Addington Symonds, [c. 19 November 1882], *Letters*, IV, p. 28.
[29] Linguistic analysis has shown that 'assommer' was one of Zola's key verbs. See John A. Frey cited in Alain Pagès and Owen Morgan, eds, *Guide Émile Zola* (Paris: Ellipses, 2016), p. 201.
[30] Norquay, *Robert Louis Stevenson, Literary Networks and Transatlantic Publishing in the 1890s*, p. 89.

Le Pauvre Thomson, il a été bien bas, savez-vous; il ne valait pas un fétu, lui; coquin de dieu, ce qu'il a dégueulé de sang, ce qu'il a sué – pis qu'un fromage de Suisse, ce qu'il a pâti, nom de Dieu – vrai, là, c'était assommant, je ne vous dis que ça. Avec ça, l'apoplexie; seulement ce n'était pas le vrai, vraie apoplexie – c'était de l'indigestion, quoi! Mais il se croyait foutu pour de vrai, tout d'même, allez. Mais c'est un gaillard, je n'vous dis qu'ça; il a mangé – ce qu'il a mangé, tout d'même! – et puis dormi – et pissé, par d'ssus l'marché – pour n'pas dire autre chose, par rapport aux dames. Car on est chevalier français ou on n' l'est pas, coquin de Dieu! Moi, je suis comme ça, gros comme le bras, sale comme une peigne, bête comme le Bon Dieu, je n'vous dis qu'ça – mais galant, savez vous, galant à ne pas plus pouvoir lâcher un pet que d'faire ça. Voilà comme je suis, moi, et solide! Farceur, va![31]

Meanwhile, the letter to Henley, written in May 1883, flaunts its manic playfulness from the outset, beginning as it does in faux legalese: 'R.L. Stevenson and Company, Granters of Authority, All orders promptly attended to, in duplicate, triplicate and polyplicate'. The comic bombast of this opening salvo shifts into a French that signals a drastic change in register: 'Je vous autorise de bien couilloner le Kégann'pol.' There is more raciness here: the slang 'couillon[n]er' humorously translates as 'to bollock' or 'to admonish'. The spelling of publisher Kegan Paul's name imitates how a French person would transcribe a French pronunciation of the name, while the definite article 'le' placed before it has familiar, pejorative undertones. Next, the letter lurches to a contract written in Middle French ('Je vous baille auctorité et pouvoir de très hardyment, honnestement [. . .]') before ending on a short rhyming poem about *Prince Otto* (1885). The postscript, written a week after the rest of the letter, is in sober, unadorned Standard English.[32] This irreverent letter, full of verve, is

---

[31] A complete translation of this can be found in *Letters*, IV, p. 37, n. 2: 'Poor Thomson, he was pretty low, you know; he wasn't worth a straw; God, the way he threw up blood, the way he sweated – worse than a Swiss cheese, the way he suffered, my God! – but then, it was overwhelming, I tell you. On top of that, apoplexy! only it wasn't real apoplexy, it was indigestion, that's all! But he thought he was really done for all the same. But he's a plucky one, I tell you; he ate – how he ate, all the same – and then slept – and pissed, into the bargain – not to mention something else, having to do with the ladies. For either you're a French gentleman or you're not, by God! That's how I am, as big as your arm, filthy as a comb, foolish as the Lord, I tell you – but gallant, you know, so gallant as to be no more able to drop a fart than to do *that*. That's how *I* am – tough! Go on, you joker!'
[32] [Mid-May 1883], *Letters*, IV, pp. 123–4.

a prime example of Stevenson slipping through languages, moving around in space (countries and the social spaces linked to different registers) and time (from the Middle Ages to the nineteenth century), and is an example of the 'variousness' that Richard Dury has identified as characteristic of Stevenson's style.[33] The language in these letters is not meant to be mimetic, an objective representation of an external reality; rather, it is representative of writerly subjectivity and of the different ways in which lived reality can be transfigured into a story through the use of multiple voices. It also demonstrates how reality and its perception are fragmented and how the perceiving subject is ever-changing.[34] In this sense, it presages Henry Jekyll's guess that 'man will be ultimately known for a mere polity of multifarious, incongruous and independent denizens' (p. 58).

Twenty-first-century readers are used to encountering the phenomenon of playful multilingualism in texts by bi-cultural, exiled, and/or émigré authors, but Stevenson was writing in a different era, an era when the worldview of realism (and propriety) demanded that language should be objective, and when the politics of the nation state and empire demanded that one central voice should dominate. By incorporating French (and Scots and Latin and German, for that matter) into his letters, Stevenson destabilises English, the dominant language of nineteenth-century Britain, by blurring its linguistic and national limits, and opts instead for a polyphonic voice. As a Scottish writer who published in Britain and the United States and who lived in England, France, New York, California and Samoa, Stevenson can hardly be qualified as a representative nineteenth-century 'British' author, or at least not as an author representative of the London literary centre. The lively multilingualism of some of his private letters shows that sticking to the 'Queen's English' and the 'Queen's Highway' was not the natural route for a writer who wrote from the periphery in terms of nationality, geography, language and genre. In this respect, Stevenson's playful experimentation with French signals an attempt to find a voice that was not limited to the confines of national literatures and literary languages, to prescriptive rules and ideas about correctness. Part of his development as an author

---

[33] In particular, variousness as evidenced in 'shifts in spatial and temporal closeness' (p. 59). 'Stevenson's Essays: Language and Style', *Journal of Stevenson Studies*, 9 (2012), 43–91 (pp. 57–64).
[34] See Richard Dury, 'Stevenson's Shifting Viewpoint', *The Bottle Imp*, 12 (2012), 1–2, available at <https://www.thebottleimp.org.uk/issues/page/2/>.

entailed learning to fictionalise his own life by adopting and integrating foreign voices.

French in Stevenson's Published Works: (Anti-)Realism

Experimenting with French was a source of pleasure for Stevenson, even before he embarked on a career as a writer. This pleasure did not disappear once he decided to commit to a literary life – far from it. In his correspondence, Stevenson approaches language contact as an adventure, an escape into variety beyond the rules of discrete national languages, where writing becomes a performance and a *mise-en-scène* of lived experience. Many of the playful uses of French that are found in Stevenson's letters are also found in his publications, including phonetic spellings, calques and occasional French words, but the language here is necessarily more measured and artistically shaped than the language in his letters. The multilingual voice through which he often speaks in his letters bubbles over into his published works in different ways and bears certain similarities to postmodern metatexts in their self-reflexiveness. Stevenson grapples with creating his new kind of romance while simultaneously experimenting with form. An important part of this process entailed a refusal to accept one of the cornerstones of realist technique: the unifying, objective, omniscient narration in which one voice and one perspective dominates a story. French has a role in this. Integrating French structures into his books allows Stevenson to interrogate the relationship between national, linguistic and literary identity and the creative act. It also allows him to experiment with realist representation within the framework of different genres.

Given the close cultural connections between Britain and France in the nineteenth century, examples of French in Victorian fiction are not hard to come by. Juliette Atkinson notes that even in the first half of the nineteenth century, 'aristocratic Francophilia' among the upper classes in Victorian Britain manifested itself in 'dizzying displays of bilingualism' in Silver Fork novels.[35] The trend persisted beyond the Silver Fork novel into the second half of the century, as books like Edward Bulwer-Lytton's *The Parisians* (1873) and George Moore's *Confessions of a Young Man* (1888) and countless others attest. According to William A. Cohen, for 'English-speaking

---

[35] *French Novels and the Victorians*, p. 213.

Victorian authors [. . .] French testifies to an English writer's social class, cultural prestige, and educational attainment – in short, it provides signs of cultural capital'.[36] French vocabulary is often incorporated into Victorian texts for socio-cultural reasons, but the practice also contributes to a situation in which language and literary forms and genres are themselves under the microscope.

French may add local colour, create an *effet-de-réel* or add to a story's verisimilitude, as is the case in many realist novels where precise details were purported to recreate an external, observed reality. In other cases, French may contribute to characterisation or to plot points. Quite often the use of French by characters in Victorian novels is linked to middle-class social climbing and aristocratic pretensions to cultural superiority. Stevenson alludes to the latter in *Prince Otto*, where one of the many criticisms meted against the Prince by an English traveller is that 'he writes intolerable verses in more than doubtful French' (p. 53). Likewise, Princess Seraphina's falsity is discernable in her pretentious French: 'Her manners, her conversation, which she interlards with French, her very ambitions, are like assumed; and the assumption is ungracefully apparent' (p. 53). However, French is sometimes used in English novels for reasons that have little to do with the fictional world itself and everything to do with the market into which it was to be launched. The use of French defines the intended audience as readers who would understand it.[37] Thus, even when British novels feature plots that take place partly in France, they may or may not feature French, as some of Stevenson's own books prove.

Given what we know of Stevenson's playful use of French in his correspondence, it comes as something of a surprise that he reportedly told an American journalist that he had 'a special distaste' for 'the use of any foreign word . . . The great instance of the folly of reading to get new words was Gautier.'[38] This seems to discount the degree to which French is a presence in his writing. It cannot credibly be claimed that Stevenson sought to dazzle his readers with his lexical erudition and

---

[36] 'Why is there so much French in *Villette*?', ELH, 84 (2017), 171–94 (p. 172).
[37] Elisabeth Jay, *British Writers and Paris: 1830–1875* (Oxford: Oxford University Press, 2016), p. 251–2. Jay analyses the lack of French in *A Tale of Two Cities* as an example.
[38] Quoted in Barry Menikoff, 'Introduction', in Robert Louis Stevenson, *The Complete Stories of Robert Louis Stevenson*, ed. by Barry Menikoff (New York: Modern Library, 2002), pp. v–liii (p. xix).

knowledge of French, so the question then becomes to what extent Stevenson uses French in his books and, more importantly, why he does so. There is not enough space to look at each of Stevenson's books here, so I propose to draw illustrative examples from his first books, the travelogues *An Inland Voyage* (1878) and *Travels with a Donkey* (1879); his first volume of fiction, *New Arabian Nights* (1882); and one of the novels he was working on when he died, *St. Ives: Being the Adventures of a French Prisoner in England* (1897).

An Inland Voyage and *Travels with a Donkey* were Stevenson's first major publications before he had established his reputation as a novelist, and they were written at a stage when he was spending extended periods of time in France. Although both books describe voyages through French-speaking spaces, Stevenson does not rely particularly heavily on French for local colour. He does, however, use French as a means of examining the natives' conception of language difference and his own relationship to language, writing and identity. *An Inland Voyage* takes place in Belgium and France, but most of the French that is used in the book is explained, either through direct translation or through the context in which it appears, so its purpose is not to impress readers through linguistic posturing. In *Travels with a Donkey*, there are occasional phonetically rendered spellings that draw attention to accent – à la '*pas bong prêtres ici*' (p. 135) – but on the whole there are surprisingly few: mocking the locals was not at the top of Stevenson's agenda either. Nonetheless, when French is used in these books, it is more than an adornment.

In the intended introductory chapter of *Travels with a Donkey*, 'A Mountain Town in France',[39] French initially appears to function as a straightforward setting of scene. Lending an air of reality to this work of non-fiction allows Stevenson to situate the text and his travels geographically and give readers a taste of this foreign land. That said, Stevenson disorients his readers by telling them that 'on the whole, this is a Scottish landscape, although not so noble as the best in Scotland; and by an odd coincidence, the population is, in its way, as Scottish as the country' (p. 134). This passage is typical of his cultural comparisons, but by conflating Scotland – to which he belongs – and France – to which he does not – it becomes clear that reflections on national and writerly identity are on the cards in the pages that follow. At one point in 'A Mountain Town in France', he

---

[39] 'A Mountain Town in France' was only published posthumously in 1897, first separately, but since then often in editions of *Travels with a Donkey*.

addresses linguistic issues directly. Stevenson records the following exchange:

> They [the lacemakers] were filled with curiosity about England, its language, its religion, the dress of the women, and were never weary of seeing the Queen's head on English postage-stamps or seeking for French words in English journals. The language, in particular, filled them with surprise.
> 'Do they speak *patois* in England?' I was once asked; and when I told them not, 'Ah, then, French?' said they.
> 'No, no,' I said, 'not French.'
> 'Then,' they concluded, 'they speak *patois*.'
> You must obviously either speak French or *patois*. (p. 136)

The local lacemakers think that the whole world speaks either French or *patois*, an assumption that derives from limited experience. In contrast, Stevenson's identification of an affinity between Scotland and the Auvergne is an attempt to arrive at an empathetic understanding of a foreign culture – he does not mean that one is identical to the other, but that significant similarities are present to those who look beyond surface difference. The above exchange is not simply Stevenson gently poking fun at the Auvergnat peasant women's lack of awareness; this is Stevenson recognising something in the complex dynamic between languages and cultures. He tells the women that neither French nor *patois* is the language of England, and in the end he speaks to them in his 'native jargon', which is neither French, nor *patois*, nor the English of England.

The narration in this episode is further nuanced by two things: firstly, by the fact that Stevenson is writing in English about conversations that would have taken place in French; secondly, by the fact that a few paragraphs later he tells readers how George Sand incorporated the local *patois* into her novels of the Auvergne. This *patois* is therefore subject to being fictionalised and integrated into French novels, presumably in the same way that Stevenson's 'native jargon' is subject to being textualised (given authority), as well. This foregrounds the writing process and the fact that the whole of the 'real' (non-fictional) situation that Stevenson is describing in his travelogue is filtered through an artistic vision that is very conscious of language and how it creates meaning, but also of textuality and how it legitimises languages. The Scotland–Auvergne affinities and fluid linguistic identities all contribute to destabilising fixed categories. Stevenson calls attention to the relationship between French, patois,

English and his 'native jargon' within a space that is both France and Scotland, non-fiction and fiction, where everything is fluid and changing.

French plays an equally destabilising role in Stevenson's fiction, from his earliest publications to his last. In the second volume of *New Arabian Nights* (1882), Stevenson uses French to question the representational qualities of language and the ability of realist techniques to describe other times and places (specifically places that do not reflect Victorian life). Take the example of 'The Sire de Malétroit's Door', a story based in Château Landon in September 1429, almost a full century before French became the *de facto* official language of France. As a historical tale set in another country before that country's national language had been adopted and standardised, 'The Sire de Malétroit's Door' poses difficulties from the perspective of realist representation, which is premised upon the transparency and neutrality of language. So-called neutral language avoids calling attention to itself in order to better represent the world it describes. 'The Sire de Malétroit's Door' is virtually devoid of French, yet it is brimming with calques and Gallicisms. The story is set during the Hundred Years War, and the town is 'full of the troops of Burgundy and England' (p. 243). Late one night, the protagonist, Denis de Beaulieu, attempts to '*regain* his inn' (p. 244), but he 'was reckoning without that *chapter of accidents* which was to make this night memorable above all others *in his career*' (p. 245).[40] Soldiers in pursuit of him '*debouched* upon the terrace' (p. 246). 'Darkness', we learn, 'threatens an *ambuscade*' (p. 244). When Denis leans on a door that mysteriously gives way behind him, he enters the home of the Sire de Malétroit, who tells him 'I have been expecting you all *the* evening' (p. 249). Believing there to be some sort of mistake, Denis tells him in frustration 'you *persist in* error' (p. 250) and 'you *lie in your throat*!' (p. 251). Some of this vocabulary has been literally translated by Stevenson into English (e.g. 'toute la soirée', 'mentir par la gorge'); other words are either unidiomatic Gallicisms or archaisms that entered English through Middle French ('chapter of accidents', 'ambuscade').

The calques and Gallicisms are deliberate, and they play a specific representational role. Essentially, they fulfil what we could call an anti-realist realist function: they 'Frenchify' a story that takes place

---

[40] All italics in this paragraph are mine.

in France without having recourse to French; they ensure that readers know where the action is occurring, but they do so while calling attention to the linguistic façade of English in which the story is narrated. Paradoxically, this undermines the realism of the text and gives the impression that Stevenson is writing in translation, writing across languages and cultures. The Gallic turns of phrase also add an unsettling element of strangeness, which is entirely fitting given the bewildering, implausible events at the heart of this unrealistic tale. In the end, the pseudo-French structures disrupt the narrative because they belong to neither English nor French. As a result, they draw attention to the way that literary representation in the Victorian era relied on monophonic voices, voices that are undermined by the complex narration of the 1882 stories.

In 'A Lodging for the Night', another story from volume two of *New Arabian Nights,* French is notable for its absence, which has little to do with catering to the widest possible readership. 'A Lodging for the Night' is about the French writer François Villon, so by rights it could feature occasional French words without setting critical alarm bells ringing or drawing charges of ostentatious Frenchness. Admittedly, there is some humour derived from French word play in the story: the soldier with whom Villon spends the night is called Enguerrand de la Feuillée, seigneur du Brisetout, bailly du Patatrac – a bombastic name that evokes war ('guerre'), destruction ('brisetout' = break everything) and loud crashing sounds ('patatrac'). As in 'The Sire de Malétroit's Door', there are even calques. That said, given the subject matter and the setting of the story, readers would almost expect French here, as a way of adding local colour; instead, they get English. Once the absence of French is noticed, its effect is disconcerting.

Instead of walking along rue Saint-Denis – a place name that poses no interpretative difficulty to monolingual English speakers – Villon walks along 'St. Denis Road'. By contrast, 'Story of the House with the Green Blinds', from the Florizel stories, alludes to rue Richelieu, rue Drouot, rue des Martyrs, rue Lepic. Instead of describing the Cimetière St.-Jean, Stevenson describes the 'cemetery of St. John'. Instead of showing Villon writing in French, he writes a French 'ballade' in English: the reader is treated to two lines in English from the imagined 'Ballade of Roast Fish'. In fact, beyond occasional calques, the only real French in 'A Lodging for the Night' (1877) is the word 'papa', which suggests a parentage between the indignant retired soldier who lodges Villon and the poet himself – but 'papa' is also an English word, so its linguistic affiliation is unclear. Why does Stevenson do this? It is perhaps a case of switching voice, which he liked to do, or of double-bluffing his readers, who expect French words and cultural references and find themselves outplayed. Either way, the choice not to use French in the Villon story is calculated, another instance of Stevensonian play. The missing French transforms Villon into an English-speaking writer within a story that unequivocally and explicitly takes place in Paris. This is an effective means of blurring linguistic, literary and national boundaries and of questioning how a text in one language can realistically represent a reality in another, and how an author belonging to one literary tradition can be represented in another.

By and large, the various tales of *New Arabian Nights* integrate French through irregularities of phrasing in such a way as to draw attention to textuality. By playing with language like this, the stories subvert the aims of realism. In his early fiction and non-fiction, Stevenson uses French in ways that complicate notions of realism by foregrounding the creative process. But his use of French also complicates notions of linguistic, literary and national identity. French continues to play a significant role in terms of the plot, characterisation and themes of some of Stevenson's later novels, like *Catriona* (1893), where the final events take place in France,[41] but it is particularly important in *St. Ives*. As in *Catriona*, bad French is mocked in *St. Ives* and positive characters – despite their many flaws – are able to negotiate different languages because their lack of fixed and simple identity allows them to switch voices with confidence.

Completed by Arthur Quiller-Couch, *St. Ives* is a romance set during the Napoleonic Wars. It tells the story of a French prisoner who escapes from Edinburgh Castle, only to become involved in a series of incidents in Britain and France that culminate in him securing both his inheritance and the hand of his Scottish love, Flora. French is therefore necessary to the plot. As Harriet Dorothea MacPherson writes,

> In *St. Ives* the very root of the tale is French. If the hero had been a prisoner of some other nationality, or of some other war, how different might have been the plot. In *St. Ives* each French incident or trait fits into the next like the points of a jig-saw puzzle.[42]

---

[41] In *Catriona*, the outlawed Alan Breck ridicules a spying English seaman's inability to properly pass as a Frenchman. The final events of the novel contrast Alan's seemingly inborn ability to code-switch and James More Drummond's use of French to betray his fellow Highlander and Jacobite sympathiser to the English, while living in France. Alan overhears James More 'colloguing with some one in French' (p. 282) and it transpires that this is part of James's plot to sell Alan to the English as a result of an ongoing clan feud in Scotland.

[42] *R.L. Stevenson: A Study in French Influence*, p. 58.

Beyond its significance to the plot, French is important in terms of both characterisation and themes relating to linguistic identity. The novel features phonetically rendered speech, quotations from French poetry in French (Lafontaine), references to French street names (a Napoleonic spy goes by the name Rue Grégoire de Tours), and the role of language in creating a performative identity is underscored through its first-person narration in English by an aristocratic French soldier.

The first signs that language and identity are intermingled in the novel are found in the protagonist's names: his birth name Vicomte Anne de Kéroual de St.-Ives is gender subversive; his pseudonym, Champdivers, phonetically plays on meaning in French: it evokes 'champs divers' (diverse fields). As the pseudonym suggests, the protagonist performs several roles in his story and the events of the novel unfold on various figurative battlefields. His fluid identity is possible because although he is French, he 'had an English nurse' and English 'has been a second language to [him] from a child' (p. 32). His linguistic competence is at the heart of the novel, and he goes so far as to state that his freedom in Britain – or at least in England – depends on not using French: 'I kept my liberty and life by my proficiency' (p. 32).[43] Variation is the norm for Champdivers/St. Ives: he constantly switches between languages and therefore cultures, such that his language use is a performance that makes of his identity a performance too. This, in turn, makes his first-person narrative a performance, as well. As Glenda Norquay rightly remarks, in this 'criss-crossing [of] national and cultural borders', *St. Ives* 'develops a model of hybridity that goes beyond the linguistic'.[44]

Even though hiding his French is a life and death matter for St. Ives, he is still able to find humour in the linguistic shortcomings of others. His English valet comically fails to master French, despite endless lessons: he is 'seeming capable of anything in the world but the one thing I had chosen – learning French' (p. 208). Furthermore, in keeping with a novelistic tradition of lampooning middle-class pretensions to sophistication, St. Ives's descriptions of Flora's aunt poke fun at her English-accented French:[45]

---

[43] See also Norquay, *Robert Louis Stevenson, Literary Networks and Transatlantic Publishing in the 1890s*, p. 142.
[44] *Robert Louis Stevenson, Literary Networks and Transatlantic Publishing in the 1890s*, p. 142.
[45] On this phenomenon, see Atkinson, *French Novels and the Victorians*, p. 208.

> She had a way of standing in our midst, nodding around, and addressing us in what she imagined to be French: '*Bienne, hommes! ça va bienne?*' I took the freedom to reply in the same lingo: '*Bienne, femme! . . . ça va couci-couci tout d'même, la bourgeoise!*' (p. 7)

This mockery is not unlike Stevenson's transcriptions of heavily accented French in his letters, where there are layers of irony at play. The added complication here stems from the first-person narration: St. Ives, a native French speaker, makes fun of Mrs. Gilchrist's French within a story that he is narrating in English, but he himself is being written by Stevenson, a native English speaker, who has invented a French-speaking narrator. There are layers of translation and role-playing at work. Thus, what might have seemed a realistic linguistic detail in fact introduces an element of textual instability. Cohen observes a similar phenomenon in Charlotte Brontë's *Villette* (1853):

> French has an element of unreality or counter-reality for Brontë and so every time it appears it raises questions about the status of the real that are, ordinarily, held in suspension by the conventions of fiction and by the transparency of a native language. The alternation of languages itself evokes the question of what is real, what is imaginary, and how we as novel readers balance the forms of knowledge associated with each.[46]

Stevenson's use of French in his published books pushes the boundaries of realism and interrogates the role and stability of linguistic, literary and national identity. He is less interested in using French as part of an *effet-de-réel* that reinforces the mimetic function of realist literature, or in using French as an expression of class-related themes that are typical of Victorian realist fiction; he is more interested in confronting the challenge of accurately representing imaginary worlds and probing the relationship between language and identity in the creative process. In the sections that follow, the emphasis will be more squarely on how Stevenson's style developed in response to his reading of key French authors and how his relationship with French and French style relates to broader issues in nineteenth-century comparative literature.

---

[46] 'Why is there so much French in *Villette*?', p. 184. Furthermore, while Mrs. Gilchrist is initially mocked for her French pretensions and bourgeois Britishness, her Britishness is itself a role she plays: this 'terrible British old maid' (p. 7) helps St. Ives escape British soldiers.

French Style and English Literature

One *idée reçue* about the differences between French and English literature in the nineteenth century was that French authors were inherently more concerned with matters of style, in part because the French language was supposedly better suited to stylistic precision. According to Gilles Philippe, the English sense of stylistic deficiency vis-à-vis the French was well in place by 1880.[47] Walter Pater's description of English as 'our somewhat diffuse, or slipshod literary language [that] hardly lends itself to the concentration of thought and expression' is representative of this general view.[48] In fact, imitation of French style is associated with English versions of Aestheticism after 1850 and with Decadentism in the last decades of the century. In an 1892 essay on 'The Contrasts of English and French Literature', George Saintsbury cited 'sobriety' and 'mechanical inventiveness' as two of the intrinsic features of the 'genius of the French language'. Elsewhere, Saintsbury lamented that in England 'it would be easy to count on one hand the living writers who think of anything but of setting down the first words which occur to them as capable of clearly and grammatically expressing their thought'.[49] In the 1890s, Stevenson seemed to be of the same opinion, for he was sceptical about the success of any movement towards emphasis on form and style in English literature. He wrote to Rhymers' Club member and *Yellow Book* contributor Richard Le Gallienne, stating:

> The little, artificial popularity of style in England tends, I think, to die out; the British pig returns to his vomit – to his true love, the love of the style-less, of the shapeless, of the slapdash and disorderly. Kipling with all his genius, with all his Morrowbie Jukeses, and At-the-End-of-the-Passages, is still a move in that direction, and it is the wrong

---

[47] *French Style: l'accent français de la prose anglaise* (Brussels: Les Impressions Nouvelles, 2016), pp. 9–10.

[48] 'Prosper Mérimée', *Fortnightly Review*, 48 (December 1890), pp. 852–64 (pp. 861–2).

[49] 'The Contrasts of English and French Literature' [1892], *The Collected Essays and Papers of George Saintsbury, 1875–1923, volume IV: Essays in French Literature* (Freeport, NY: Books for Libraries Press, 1924), pp. 221–49 (p. 238); 'Charles Baudelaire' [1875], *The Collected Essays and Papers of George Saintsbury, 1875–1923, volume IV*, pp. 1–29 (p. 27). Stevenson was interested in this question and in late August 1890 asked Edward L. Burlingame to send him W.C. Brownell's book, *French Traits: An Essay in Contemporary Criticism*. See *Letters*, VI, p. 412.

one. There is trouble coming, I think; and you may have to hold the fort for us in evil days.[50]

Stevenson is not critiquing stylistic artifice here but is instead suggesting that the contemporary predilection for style was simply a passing phase. The implication, of course, is that 'style' was somehow un-English. As Stevenson prophesied, trouble was, indeed, on the way, but it was not for the reason he anticipated: following the trial against Oscar Wilde in 1895, art for art's sake, heavily influenced by both the stylistic and thematic preoccupations of French literature, became an increasingly less popular worldview for British writers and publishers, many of whom would henceforth seek to distance themselves from the aesthetic-Decadent movement.

Stevenson's comments are worthy of remark precisely because he was frequently cited as one of the British stylists who had been influenced by French literature. In the *Fortnightly Review*, Grant Allen described *Travels with a Donkey* as having been written with a 'light and graceful touch, as if Mr. Stevenson were rather a Frenchman born out of place, than a Scotsman of the Scots'.[51] Even French critics were cognisant of Stevenson's apparently French qualities: Georges Grappe asserted in his early biography of Stevenson that 'l'œuvre entière de Stevenson écrite en langue anglo-saxonne, donne souvent l'impression qu'elle fut pensée et ouvrée par un Français'.[52] In his seminal retrospective, *The Eighteen Nineties*, Holbrook Jackson expressed admiration for Stevenson's 'meticulous prose', but was careful to specify that

> all this concern for language as language, for the set and balance of words, was not, however, entirely of native origin. It was, as in the

---

[50] 28 December 1893, *Letters*, VIII, p. 212. Le Gallienne later published a collection called *Robert Louis Stevenson, an Elegy; and Other Poems Mainly Personal* (London: John Lane, 1895). It was originally published in the *Daily Chronicle* on 25 December 1894.
[51] Review of *Travels with a Donkey in the Cévennes*, *Fortnightly Review*, July 1879, pp. 153–4, in *Robert Louis Stevenson: The Critical Heritage*, ed. by Paul Maixner (London: Routledge & Kegan Paul, 1981), pp. 64–6 (p. 65).
[52] *R.L. Stevenson: l'homme et l'œuvre*, p. 28. ('Stevenson's entire body of work, written in the Anglo-Saxon language, frequently gives the impression of having been thought through and worked over by a Frenchman.') Grappe also commented that 'il lui semblait suffisant de peindre, d'animer des personnages en un style nerveux, très clair et presque latin par la syntaxe' (p. 30).

case of so much that was new and strange, partially derived from the French decadent movement which was influencing the whole of Europe.[53]

In hindsight, it is probably not entirely accurate to say that Stevenson was influenced by French Decadence *per se*: he was writing concurrently with the Naturalists and Decadents of the 1880s and 1890s and was, as we shall see in the next chapters, identified as an antidote to Naturalism and Decadence by the emerging generation of French authors. It is, however, accurate to say that Stevenson's stylistic apprenticeship took place at least in part within the structures of the French language and within the pages of the French literature of the previous generation and his reading of authors like Flaubert and Baudelaire. In this respect, he is very much a part of what has been called the '"moment français" de la littérature anglaise'.[54]

Whether the alleged French influence in Stevenson's published works was considered positive or negative depended entirely on who was doing the commenting. Some critics perceived Stevenson's style as affected and as too French; others thought the emphasis on form and on language was a positive refinement. A good example of these contradictory assessments is the critical reaction to *New Arabian Nights*, which we looked at in the previous section. A *Westminster Review* article claimed that 'the style [of *New Arabian Nights*] is frequently forced and affected; one pervading affectation being the use of French idioms literally translated into English'.[55] Conversely, Saintsbury praised the 'thoroughly literary character of [the] apparently childish burlesque' in this same book, and noted that there were 'no conceits of phrase, or at least very few, most of which are simple Gallicisms'.[56] The widespread view of the artistic literati of the Nineties on Stevenson is perhaps best encapsulated by Oscar Wilde, who shared many of Stevenson's anti-mimetic views (romance and aestheticism being two of the reactions against realism at the end of the century).[57] Wilde referred to Stevenson as a 'delicate artist in

---

[53] *The Eighteen Nineties: A Review of Art and Ideas at the Close of the Nineteenth Century* [1913] (London: Grant Richards, 1922), pp. 135–6.
[54] Philippe, *French Style*, p. 6.
[55] Review of *New Arabian Nights*, *Westminster Review*, January 1883, p. 284, in *Robert Louis Stevenson: The Critical Heritage*, ed. by Maixner, p. 118–19 (p. 118).
[56] 'New Arabian Nights', *Pall Mall Gazette*, 4 August 1882, p. 4.
[57] See Stephen Arata, 'Realism', in *The Cambridge Companion to the Fin de Siècle*, ed. by Gail Marshall (Cambridge: Cambridge University Press, 2007), pp. 169–87 (pp. 183–4).

language', and when he requested books to build his library upon leaving Reading Gaol, he included Stevenson in a list that was otherwise largely dominated by French-language authors who – now as then – are considered masters of style (the exception being Dumas): 'You know the sort of books I want', Wilde writes to Rupert Ross, 'Flaubert, Stevenson, Baudelaire, Maeterlinck, Dumas *père*, Keats, Chatterton, Coleridge, Anatole France, Gautier, Dante and all Dante literature'.[58]

If truth be told, it is tempting to put inverted commas around the word 'style', since any discussion of it is fraught with definitional difficulty and seemingly impossible burdens of proof; consequently, there is a real danger of not knowing exactly what is under discussion when one is discussing an author's 'style'. We can say that style is not simply a question of grammar or vocabulary, or the transcription of realist details, but of the ebb and flow of sentences, of the turns of phrase that make one author recognisably different from another. It is personal, something that distinguishes one writer from the crowd and raises some works above others as far as critical esteem is concerned. For example, when *Treasure Island* was published in 1883, a review in *Graphic* made a claim for Stevenson's 'perfect mastery of style, a mastery which entitles Mr. Stevenson almost alone among living writers to be called classic'.[59] We have an intuitive sense of what a 'perfect mastery of style' might mean here, but would probably stumble if asked to articulate it clearly. This is doubly true when trying to assess stylistic cross-pollination over national, linguistic and generic borders.

In his essay on style in Stevenson's essays, Richard Dury defines style as 'distinctive foregrounded manner';[60] Barry Menikoff writes that for Stevenson 'style *is* art'.[61] These are both useful in different ways: Dury's approach allows for an analysis of specific features of Stevenson's writing, while Menikoff's draws attention to style as a philosophy of art and the very essence of artistic production. One insight into what Stevenson's contemporaries meant by his 'style' is

---

[58] *The Complete Letters of Oscar Wilde*, ed. by Merlin Holland and Rupert Hart-Davis (New York: Henry Holt, 2000). Letter to Oswald Sickert, [early May 1892], p. 525; Letter to Rupert Ross, 6 April 1897, p. 791.
[59] Review of *Treasure Island*, *Graphic*, 15 December 1883, p. 599, in *Robert Louis Stevenson: The Critical Heritage*, ed. by Maixner, pp. 140–1 (p. 140).
[60] 'Stevenson's Essays: Language and Style', p. 44.
[61] 'Stevenson on Style', *The Bottle Imp*, 12 (2012), 1–4 (p. 4), available at <https://www.thebottleimp.org.uk/2012/11/stevenson-on-style/>.

found in a letter from W.E. Henley to Stevenson in which Henley discusses *Virginibus Puerisque* (1881), which Stevenson had dedicated to him. Henley makes a distinction between 'style' and 'personality', and his comparison provides a framework for understanding what 'style' might have meant to both Stevenson's admirers and his detractors. Henley's explanation of style suggests that it is less idiosyncratic, less individual, and more impersonal and detached from a work than is 'personality'. According to Henley, the style of the newer essays in *Virginibus Puerisque* – by which he presumably meant 'Ordered South', 'Walking Tours' and 'Virginibus Puerisque' – is better than the style in 'the earlier ones. It is clearer, more sufficient, less foppish or rather less tricksy (not tricky, mind) and more like Style; has more distinction, in fact, and less personality.' Stevenson has 'Style' – note the capital – which is 'that union of the Personal with the Absolute in art'.[62] Arthur Quiller-Couch, who wrote the final chapters of *St. Ives*, seems to concur, at least on some points. He describes the paradoxes of style in terms of an opposition between the personal, on the one hand, and rules and norms, on the other, but also states that the writer must remain somewhat detached.[63]

These juxtapositions foreshadow Michael Wood's comparison of a writer's 'style' and a writer's 'signature'. Wood makes the comparison in the context of a study on Vladimir Nabokov – a well-known admirer of Stevenson's – but his analysis of style and signature is framed quite broadly. According to Wood, an author's style 'works largely through syntax and small words'. He elaborates: 'signature is their habit and their practice, their mark, style is something more secretive, more thoroughly dispersed among the words, a reflection of luck or grace, or of a moment when signature overcomes or forgets itself'.[64] Part of what comes through in these models is that Style implicates a shedding of self-awareness, a shaking off of authorial self-consciousness, which is curious indeed given the extreme artistic self-awareness that pervades Stevenson's writing (not to mention Nabokov's). Yet, as should be becoming clear, the Style/personality

---

[62] W.E. Henley letter to Stevenson, April 1881, quoted in *Robert Louis Stevenson: The Critical Heritage*, ed. by Maixner, p. 76. A *Spectator* reviewer thought the exact opposite, claiming that 'the later ones are less fresh than the earlier'. See Review of *Virginibus Puerisque and Other Papers*, *Spectator*, 11 June 1881, pp. 775–6, in *Robert Louis Stevenson: The Critical Heritage*, ed. by Maixner, pp. 82–6 (p. 86).
[63] *On the Art of Writing* (Cambridge: Cambridge University Press, 1921), p. 246.
[64] *The Magician's Doubts: Nabokov and the Risks of Fiction* (London: Pimlico, 1994), pp. 27 and 23.

contrast (to use Henley's terms) relates to Stevenson as a writer of French in different, but equally illuminating ways, ways that point at one and the same time to writerly freedom – as evidenced in his letters – and writerly control – as evidenced in his published works and the texts he produced during his stylistic apprenticeship. It also relates, of course, to the issue of stylistic affectation – and Stevenson was certainly not immune from criticism on this front, with many early twentieth-century critics thinking that his style disguised a lack of substance. As MacPherson noted, 'we find his most drastic critics today among those people who maintain that Stevenson is all form with little content'.[65]

Although the critical tide turned against Stevenson in the early twentieth century, accusations of affectation and complaints about Stevenson's Gallic turns of phrase were also made in reviews of his early works. As time went on, comments on his 'Frenchness' become less frequent (although there was still criticism on the grounds of affectation and preciosity). How do we account for the decreasing number of complaints about Stevenson's 'Frenchness' in reviews of his work as time went on? The change in attitude can be attributed to at least three things, the first and most obvious of which is Stevenson's maturation as an author: as he becomes more comfortable, he no longer needs to imitate others so directly. This explanation would account for his dismay that William Archer did not discern a change in his style in *A Child's Garden of Verses* (1885) compared with his earlier works.[66] The second explanation is that British critics were increasingly conversant with French theories of the novel, especially the very public debate over the relative merits of the stylistic precision and possible affectation of *écriture artiste*, with its focus on perception, versus the Naturalist experimental method in fiction. As Chapter 1 illustrated, in Britain these debates had spilled over into debates over realism in the English novel. Indeed, Archer's comments on *Memories and Portraits* (1887) implicitly draw attention to French preoccupations, but he never names (or blames) the French. He writes that it

> says much, in our opinion, for [Stevenson's] inborn faculty that it survived his early course of 'sedulous aping'. We may perhaps trace to it one of the faults of his style, its ever-present self-consciousness.

---

[65] *R.L. Stevenson: A Study in French Influence*, p. 73.
[66] Letter to William Archer, 28 October 1885, *Letters*, V, p. 141.

> When at its best it is perfect in purity and variety of cadence, but not always in choice of words. A word may become wrong by being too right, or rather too obtrusively right. The perfection of style, we conceive, is that it should delight without surprising; Mr. Stevenson often surprises while he delights. He is a little too much of the conjurer of words.[67]

Conjuring with words is connected to the 'variousness' and 'strangeness' of Stevenson's style, as analysed by Dury,[68] but it is also intimately related to the French emphasis on the *mot juste*, which was so much a part of the aesthetic theory of writers like Flaubert and the Goncourt Brothers. Flaubert explained the importance of lexical precision in a letter he wrote to Louise Colet: 'Tout le talent d'écrire ne consiste après tout que dans le choix des mots. C'est la précision qui fait la force.'[69] On this, MacPherson has noted how 'Stevenson, in his early days, particularly admired that never-ending pursuit of Flaubert for the exact word which he desired.'[70] A third possible explanation for a decrease in the number of complaints about Stevenson's Frenchness is that by the late 1880s and the 1890s, British literature had developed its own Decadent movement and its authors were writing in a style that was very much more self-consciously, ostentatiously 'artificial' and 'French' than Stevenson's.

Thanks to essays like 'A College Magazine', published in *Memories and Portraits* in 1887, a fair amount is known about Stevenson's literary apprenticeship and how he developed his stylistic skills in texts that were 'written consciously for practice' (p. 28). Some of the authors he cites in 'A College Magazine' are French: Michel de Montaigne, Étienne Pivert de Senancour and Charles Baudelaire. In the early twentieth century, Charles Sarolea analysed the connections between Stevenson and Montaigne in one of the first books on Stevenson and France. The connection to Senancour is not relevant to the present discussion, as it likely relates to the themes of his 1804 novel, *Obermann*, and its general sense of romantic ennui. This leaves Baudelaire, who is not the first French

---

[67] Review of *Memories and Portraits*, *Pall Mall Gazette*, 1 December 1887, p. 3, in *Robert Louis Stevenson: The Critical Heritage*, ed. by Maixner, pp. 286–8 (p. 288).
[68] 'Stevenson's Essays: Language and Style', pp. 57–64 and 70–1.
[69] 22 July 1852, *Correspondance électronique de Flaubert*, ed. by Yvan Leclerc and Daniel Girard, Laboratoire Cérédi, Université Normanie Rouen, available at <https://flaubert.univ-rouen.fr/correspondance/>.
[70] *R.L. Stevenson: A Study in French Influence*, p. 37.

author with whom readers might associate Stevenson, even though Stevenson lists him among those he 'sedulously aped' and admired. Yet, there is nothing particularly unusual in Stevenson citing Baudelaire: along with authors like Gustave Flaubert, Théophile Gautier and the Goncourt Brothers, he was one of the godfathers of style in nineteenth-century France and became a presence in English literature thanks to Swinburne's essays and poems in the 1860s. After the publication of *Les Fleurs du mal* (1857), Baudelaire had a cult-like status among authors who considered themselves artists rather than hack writers. On the other hand, generic differences would seem to separate Stevenson and Baudelaire: while the former was associated with a renewal of romance, the latter was the consummate dandy, an observant *flâneur* who leisurely wandered the streets of Paris, a painter of modern life in poetry and art criticism, a writer who was charged with outrages against religion and public morals. Despite these apparent differences, however, Baudelaire was nonetheless a poet with whom Stevenson had certain affinities, in terms of both artistic outlook and style. Baudelaire's *Petits Poèmes en Prose* (1869) – innovative in their length, their lyricism and their thematic modernity – led Stevenson to write his own prose poems, and Baudelaire's fable-like 'Le Mauvais vitrier' clearly influenced two of Stevenson's fables: 'The Two Matches' (1896) and 'The Sinking Ship' (1896).

What interests me, beyond shared artistic vision and common approaches to managing the career of writing, is how a novelist like Stevenson could have taken as a model a poet like Baudelaire and what this reveals about Stevenson's development as a writer. The answer lies at least partly in the April 1885 essay 'On Some Technical Elements of Style in Literature', published in the *Contemporary Review*.[71] In this essay, Stevenson takes as his premise that 'all our arts [. . .] lie wholly on the surface; it is on the surface that we perceive their beauty, fitness and significance' (p. 33). Observations like this go some way to explaining how Stevenson could be accused of being a superficial writer by his critics. The parallel to Baudelaire, though, relates more specifically to Stevenson's conception of the relationship between music and literature. While the tendency in the late nineteenth century was to equate literature with painting, both Stevenson and Baudelaire also see close connections between literature and music, with Stevenson referring to them as 'the two temporal arts' because both 'contrive their pattern of

---

[71] It is included in *Essays Literary and Critical*, pp. 33–50. Hereafter TES.

sounds in time' (p. 35). According to Stevenson, 'in all ideal and material points, literature, being a representative art, must look for analogies to painting and the like; but in what is technical and executive, being a temporal art, it must seek for them in music' (p. 40). Ideally, writing should be musical in its style and painterly in its representational qualities. According to 'On Some Technical Elements of Style', good writing merges a 'contrast of the words employed' and 'a pattern of sounds in time', and the inherent musicality of words means that good writers can 'make of [words] a drum to rouse the passions' (pp. 34–5).[72]

The phrasing here recalls another author with cult status in the nineteenth century: Gustave Flaubert – the 'martyr of literary style'[73] – who famously wrote in *Madame Bovary* that 'la parole humaine est comme un chaudron fêlé où nous battons des mélodies à faire danser les ours, quand on voudrait attendrir les étoiles'.[74] Indeed, Philippe describes 'On Some Technical Elements of Style in Literature' as dealing with 'des problématiques toutes flaubertiennes'.[75] Flaubert, whose available correspondence Stevenson read, repeatedly likened prose to music. In a letter to Louise Colet in 1852 he explained:

> J'en conçois prtant un moi, un style: un style qui serait beau, que quelqu'un fera à qq jour, dans dix ans, ou dans dix siècles, et qui serait rythmé comme le vers, précis comme le langage des sciences, et avec des ondulations, des ronflements de violoncelle, des aigrettes de feux, un style qui vous entrerait dans l'idée comme un coup de stylet, et où [. . .] votre pensée enfin [. . .] voguerait sur des surfaces lisses, comme lorsqu'on [. . .] file dans un canot avec bon vent arrière. La prose est née d'hier, voilà ce qu'il faut se dire. Le vers est la forme

---

[72] Compare this with Pater's contention that 'Music and prose literature are, in one sense, the opposite terms of art; the art of literature presenting to the imagination, through the intelligence, a range of interests, as free and various as those which music presents to it through sense [. . .] If music be the ideal of all art whatever, precisely because in music it is impossible to distinguish the form from the substance or matter, the subject from the expression, then, literature, by finding its specific excellence in the absolute correspondence of the term to its import, will be but fulfilling the condition of all artistic quality in things everywhere, of all good art'. 'Style' [1888], in *Appreciations, with an Essay on Style* (London: Macmillan, 1889), pp. 1–36 (p. 35).
[73] Pater, 'Style', p. 24.
[74] [1857], ed. by Bernard Ajac (Paris: Garnier-Flammarion, 1986), p. 259. ('Human speech is like a cracked cauldron on which we beat out tunes for bears to dance to, when we long to move the stars.')
[75] *French Style*, p. 35.

par excellence des littératures anciennes. Toutes les combinaisons prosodiques ont été faites, mais celles de la prose, tant s'en faut.[76]

Flaubert returned to the same idea a few months later:

> Quelle chienne de chose que la prose! Ça n'est jamais fini; il y a toujours à refaire. Je crois prtant qu'on peut lui donner la consistance du vers. Une bonne phrase de prose doit être comme un bon vers, *inchangeable*, aussi rythmée, aussi sonore.[77]

Style, for Stevenson, is 'synthetic' (TES, p. 37), constructed, and he believed that distinctive style emerges through the attentive patterning of words and sounds. As Raphaël Luis observes, synthetic style engages the ear and the intellect, 'sans sacrifier ni le plaisir musical, ni la conduite du récit'.[78] The difficulty for a writer of prose, as opposed to a writer of poetry – who in the nineteenth century most often worked within the constraints of pre-established fixed forms, metre and rhyme schemes – is that in prose 'the pattern itself has to be invented' (TES, p. 38). In other words, the writer of prose has to invent not only the story, but the form; the writer of prose has to develop synthetic stylistic features, what Stevenson refers to as 'those phrases, such as prose is built of, which obey no law but to be lawless and yet to please' (TES, p. 41). The challenge therefore is to

---

[76] 24 April 1852, *Correspondance électronique de Flaubert*, ed. by Leclerc and Girard. ('I envision a style: a style that would be beautiful, that someone will invent some day, ten years or ten centuries from now, one that would be rhythmic as verse, precise as the language of the sciences, undulant, deep-voiced as a cello, tipped with a flame: a style that would pierce your idea like a dagger, and on which your thought would sail easily ahead over a smooth surface, like a skiff before a good tail wind. Prose was born yesterday: you have to keep that in mind. Verse is the form par excellence of ancient literatures. All possible prosodic variations have been discovered; but that is far from being the case with prose.' Translation from *The Letters of Gustave Flaubert*, ed. by Francis Steegmuller (London: Picador, 2001), pp. 219–20.)

[77] Letter to Louise Colet, 22 July 1852, 4 p.m., *Correspondance électronique de Flaubert*, ed. by Leclerc and Girard. (Steegmuller's translation (p. 228): 'What a bitch of a thing prose is! It is never finished; there is always something to be done over. However, I think it can be given the consistency of verse. A good prose sentence should be like a good line of poetry – *unchangeable*, just as rhythmic, just as sonorous.')

[78] *La Carte et la fable. Stevenson modèle de la fiction latino-américaine (Bioy Casares, Borges, Cortázar)* (doctoral thesis, l'université de Lyon, Université Jean Moulin (Lyon 3), 2016), p. 238, available at <http://www.theses.fr/2016LYSE3040>. ('While sacrificing neither the musical pleasure nor the train of the story.')

write poetical prose, which was doubly difficult given that Stevenson was simultaneously trying to resuscitate romance and experiment with other genres. While poetry was at the top of the nineteenth-century aesthetic hierarchy, the prose genres in which Stevenson experimented were considered popular and therefore not valid as serious literature. This is further amplified by Stevenson's rejection of the realist novel, which was considered the serious novelistic genre that could potentially compete with poetry in terms of artistic legitimacy.[79] Stevenson's experiments with 'petits poèmes en prose' were therefore fitting, as the prose poem itself is generically unstable.

The challenge of writing poetical prose brings us squarely to Baudelaire and his posthumously published *Petits Poèmes en Prose*, which he referred to as *Le Spleen de Paris* – differences in title that point both to formal innovation (short prose poetry) and to the profound malaise of modern life (Baudelairian spleen). Stevenson specifically admired *Petits Poèmes en Prose*: he recommended the volume to his cousin Katharine de Mattos and imitated it in a series of prose poems that he composed in the spring of 1875. George Saintsbury would no doubt have approved of Stevenson's sedulous aping of Baudelaire, for in his 1875 essay on the French poet, he suggested that

> it is not merely admiration of Baudelaire which is to be persuaded to English readers, but also imitation of him which is with at least equal earnestness to be urged upon English writers. We have had in England authors in every kind not to be surpassed in genius, but we have always lacked more or less the class of écrivains artistes – writers who have recognised the fact that writing is an art, and who have applied themselves with the patient energy of sculptors, painters, and musicians to the discovery of its secrets.[80]

Baudelaire dedicated *Petits Poèmes en Prose* to newspaper editor and fellow poet Arsène Houssaye, who had published some of the poems in *La Presse*. Although the dedication contains neither the elaborate detail nor the close textual analysis of an essay like 'On Some Technical

---

[79] For an overview of the issues raised by the serious literature/genre fiction opposition, see Luis, *La Carte et la fable*, pp. 187–8.
[80] 'Charles Baudelaire', pp. 26–7. The term 'écrivains artistes' likely alludes to the Goncourt brothers' *écriture artiste* – a term used to refer to their nervous, painterly style.

Elements of Style in Literature', the language Baudelaire uses prefigures the language Stevenson uses in his essay and the dedication functions as a sort of manifesto:

> Quel est celui de nous qui n'a pas, dans ses jours d'ambition, rêvé le miracle d'une prose poétique, musicale sans rythme et sans rime, assez souple et assez heurtée pour s'adapter aux mouvements lyriques de l'âme, aux ondulations de la rêverie, aux soubresauts de la conscience.[81]

This passage from the dedication was used by Arthur Symons in 1896 to compare Walter Pater to Baudelaire, which shows that the vision behind the *Petits Poèmes en Prose* was still relevant in discussions of British Aestheticism and Decadence in the 1890s.[82]

Although Stevenson advised his cousin Bob – perhaps in jest – not to let his sisters read Baudelaire for 'he would have corrupted St. Paul',[83] on reading a draft of a paper by his cousin Katharine de Mattos in 1874, Stevenson told her that he was going to send her a copy of *Petits Poèmes en Prose* 'because it is just one of those specimens of consummate polished perfection [. . .] that I think you would do best to read at present'.[84] The assumption that her study of French prose poems would help her English writing is not as surprising as it may at first appear, given what Stevenson says of the nature of poetic and prose style in 'On Some Technical Elements of Style in Literature', and given his rather sweeping contention that 'French prose is distinctly better than English' (p. 44).

---

[81] *Le Spleen de Paris* [1869], ed. by Aurélia Cervoni and Andrea Schellino (Paris: Garnier-Flammarion, 2017), p. 239. ('Who among us has not, on ambitious days, imagined the miracle of poetic prose, musical without rhythm and rhyme, supple and agile enough to adapt to the lyrical movements of the soul, to the meanderings of daydreams, and to the paroxysms of consciousness.')

[82] 'Walter Pater: Some Characteristics', *Savoy*, 8 (December 1896), pp. 33–50 (p. 34). For a fuller appreciation, see Clements, *Baudelaire and the English Tradition*.

[83] 29 March 1870, *Letters*, I, p. 194. Stevenson or Colvin apparently cut out some of the pages. See 'Longer Comments on Individual Items', EdRLS: Stevenson's Library Database.

[84] Letter to Katharine de Mattos, [? October 1874], *Letters*, II, p. 63. On de Mattos's literary career, see Hilary J. Beattie, 'The Enigma of Katharine de Mattos: Reflections on her Life and Writings', *Journal of Stevenson Studies*, 14 (2008), 47–71.

A few weeks after his initial recommendation to Katharine, Stevenson warned her, possibly remembering what he had counselled Bob:

> The book, you will receive shortly. Do not run away with the idea that I think it specially commendable. Only I think he might be suitable at this moment for you.
> Note the following.
> III, IV, XIII, XIV (O admirable), XVII, XVIII, XXIV, XXV, XXVII, XXXVII. Some of these are really very excellent; and (it was that paper of yours that made me think of the book) will show you I think how you may approach such slight and essentially exotic ideas in prose, and yet retain for them some of the immunities that go with verse.[85]

No doubt, the themes of the *Petits Poèmes en Prose* are pertinent to Stevenson's opinion of them, and one of Baudelaire's chief innovations was to introduce the 'modern' into an older literary form.[86] From the artist's Confiteor (III) at the beginning of the collection, in which 'solitude, silence' and 'irrémédiable existence' express themselves 'musicalement et pittoresquement, sans arguties, sans syllogismes, sans déduction'; to the aged circus entertainer who is misunderstood by the younger generation (XIV: 'Le Vieux saltimbanque'); to the power of the artist before the abyss (XXVII: 'Une mort héroique'): artistic creation is a central theme of Baudelaire's collection, and it is also a theme that Stevenson dealt with in stories like 'Providence and the Guitar' (1878) and *The Wrecker* (1892). But Stevenson also recommended poems where Baudelaire rails against bourgeois vulgarity (IV: 'Un plaisant'); where he exults in sensuous exotic reveries in which imagination reigns over reality, allowing the poet to exist in two places at once (XVII: 'Un Hémisphère dans une chevelure', XVIII: 'L'Invitation au voyage', XXIV: 'Les Projets'); where he ruminates on the existential angst and the tragedy of unfulfilled dreams and ruined lives (XIII: 'Les Veuves'). Still, Stevenson is careful to specify to de Mattos that *Petits Poèmes en Prose* as a whole is not 'specially commendable'. His recommendation seems to relate specifically to style and how to treat prose poetically, since he qualifies the poems as 'consummate polished perfection'. In other words, the

---

[85] Letter to Katharine de Mattos, [7 November 1874], *Letters*, II, p. 80.
[86] See Steven Monte, *Invisible Fences: Prose Poetry as a Genre in French and American Literature* (Lincoln: University of Nebraska Press, 2000), pp. 20–2.

poems model poetic freedom in prose form, and they respect neither the rules of regular versification nor the conventions of storytelling.

From *Petits Poèmes en Prose* to Novels

Like his conflicting messages about Baudelaire's collection, Stevenson's messaging on his own prose poems was mixed. On the one hand, he admits that 'they'll remind people of Baudelaire, but I think they're really quite unlike'; on the other, he remarks 'I am writing, *Petits Poèmes en Prose*. Their principal resemblance to Baudelaire's is that they are rather longer and not quite so good.'[87] In the first instance, he is attempting to distance himself from Baudelaire and assert his own artistic independence; in the second instance, he is openly acknowledging a debt to Baudelaire by referring to his own poems using Baudelaire's title – a rhetorical move that should be interpreted as humility or defensive modesty (à la Baudelaire was here before me and I am a mere imitator). In both cases, Stevenson is inviting comparisons between his poems and Baudelaire's.

Only six of Stevenson's prose poems have survived: 'The Quiet Waters By', 'A Summer Night', 'On the Lighthouse Roof', 'In the Lightroom', 'Sunday Thoughts' and 'Good Content'. Stevenson's prose poems do not have much of the modern urban or sexually *troublant* subject matter of Baudelaire's. In fact, at first glance only one of the six – 'A Summer Night' – deals with a situation that could be deemed overtly Baudelairian.[88] In this prose poem, Stevenson paints an urban nightscape where the speaker and his 'friend' (Stevenson and his cousin Bob) sit on a wall observing a city in motion (Edinburgh), all the while surrounded by the weighty permanence of the hills. This is a textbook Baudelairian scenario, calling to mind the following passage of *Le Peintre de la vie moderne* (1863; *The Painter of Modern Life*):

> Pour le parfait flâneur, pour l'observateur passionné, c'est une immense jouissance que d'élire domicile dans le nombre, dans l'ondoyant dans le mouvement, dans le fugitif et l'infini. Être hors de chez soi, et pourtant se sentir partout chez soi; voir le monde, être au centre du monde et

---

[87] Letter to Frances Sitwell, [28 May] 1875, *Letters*, II, p. 138; Letter to Sidney Colvin, [7 or 8 June 1875], *Letters*, II, p. 142.
[88] The texts can be found in *Letters*, II, pp. 332–8.

rester caché au monde, tels sont quelques-uns des moindres plaisirs de ces esprits indépendants, passionnés, impartiaux, que la langue ne peut que maladroitement définir.[89]

In the same paragraph, Baudelaire writes that 'l'observateur est un prince qui jouit partout de son incognito' ('the spectator is a *prince* who everywhere rejoices in his incognito') – there is nobility in detachment. This seems an apt description of the two men in 'A Summer Night', and it would also serve as an apt description of Prince Florizel of Bohemia whom Stevenson created in *New Arabian Nights*.[90]

In 'A Summer Night', Edinburgh is 'dotted with lamps' and unfolds before the spectator-cousins in 'wide ways [that] crossed each other on the ridge'. While the *flâneurs* stay still, the streets bustle with activity, crowds pass them by, and there is a general sense of disembodiment and unreality: 'pale faces leaped out of the crowd as they went by the lights, and passed away like a dream in the general dream of the pallid and populous streets'. The city is a sensory feast. City noises are catalogued in images of a 'coarse brass band', 'the pulse of drums and the brazen call of bugles', 'the last tramway' and the 'sound of traffic'. The night symbolises freedom: Stevenson writes that when morning comes 'the day found us slaves, whom the night had left freemen reckoning the treasure of time'. Night represents escape from the constraints of bourgeois materialism, from work, and from obligations to usefully occupy oneself: it enables the two observers to 'make free with the treasure of time'. The phrase 'longing night', for example, suggests both a lengthy night and the passage of time as dawn approaches, but also the sensuous pleasures of languorous physical 'longing'. Indeed, in fine Baudelairian tradition – *The Painter of Modern Life* contains a section on prostitutes – 'A Summer Night' describes the movement and gaze of 'harlots' whose 'dresses [. . .] swayed and swished upon the pavement'. Moreover, amongst the faces that stand out 'the eyes

---

[89] [1863], in *Œuvres complètes de Charles Baudelaire*, 7 vols (Paris: Calmann-Lévy, 1885), III, p. 64. ('For the perfect *flâneur*, for the passionate spectator, it is an immense joy to set up house in the heart of the multitude, amid the ebb and flow of movement, in the midst of the fugitive and the infinite [. . .]; to see the world, to be at the centre of the world, and yet to remain hidden from the world.' Translation from *The Painter of Modern Life*, in *Art in Theory, 1815–1900: An Anthology of Changing Ideas*, ed. by Harrison and Wood with Gaiger, pp. 493–506 (p. 496).)

[90] MacPherson observes that although Florizel is a Prince of Bohemia, all of his adventures take place in England and France. As such, he is the perfect rootless Bohemian. See *R.L. Stevenson: A Study in French Influence*, p. 50.

stood forth with a sordid animal invitation'. There is no question that this particular prose poem 'remind[s readers] of Baudelaire'.

The two men are at the centre of a revolving world in 'A Summer Night'. It would be easy to associate this attitude of observation with an attitude of self-centredness, but it is also associated with an interpretation of reality as perceived phenomena. This arises in other works by Stevenson, as well. In *Edinburgh: Picturesque Notes* (1878), the final paragraph of the 'Calton Hill' chapter once again positions an observer in the city. It is no coincidence that a *Scotsman* review referred to Stevenson's tone here as

> that of a well-bred lounger, a *flaneur*, not deeply interested in anything, sympathising with well-bred languor in the misery or welfare of the people he observes and describes, but not much moved by either, or, if moved at all, showing emotion lightly, as becomes a philosopher and a man of the world.[91]

The difference in the 'Calton Hill' chapter, however, is that now the observer is the simultaneously personal and impersonal 'you',[92] and the emphasis is on connecting the city to the heavens: the lantern lights extending across the landscape function as substitute stars (pp. 180–1). In other texts, Stevenson broadens the perspective. Although not concerned with the flow of perception, the title character of the story 'Will o' the Mill' finds himself the centre of a world that extends outward from his mill. Will is no *flâneur*, but there is still an overriding sense of him being a fixed point in time and space, around which life occurs.

In Stevenson's other prose poems, the influence of Baudelaire is more subtle. The shortest, the controlled one-paragraph 'In the Lightroom',[93] while geographically far removed from the thematics of the Baudelairian modern city, is highly successful in its contrast of day and night, existential hope and hopelessness, as well as in its accentuation of the reading process – an emphasis that is frequently

---

[91] Review of *Edinburgh: Picturesque Notes*, *Scotsman*, 21 January 1879, in *Robert Louis Stevenson: The Critical Heritage*, ed. by Maixner, pp. 59–61 (p. 60).
[92] The same pronoun shift occurs in 'Forest Notes', where it contributes to the 'indeterminate nature of the narration'. Richard Dury, 'Reading "Forest Notes"', *Journal of Stevenson Studies*, 13 (2017), 5–34 (p. 16).
[93] In 1869–70, Stevenson wrote a poem called 'The Light-Keeper', with which this prose poem can be usefully compared. See *The Collected Poems of Robert Louis Stevenson*, ed. by Roger C. Lewis (Edinburgh: Edinburgh University Press, 2003), pp. 252–3.

found in Baudelaire's prose poems. Through a deft doubling of key words ('frame', 'lenses', 'pane'; 'light', 'night') and repetition of initial consonants (/b/, /f/, /l/), form becomes content: the poem reflects and refracts words and sounds in the same way that the glass lenses of a lighthouse reflect light. In this way, the surface of the poetry is foregrounded, and it becomes a figurative light that readers see. What is more, the repetition of the sound /aɪ/ – not only in the assonance created by 'bright', 'light', 'night', 'sights', but in the words 'chimes', 'fly', 'blind', 'strike' and 'sunrise' – puts the concepts of the 'I' and the 'eye' phonologically at the heart of the poem. In this way, sound creates images. Although 'In the Lightroom' is not a Baudelairian cityscape, it deals explicitly with individual perception of variegated reality. Indeed, the 'lightroom' itself can be interpreted as a room in a lighthouse where 'the patient and serious watchman holds his vigil', and also as a place in the mind's eye where poetic beauty can be both perceived and conceived.

The richly textured, three-paragraph-long 'The Quiet Waters By', dedicated to Frances Sitwell, applies similar style to Psalm 23: 'in pastures green he leadeth me the quiet waters by'.[94] The poem condenses and combines rhythmical repetition and slight paronomastic changes of phrasing. These surprising changes add a leisurely lolling quality to the poem as a whole and simultaneously call back to the 'quiet waters' of the title. Similarly, the phrase 'the green pastures' transmutes into 'the pastures are green', 'among the pastures', 'pastime', 'carpet of sweet green' and 'pasturing'; similar shifts affect the words 'water' and 'lilies and leaping fish'. One striking example affects 'the windmill [that] turns and turns its arms, and bickers away before the big soft wind'. The simple, childlike monosyllables of 'big soft wind' and the alliterative /b/ serve to highlight the key word 'bicker', which is subsequently subjected to an adept play on words thanks to its triple meaning relating to movement, perception and attitude. The personified windmill does not simply spin quickly; it is a petulant, glittering 'bickering windmill' that draws attention to itself. It silently disrupts the 'quiet' of the title while highlighting the passage of time and the contrasting placidity of the surroundings. Further surprising effects are created through reversals of perspective, such that up becomes down, as in the following example: 'The face of the flush river is all dipped and skimmed about by two-winged martins. The dark trees on the hilltop sink into a great bright

---

[94] 'The Quiet Waters By', *Letters*, II, pp. 332–3.

cloud.' Here both reality and its reflection are visible at once and, because the passage suggests sinking upward, it is unclear whether the poem describes clouds or their reflection in the river.

Intensely lyrical in tone, the paragraphs grow shorter as they approach the speaker's calm acceptance of his insignificance before nature's timelessness. The decentring of the speaker is ultimately confirmed in the final line where interpretative responsibility shifts to 'you', a second-person subject that represents both Sitwell, as dedicatee, and the reader: 'But my sorrow was no more. It had gone like dew, or frost, or a shadow, or what you will.' 'What you will' is ambiguous, implying both the somewhat flippant 'and what have you' and the gratification inherent in 'what you desire'. In common with many of Baudelaire's prose poems, 'The Quiet Waters By' puts the onus on the reader to address their own 'will' and decide whether they are seeing reality or a reflection of it that has been filtered through an artistic vision.[95]

The six prose poems represent some of Stevenson's earliest creative works and were written before Stevenson had been long exercising the art of writing. The influence of Baudelaire can be seen in the example of brief, self-contained lyrical prose pieces, and in the importance of perception and artistic vision. They were written at the same time that Stevenson's reputation as an essayist was growing; indeed, they contain many of the hallmark stylistic traits that Richard Dury has pinpointed in Stevenson's essays, notably lightness, variousness, playfulness and strangeness.[96] Henley even detected instances of 'verse-in-prose' in the *Virginibus Puerisque* essays: 'Here and there too – *passim* – I came upon odds and ends of verse: chiefly to round off sentences!'[97] The prose poem was not a genre that Stevenson pursued, though. Nonetheless, the poetic techniques used here resurface in other works, and it is particularly interesting to see how Stevenson wields them in works of longer fiction, where a balance needs to be found in terms of manner and matter. This is all the more interesting because while Stevenson was a stylist, he was simultaneously experimenting with novelistic genres in an effort to revive the art of storytelling.

---

[95] For more on this in Baudelaire, see Kara Rabbitt, 'Reading and Otherness: The Interpretative Triangle in Baudelaire's *Petits poèmes en prose*', *French Studies*, 33.3–4 (Spring–Summer 2005), 358–70.
[96] 'Stevenson's Essays: Language and Style', passim.
[97] W.E. Henley letter to Stevenson, April 1881, in *Robert Louis Stevenson: The Critical Heritage*, ed. by Maixner, pp. 75–7 (p. 76).

Stevenson's Baudelairian apprenticeship can be discerned beyond his prose poems, and traces of his early education in style reappear in his essays – particularly (and unsurprisingly) those dealing with art. These include 'Forest Notes' (1875) and 'An Autumn Effect' (1875), where he is probably trying to imitate Impressionist painting, and 'Fontainebleau' (1884). There are also traces of his early stylistic experimentation in his travel writing and his fiction, sometimes in unlikely places. *An Inland Voyage*, published in 1878 but based on journals he kept during his trip to Belgium and France in 1876, offers a representative example. The chapters that deal with canoeing on the river Oise contain multiple descriptions of willows and reeds that are linked to impressions of movement through the repetition of words like 'running' and 'rushing'. A connection is also established between man and the landscape when the same vocabulary ('quivering') is used to describe veins and rivers. The style in this book was not uniformly well received; in fact, George Meredith, whom Stevenson admired, singled out these chapters for criticism, alleging – somewhat oddly – that they were in the style of Dickens because they were deprived of their beauty through being 'overinform[ed] with [Stevenson's] sensations'.[98] Too much 'personality' and not enough 'Style' perhaps? On the other hand, 'sensations' and 'nervosité' were central to *écriture artiste*, which brings Impressionist techniques to bear on prose, so the French comparison may be equally fitting. We need only look at Stevenson's appreciation of Paul Bourget's *Sensations d'Italie* for confirmation.[99]

A still more surprising example of the way in which Stevenson's reading of French literature, and his exposure to Impressionist painting in 1874–6, may have contributed to his literary voice can be found in *The Black Arrow: A Tale of the Two Roses*. *The Black Arrow* was first serialised in *Young Folks* in 1883 and can hardly be accused of having style as its 'engendering idea'. Certain chapters – notably 'In the Fen' and 'The Fen Ferry' – contain descriptions that recall prose poems in general and 'The Quiet Waters By' in particular. Chapter III, 'The Fen Ferry', opens on this description:

---

[98] George Meredith letter to Stevenson, 4 June 1878, in *Robert Louis Stevenson: The Critical Heritage*, ed. by Maixner, pp. 53–5 (p. 54).

[99] Dury speculates that one of the things that might have attracted Stevenson to Bourget was the latter's 'impressionistic descriptions'. See 'Stevenson and Bourget: An Enigma'.

> The river Till was a wide, sluggish, clayey water, oozing out of fens, and in this part of its course it strained among some score of willow-covered, marshy islets.
> It was a dingy stream [. . .] The wind and martens broke it up into innumerable dimples; and the reflection of the sky was scattered over all the surface in crumbs of smiling blue.
> A creek ran up to meet the path, and close under the bank the ferryman's hut lay snugly. It was of wattle and clay, and the grass grew green upon the roof. (p. 36)

This short passage is alliterative (/s/ and /g/), repeats words and assonant sounds (clayey, clay; water, wattle; dingy, dimples), and contains personifications (the 'creek ran up') – evidence of similar stylistic techniques to those used in the prose poems. What is different is that the descriptions in these two chapters are interwoven into an adventure narrative in which the central character, Richard Shelton, helps 'Jack Matcham' – the disguised Joanna Sedley – flee her Lancastrian pursuers. Accordingly, these opening paragraphs are followed by a conversation between Shelton and a reluctant ferryman, which is then briefly suspended by a second description that recycles the language from the beginning of the chapter and makes use of similar techniques, such as the breaking up of idioms (in this case, 'to open up'):

> They were by that time at the mouth of the creek, and the view opened up and down the river. Everywhere it was enclosed with islands. Clay banks were falling in, willows nodding, reeds waving, martens dipping and piping. There was no sign of man in the labyrinth of waters. (p. 37)

The obvious parallels with 'The Quiet Waters By' can likely be attributed to the fact that the novel takes place in England, where Stevenson had spent time with Frances Sitwell (in Suffolk in 1873) – windmills are also a presence in *The Black Arrow*, where their sails spin rather than bicker.[100] What is more interesting, though, is the patterning, the calling back to previous descriptions, and the repetition of phrases,

---

[100] A windmill is a leitmotif in chapter 30 of *Catriona*, where each time it is described it anticipates or reflects a change in the course of events. For example, 'it seemed there was trouble afoot; the sails of the windmill, as they came up and went down over the hill, were like persons spying' (p. 276). It is then revealed that there are spies about.

which collectively weave the chapter – and, in turn, the novel – together. This can be seen, for example, in 'islands' and 'islets', in the 'clay', the 'martens' and the 'willows'. While some of the images in the novel are decidedly painterly – the 'crumbs of smiling blue' suggest dabs of a painter's brush on a canvas – their repetition and their iambic rhythm is musical. Similar techniques are used in other places as well, notably in the descriptions of falling snow in Book IV: The Disguise. Chapter 1 of Book IV, which takes place in January, contains the following descriptions, some of which are effective but unremarkable ('the snow was falling, without pause or variation, in one even, blinding cloud'; p. 161), others of which surprise through unexpected use of articles and prepositions ('out of sight among the falling snow'; pp. 167–8), or through painterly evocations ('the whole world was blotted out and sheeted down below that silent inundation'; p. 161). The repetitive nature of these descriptions creates a lulling effect frequently found in short prose poems, but here the incantation is disrupted by adventure. This texturing is likely what prompted William Archer, in an otherwise unfavourable review, to comment favourably on the novel's descriptions. Archer had no reason to associate the descriptions with prose poems – Stevenson's prose poems were still unpublished and Baudelaire's were still untranslated – but he does consider the style of the descriptions a hallmark of Stevenson's voice:

> There are little bits of fresh and crisp description here and there. In the opening chapters we breathe the very air of the woodland glades through which Dick and 'Matcham' pursue their adventurous way, and the snow scenes of the wintry close are no less happily touched. In short, we never forget for many minutes together that it is Mr. Stevenson we are listening to.[101]

The Black Arrow is a plot-driven novel written for an audience of young readers, and its careful succession of short chapters is a function of the demands of serialisation. Nevertheless, it also contains artistry in its patterning and in the texture of its descriptions, which echo and repeat throughout the novel in the same way that prose poems do. *The Black Arrow* was one of Stevenson's least critically successful novels.[102] Despite its flaws, it demonstrates the ways in

---

[101] Review of *The Black Arrow*, Pall Mall Gazette, 13 August 1888, in *Robert Louis Stevenson: The Critical Heritage*, ed. by Maixner, pp. 320–3 (p. 321).
[102] For examples of unfavourable reviews, see *Robert Louis Stevenson: The Critical Heritage*, ed. by Maixner, pp. 320–8.

which Stevenson incorporated techniques learned from his prose poems – evocative repetition, musical variation – into an adventure narrative that is not only distinctly un-Baudelairian in theme, but that also seems in no way connected to the thematic concerns of Naturalism, Decadence or Aestheticism – this in itself is innovative.

I chose *The Black Arrow* as an example of Stevenson's style because the descriptions of the fens have affinities with descriptions Stevenson had used in his earlier prose poems. This is not an isolated phenomenon in Stevenson's writing. Stevenson's most successful extended attempt at writing a poetic novel was *Prince Otto* (1885), a book whose style he found difficult to sustain. The descriptions of forests, rivers and nightscapes that are woven through the tissue of the novel are incantatory. *Prince Otto*'s debt to other works has been comprehensively documented by Robert P. Irvine,[103] but the remnants of the style of his prose poems can be felt in the repeated descriptions that function as variations on a theme. In this respect, *Prince Otto* can be considered an extended experiment with poetic prose in the novel. It was unpalatable to many critics because of its fantastical, poetic qualities, but the style works – in my opinion at least – because the story bears no relation to external reality and has instead dreamlike qualities.

Subsequently, the patterning and variations that feature in Stevenson's prose poems and in descriptive passages in novels like *The Black Arrow* and *Prince Otto* take on a more diffuse form (that is, they are less 'added-on', less concentrated). The recurring image of the windmill at the end of *Catriona* is a good example because the description of the windmill interacts with the action that is taking place. Vernon Lee (Violet Paget) describes a passage from *Catriona* as 'an adjective on a large scale', an interpretation that shows the relationship between style and form, between small details and the larger shape of the text. This leads her into a discussion of 'construction – that is to say, co-ordination' and the way in which movements and themes are ideally subject to variation. Like Stevenson in 'On Some Technical Elements of Style in Literature', Lee evokes music when discussing literary composition:

> For, remember, such a movement does not die out at once. It continues and unites well or ill with its successors, as it has united well

---

[103] See the 'Introduction' to *Prince Otto*, ed. by Robert P. Irvine, New Edinburgh Edition of the Works of Robert Louis Stevenson (Edinburgh: Edinburgh University Press, 2014), pp. xxiii–liv (pp. xxxv–xlix). On *Prince Otto* and Meredith specifically, see Sandison, *Robert Louis Stevenson and the Appearance of Modernism*, pp. 156 and 172.

or ill with its predecessors. You must remember that in every kind of literary composition, from the smallest essay to the largest novel, you are perpetually, as in a piece of music, introducing new themes, and working all the themes into one another. A theme may be a description, a line of argument, a whole personage; but it always represents, on the part of the reader, a particular kind of intellectual acting and being, a particular kind of mood. Now, these moods, being concatenated in their progression, must be constantly altered by the other moods they meet; they must never be quite the same the second time they appear as the first, nor the third as the second; they must have been varied, and they ought to have been strengthened or made more subtle by the company they have kept, by the things they have elbowed, and been – however unconsciously – compared and contrasted with [. . .].[104]

The language here recalls Stevenson's assertion that literature must look to musical analogies in terms of what is 'technical and executive'. Lee notices the movement and variation not in individual sounds in *Catriona*, but in the whole construction of the novel. The principles learned through the prose poems have now found full expression on the larger canvas of the historical romance. The mature Stevenson has developed his own distinctive style in which plot and style converge, and in which techniques honed through studying authors like Baudelaire, Flaubert and others fertilise English-language romances.

Despite adhering to many of the aesthetic principles of art for art's sake as far as style and form are concerned, Stevenson thought that the novel should develop in another way. This is something that his French critics picked up on. Stevenson's obvious appreciation of language for its own sake, and the pleasure he takes in its textures and sounds, was typical of proponents of *l'art pour l'art* – if not necessarily of writers of romance – and the conscious sophistication of his style was both praised and damned by his contemporaries. Stevenson's background in French language and literature contributed to the development of his writing voice, in terms of both his theory of the novel and the elaboration of his style. If he was accused in the nineteenth century of being too preoccupied with style, it is perhaps because he was living between two literatures. The next chapter will explore how Stevenson was transformed into a French writer through translation.

---

[104] 'On Literary Construction', *Contemporary Review*, September 1895, pp. 404–7, in *Robert Louis Stevenson: The Critical Heritage*, ed. by Maixner, pp. 444–8 (pp. 444 and 447–8).

Chapter 3

French Translations and Translators of Stevenson

On continue à se disputer les traductions de Stevenson.[1]

When Stevenson died, only three of his books had been published in France, but there was not much time for more to have appeared. *Treasure Island* was translated very quickly – within two years as a book, which is acceptable even by twenty-first-century standards. Stevenson died a mere four years after the first metropolitan French translation of *Strange Case of Dr. Jekyll and Mr. Hyde*, which was published only four years after the novel had appeared in English. Even so, Stevenson appeared to think he was an unknown quantity in France. In a well-known comment to Marcel Schwob, he claimed that he 'might write with the pen of angels or of heroes, and no Frenchman be the least the wiser'.[2] Echoing this sentiment, early French critics made frequent claims that Stevenson's literary qualities were undervalued except by the most culturally aware.[3] Confusingly, though, while some commentators suggested that because of his literary talents Stevenson

---

[1] Les Treize, 'Les Lettres', *L'Intransigeant*, 24 October 1920, p. 2. 'Les Treize' was the name used by a group of journalists who contributed to *L'Intransigeant*'s daily literature column. Members included Fernand Divoire, René Bizet, Léon Deffoux and Alain-Fournier. See Gaston Picard, 'Histoire des Treize', *Les Nouvelles littéraires, artistiques et scientifiques*, 17 November 1934, p. 4.
[2] 19 August 1890, *Letters*, VI, p. 401.
[3] By way of example: 'Exception faite pour quelques fervents de littérature anglaise, Stevenson est peu connu du grand public français' ('With the exception of a few English literature enthusiasts, Stevenson is little known to the general public in France'). 'Markheim', [unknown translator], *La Revue des revues*, 15 May 1900, p. 378, n. 1. Or: 'combien de gens en France, ignorent le nom de l'exquis romancier anglais qui s'appelait Stevenson, combien aussi ne le connaissent que de nom et ne

ought to have been better known in France, others sought to establish his credibility and importance by highlighting how many books he had already sold and how solid his reputation was. In 1895, the *Journal des voyages* called him 'à coup sûr le plus renommé parmi les littérateurs anglais'.[4] In 1897, *Le Gaulois* drew attention to the fact that Stevenson's books had sold by the thousands in France.[5] By the 1920s, Jules Romains could declare that Stevenson had been 'copiously' translated into French, with French versions of almost all his notable works.[6] Contradiction was in the air in terms of how to assess his reception in France. While there are gaps in Stevenson's French publishing fate,[7] the fact that many people were – as the epigraph to this chapter intimates – 'fighting to translate his books' proves that Stevenson was a known quantity in literary circles and that critics,

---

savent pas, pour en avoir joui, le charme de cet esprit délicat, de cet ironique de grande marque, petit cousin de Voltaire et de Sterne' ('how many people in France are unaware of the exquisite British novelist by the name of Stevenson, and how many only know him by name and have never enjoyed this charming, delicate spirit, this markedly ironic man, who is a younger cousin to Voltaire and Sterne?'). Philippe Gille, 'Les Livres', *Le Figaro*, 13 August 1896, p. 5. Another article states that Stevenson was hardly read in France, except by a 'petit nombre de délicats, épris de littérature exotique' ('a small number of people of discernment, enamoured of exotic literature'). M.S., '*Le Dynamiteur* de Robert-Louis Stevenson', *Journal des débats politiques et littéraires*, 3 November 1894, p. 1. This same article states, reasonably enough, that the reason Stevenson was not better known is that 'la mode ne s'est pas portée encore vers lui' ('fashion hasn't inclined toward him yet'). When Stevenson's letters were published, it was stated that he was known to a 'petit nombre d'amateurs et de lettrés'. See the editor's note accompanying 'Robert Louis Stevenson: Lettres à divers (ses idées sur l'Art et sur la vie d'après sa correspondance', trans. by Madeleine Rolland, *Minerva*, 1 March 1903, pp. 98–136 (p. 98).
[4] Edmond Neukomm, 'Un roman de Louis Stevenson', *Journal des voyages*, 30 July 1895, pp. 39–40 (p. 39). ('Assuredly the most renowned of the English authors.')
[5] 'L'œuvre, même en traduction française, s'est répandue à des milliers d'exemplaires.' Rzewuski, 'Le Dernier roman de Stevenson', p. 2.
[6] 'Stevenson et l'Aventure', *L'Humanité*, 16 August 1920, p. 2. He also remarked, 'De presque toutes ses œuvres notables, il existe une version française' ('There is a French version of almost all of his notable works').
[7] For instance, at the very least I think we can question why there were not more references to him in the *Revue britannique*, whose explicit aim was to publish selected writing on British art and literature in French translation: it mentioned the play of *Strange Case of Dr. Jekyll and Mr. Hyde* in July–August 1888 ('Correspondance de Londres', pp. 388–9), and contained a short, positive review of *The Dynamiter* in September 1894 ('Les Livres', p. 454), but nothing more. Tom Hubbard provides an engaging overview of some of the earliest translations in 'Dva Brata: Robert Louis Stevenson in Translation Before 1900', *Scottish Studies Review*, 8.1 (Spring 2007), 17–26.

translators and publishers wanted his books to be available in France. It also means, however, that no definitive textual version of 'RLS' was being presented to the French. This allowed his books to be marketed to very different reading publics.

The fact that Stevenson did not have one dedicated translator or publisher promoting his work likely contributed to confusion about his French presence. Translators and publishers can 'create' authors, giving them a voice and a reading public abroad. Unlike Walter Scott and his translator Auguste Defauconpret, whose translations played a decisive role in disseminating Scott's writings not only in France but throughout Europe,[8] it was more than two decades after Stevenson's death before one individual translator took on the task of translating his complete works. The task had been projected by Berthe Low: her obituary in *American Art News* states that 'it was her ambition to translate all of Stevenson's works into her native language' but offers no explanation as to why she stopped at *Strange Case of Dr. Jekyll and Mr. Hyde*.[9] Albert Savine also intended to translate many, if not all of the books, including some of Stevenson's non-fiction.[10] In the end, he translated *Kidnapped*, 'The Merry Men', *The Misadventures of John Nicolson* and *Treasure Island*.[11] The person who is generally recognised as being the first to embark on the task of translating Stevenson's complete works is Théo Varlet, whose translations started to appear in the 1920s.[12] This does not mean that Stevenson was unavailable in

---

[8] See Paul Barnaby, 'Restoration Politics and Sentimental Poetics in A.-J.-B. Defauconpret's Translations of Sir Walter Scott', *Translation and Literature*, 20.1 (2011), 6–28 (p. 6).

[9] 'Mrs. Will H. Low', *American Art News*, 7.27 (17 April 1909), p. 6, available at <http://www.jstor.org/ stable/25590444>.

[10] Les Treize, 'Les Lettres', *L'Intransigeant*, 17 August 1924, p. 2.

[11] *The Merry Men* was translated with Michel Georges-Michel as *Les Hommes joyeux* (Paris: G. Crès, 1929). According to an article in *L'Intransigeant*, *Les Hommes joyeux* contains 'Will du moulin', 'Janet la maltournée', 'Le Voleur de cadavres' and 'Olalla', in addition to the title story ('Les Lettres', *L'Intransigeant*, 13 March 1921, p. 2). *The Misadventures of John Nicolson* was also a joint translation with Michel Georges-Michel: *Les Mésaventures de John Nicolson*, Collection littéraire des romans d'aventures (Paris: Édition Française Illustrée, 1922). The publication was announced in Marcel Martinet, 'Le Roman anglais de notre temps. Quelques œuvres', *L'Humanité*, 20 July 1922, p. 5. Savine's translation of *Les Squatters de Silverado* is mentioned in L. Méritan, 'Franck Norris, Albert Savine et le roman d'aventures', *L'Homme libre*, 5 March 1921, p. 2, but I can find no evidence that he completed it.

[12] Vincent Giroud, 'Cocteau and Stevenson', in *European Stevenson*, ed. by Ambrosini and Dury, pp. 185–98 (p. 191).

French prior to this; rather, it means that his French publishing identity emerged in a way that made it difficult to chart his course through the French literary landscape, a fact that reflects the turbulence of the literary and publishing worlds at the end of the nineteenth century.

Until the 1920s, a whole constellation of translators, working independently, collectively contributed to the spread of Stevenson's works and reputation in France. Having multiple translators was not completely out of the ordinary in terms of Franco-British publishing history. George Sand's novels, for example, were translated into English by several people under the direction of a fervent supporter.[13] What distinguishes Stevenson's translators is that they were not intentionally embarking on a joint translational project. He was translated by women and men; amateurs and professionals; novelists, critics and professors – a situation that speaks volumes about the instability of the French literary field at the turn of the century. It also directs our attention to the different markets that Stevenson was reaching and the types of publishers who were willing to take a risk on an author who worked in many genres and whose output frequently defied categorisation. By detailing the earliest French translations of Stevenson and charting his publishing history during the French Third Republic, this chapter will show how Stevenson came to be positioned both as a popular author and as an example of an artist who was representative of the literary future, dispelling the early belief that his writing was undiscovered by, and unavailable to, French readers.

French *Treasure Islands*

Treasure Island was the novel that first made Stevenson's reputation in France, as it had in Britain. After it was serialised in *Young Folks*, *Treasure Island* was published as a book by Cassell in 1883. Within six weeks of the English publication, esteemed French critic and theologist Edmond Schérer urged his friend Pierre-Jules Hetzel to quickly publish the book, lest another publisher make an offer:

> Mon cher ami, laissez-moi vous rendre un service. Il vient de paraître en Angleterre (Cassel & Cie) un livre intitulé *Treasure Island*, l'île des trésors, par un M. Stevenson. C'est un récit d'aventures de mer,

---

[13] Atkinson, *French Novels and the Victorians*, pp. 102–3.

de piraterie, de trésor caché, vieux thème, comme vous voyez mais renouvelé par un don très rare d'invention. [. . .] Pressez-vous, car si vous ne prenez pas les devants, un autre demandera l'autorisation de traduire, bien certainement.[14]

Schérer is alerting Hetzel, a major publisher of novels for young people and the exclusive publisher of Jules Verne, to publish a book that he can make money on – a book that will fit into Hetzel's by then well-established product line. Schérer's description of *Treasure Island* as a classic pirate story 'renouvelé par un don très rare d'invention' is praise of the literary strength of the work. In other words, here was a quality book, like Jules Verne's, with broad popular appeal. The suggestion was acted upon.

In France, *L'Île au trésor* was serialised in the daily newspaper *Le Temps* from 25 September to 8 November 1884. On 4 October, Stevenson requested a subscription to *Le Temps*, presumably to follow its progress.[15] *Le Temps* was the French newspaper of record, and serialisation in its pages meant access to an educated adult readership. *L'Île au trésor* was subsequently published on 15 February 1885 as a book by Hetzel in the 'Bibliothèque d'éducation et de récréation' collection.[16] The books in this series belonged to the long tradition of Defoe, Dumas, Verne, Haggard and others, works in the single broad genre of the romance of adventure which had always captivated adults and children alike. Stevenson's prefatory verses 'To the Hesitating Purchaser' in the book-form version of *Treasure Island*, although not kept in Hetzel's edition, summarise this perspective, positioning *Treasure Island* precisely in this tradition.

As part of his marketing strategy for the launch of the 'Bibliothèque d'éducation et de récréation', Hetzel insisted on its quality, presumably to induce buyers to pay more for the books in the series: 'Nous osons beaucoup pour les enfants. Le luxe du fond et

---

[14] Antoine Parménie and C. [Catherine Hetzel] Bonnier de La Chapelle, *Histoire d'un éditeur et de ses auteurs: P.-J. Hetzel (Stahl)* [1953] (Paris: Albin Michel, 1985), p. 640. ('My dear friend, let me do you a favour. There has just been published in England (Cassel & Co.) a book called *Treasure Island* [. . .] by a Mr Stevenson. It is a story of sea adventures, pirates, hidden treasure – an old theme, as you see, but renewed by a rare gift of invention [. . .]. Hurry, because if you do not take the lead, another will certainly ask for permission to translate.' With thanks to Roger Swearingen for providing both the reference and the English translation.)
[15] Letter to Alfred Nutt, 4 October 1884, *Letters*, V, p. 13.
[16] See the article 'Petites nouvelles', *Gil Blas*, 15 February 1885, p. 3. Vincent Giroud also comments on Hetzel's role in 'Cocteau and Stevenson', p. 187.

de la forme, c'est fort cher; mais nous ne craignons pas d'échouer dans notre tâche si nous avons le concours de tous ceux qui aiment sérieusement l'enfance.'[17] Hetzel advertised *Treasure Island* relentlessly, publicising it as a 'livre d'étrennes' (potential gift book) in the week between Christmas and New Year 1885 (and for many years to come). It would no doubt have made an attractive gift: Tom Hubbard describes its binding as a 'gorgeously loud piece of exotica'.[18] Advertisements appeared in national and regional newspapers as diverse as *La Charente*, *Le Gaulois*, *Gil Blas*, *Le Grand Écho du Nord de la France*, *L'Intransigeant*, *L'Univers* and *Le XIXe siècle*. The novel was rarely advertised alone, most often appearing in advertisements masquerading as book review articles or in advertisements highlighting Hetzel's various collections. For example, when *L'Île au trésor* was promoted by Hetzel in *Le Figaro* on 5 December 1885, it appeared in an advertisement alongside fifteen other books, including novels by Jules Verne and Thomas Mayne Reid.[19]

Although he is not credited in *Le Temps*, the French translator of *L'Île au trésor* was André Laurie (pseudonym of Jean-François Paschal Grousset), a politician and author who collaborated with Verne on novels such as *L'Épave du Cynthia* and *L'Étoile du sud*. Laurie also wrote solo novels like *L'Héritier de Robinson* and translated the works of Mayne Reid, whom Stevenson describes in 'Rosa Quo Locorum' as a 'cheerful, ingenious, romantic soul'.[20] In a half-page advertisement that appeared in *Le Constitutionnel* and elsewhere, Hetzel put *Treasure Island* in the 'Romans d'aventure – A. Laurie' category along with *L'Épave du Cynthia* and *King Solomon's Mines*.[21] Initially, Laurie was the more famous writer and the fact that he was the translator was used to promote Stevenson's novel in France. This was a strategic decision, since Stevenson's own prior publications – *Travels*

---

[17] From an 1862 catalogue description of the Bibliothèque d'éducation et de récréation, cited in Daniel Compère, 'Hetzel et la littérature pour la jeunesse', *Europe*, 58.619 (1980), 31–8 (p. 32). ('We're taking a big gamble on children. Premium content and premium form come at a cost; but we're not worried about failing in our mission if we have the help of all those who earnestly love youth.')

[18] 'Dva Brata', p. 17.

[19] Similar ads masquerading as articles appeared in other newspapers: for example, L.M., 'Livres d'étrennes', *La Charente*, 29 December 1885, p. 3; *La Charente*, 26 December 1886, p. 3.

[20] 'Rosa Quo Locorum', in *Further Memories*, p. 4, was likely drafted in 1893. It was first published in the Edinburgh Edition of Stevenson's works in 1896.

[21] *Le Constitutionnel*, 20 December 1890, p. 4. Similar advertisements appeared in *Le Grand Écho du Nord de la France* in December 1892 and December 1905.

with a Donkey (1879), *An Inland Voyage* (1878) and the essays – would not be published in French for many years to come, and *New Arabian Nights* (1882), volume one of which was also translated in 1885, was not yet widely enough known in France to be used as a marketing hook.[22]

The *Île au trésor* serial was printed without any critical apparatus, as was usual, but the book contained a preface signed 'J. Hetzel et Cie' in which the novel's credentials were established, presumably the better to market it to parents buying for their children (but also to readers of *Le Temps*). The preface drew attention to the novel's immediate success in Britain and to the fact that Prime Minister Gladstone and Edmond Schérer both approved of it, which was clearly a means of attracting adult purchasers:

> Un très vif succès a déjà accueilli comme livre charmant *L'Île au Trésor*, en Angleterre et dans le feuilleton du *Temps*. Ce succès n'est pas venu exclusivement des jeunes lecteurs à qui l'ouvrage semblait d'abord destiné. Grandes sœurs et grands frères, maîtres et parents l'ont dévoré avec un égal appétit. Cela n'a rien qui puisse étonner, en présence de l'intérêt saisissant du sujet et de l'accent si personnel du style. [. . .]
>
> L'illustre homme d'État [Gladstone] ne saurait passer pour un esprit naïf ou illettré, accessible aux impressions vulgaires. Tout le monde connaît son érudition profonde et les beaux travaux qui l'auraient placé au premier rang des hellénistes, si l'éloquence ne l'avait mis au premier rang des politiques.
>
> Eh bien! dès les premières pages, le charme subtil de *L'Île au Trésor* agit si vivement sur cette haute intelligence que M. Gladstone en oublia tout le reste. [. . .]
>
> Nous ne nuirons pas aux mérites de l'ÎLE AU TRÉSOR en disant que c'est sur la recommandation de l'éminent critique, M. *Edmond Schérer*, que nous l'avons lu et que nous avons acquis, à l'exclusion de tous autres, le droit de le traduire en langue française.[23]

---

[22] *Travels with a Donkey* was translated and adapted in 1901 and translated in 1925: *Voyage à travers les Cévennes avec un âne*, trans. and adapted by A. Moulharac (Paris: Club cévénol, 1901); *Voyage avec un âne dans les Cévennes; Au fil de l'Oise*, trans. by Fanny W. Laparra, Bibliothèque cosmopolite (Paris: Stock, 1925). *New Arabian Nights* was translated by Louis Despréaux as *Suicide-Club. Le Diamant du Rajah* (Paris: Calmann-Lévy, 1885).

[23] *L'Île au trésor*, trans. by André Laurie, illus. by Georges Roux, Bibliothèque d'éducation et de récréation (Paris: Hetzel, 1885), pp. i–ii. ('The charming book *Treasure Island* has already met with a lively success in England and as a serial in *Le Temps*. This success isn't only down to the young readers to whom the work seemed at first to be geared. Older sisters and older brothers, schoolmasters and

This preface was quoted almost verbatim in an announcement (read: advertisement) for the book that was published in the Angoulême newspaper, *La Charente*, and elsewhere on 31 December 1885. The newspaper mentions its success in both Britain and in *Le Temps*, calling the book a 'chef-d'œuvre' and commenting on its 'allure tout à fait originale'.

Several other French translations of *Treasure Island* have been published since Laurie's for Hetzel, including most notably Théo Varlet's for highbrow Éditions de la Sirène, and Albert Savine and Albert Lieutaud's for Albin Michel (1924); the latter also included a translation of Stevenson's essay 'My First Book'. *L'Île au trésor* has been serialised several times, too. In 1908, Laurie's translation was published in *Le Petit Parisien*; in 1916, it appeared in the extreme right daily newspaper, *L'Action Française*, a self-described 'organe du nationalisme intégral' run by Léon Daudet who, notwithstanding his frequently repugnant politics and early anti-Semitism, was an observant reader of Stevenson. In 1921, Varlet's translation was serialised in the socialist international newspaper, *Le Populaire*, which published it at the same time that it serialised Zola's *Travail*, a detail that would surely have amused Stevenson given his ambivalent feelings about Zola and his less ambivalent views on idleness.[24] The fact that the same novel was serialised in such radically different venues did not fail to raise eyebrows. Another daily newspaper, *L'Intransigeant*, suggested that it was a testament to the independence of novelists, but it could just as well point to the popular – populist? – appeal of Stevenson's swashbuckling adventure tale:

parents, have devoured it with equal appetite. There is nothing surprising in this, given the thrilling interest of the subject or the very personal accent of the style. [. . .] The illustrious statesman [Gladstone] could hardly pass for naïve or illiterate, susceptible to vulgar feelings. Everyone is familiar with his profound erudition and the fine works that would have placed him among the first rank of Hellenists, if his eloquence hadn't already placed him in the first rank of politicians. Well! From the first pages, the subtle charm of *Treasure Island* acted so swiftly upon this great intellect that Mr Gladstone forgot all else. [. . .] We would not be taking away from *Treasure Island*'s merits by saying that it was on the recommendation of the eminent critic, M. Edmond Schérer, that we read it and acquired the exclusive right to translate it into French.') A lengthy article-cum-advertisement on Hetzel's 'livres d'étrennes' by Charles Clément mentions much the same thing as this preface. 'Livres d'étrennes: publications illustrées de la maison Hetzel', *Journal des débats politiques et littéraires*, 23 December 1885, pp. 2–3.

[24] *L'Île au trésor*, trans. by Théo Varlet, *Le Populaire*, 8 April–25 May 1921.

L'Île au Trésor, de Stevenson, a été publié récemment en feuilleton par *l'Action Française*. *Le Populaire* annonce qu'il va la faire paraître. Cette communauté d'accès à de si lointain extrêmes est une des choses qui peuvent rehausser le mieux l'indépendance du métier de romancier.[25]

The fate of *Treasure Island* is a first indication of the wide and diverse reading public that Stevenson would gain in France.

Stevenson was pleased with the edition that Hetzel produced, and later wrote to Berthe Low on 18 August 1886, sending her a copy of the book accompanied by the following comments:

Chère Madame Low, Nous allons faire quelques petites fautes de Français, n'est ce [sic] pas? – C'est convenu? – Alors, me voilà content: me voilà à même de vous dire tout tranquillement que ce que vous avez à la main est une petite bêtise assez mal écrite, assez bien traduite; et que je vous prie de l'accepter en souvenir du boulevard Montparnasse, de Montigny sur Loing et de la rue Vernier.[26]

Stevenson was particularly satisfied with Georges Roux's illustrations, especially their ability to quickly narrate the story: 'A picture in a storybook must be something more than a mere pretty picture; it should do more even than represent a suitably selected type; it should narrate.' The illustrations also had the distinct merit of allowing Stevenson to appreciate his own story:

The story of *Treasure Island* has been so treated, so illuminated, so condensed and is thrown up into a sort of glory by a French artist – one of

---

[25] Les Treize, 'Les Lettres', *L'Intransigeant*, 4 April 1921, p. 2. ('*Treasure Island*, by Stevenson, has recently been serialised by *L'Action Française*. *Le Populaire* is announcing that the novel is going to appear. This access to communities separated by such extremes is one of the things that best underscores the independence of the novelist's profession.') *L'Action Française* also serialised *The Master of Ballantrae* (23 May–22 July 1921).
[26] *Letters*, V, pp. 301–2. ('Dear Mrs. Low, I'm going to make a few little mistakes in French, ok? Agreed? Well, I'm pleased: I'm now able to tell you quite coolly that what you have in your hands is a little foolishness, fairly badly written, fairly well translated, that I beg you to accept in remembrance of Boulevard Montparnasse, Montigny sur Loing and Rue Vernier.' Translation contained in a footnote to the original letter.) A facsimile of this letter is printed in Low, *A Chronicle of Friendships: 1873–1900*, p. 335, available at <https://archive.org/details/achronicle frien-01lowgoog/page/n433>.

the band, if I am not in error, who did the like along with de Neuville for Jules Verne. Henceforth it may be skimmed, swift as a racer, the points seized, the story drained of such cheap virtue as it possesses in five living minutes instead of in the tedium of several hours of study. Not only that. There is one man in England with a particular liking for such boyish kickshaws, who was yet, by an unalterable law, hitherto debarred from reading *Treasure Island*; and that was the man who wrote it. His was a hard case; he thought he would like that story, it was the essence of what he had admired in so many others; and yet the gates of that penny Paradise were closed against him. He could read Shakespeare and Dumas, and Homer, thanks to Mr Lang; he could have read (if he had wanted) the whole series of foul and dreary plays that go by the name of Dodsley; and he could read *King Solomon's Mines*, and did. But not *Treasure Island*; that was shut out from him, the mist always thick down over the Spy-glass, not even the surf audible; till down stepped M. Roux with this new graphic version, reeling the whole story off in a score of spirited plates, and for the first time introducing him to his own puppets. If any man should be grateful to M. Roux, I think it should be he; if any man has a mind quite disengaged of any fear or favour, it must be he, for to him M. Roux is the inventor.[27]

Stevenson advised Charles Scribner to use the Roux illustrations: 'Should you get *Treasure Island*, remember to sack the disgusting American illustrations; and get from Hetzel, Roux's very spirited pictures – the very best of which Cassell omitted to reproduce!'[28] The Roux illustrations were picked up by both Cassell and Scribner's for their illustrated English-language versions beginning in 1885. Hetzel also recognised the quality of the illustrations: an 1886 advertisement for André Laurie's novel, *Le Capitaine Trafalgar*, mentions that Roux's illustrations for *Le Capitaine Trafalgar* are 'aussi artiste que dans L'Île au trésor de Stevenson et Laurie'.[29] This reveals a good deal about the quality of the illustrations, but it is also a good indication of how quickly the Hetzel edition made a name for itself. A year after *Treasure Island* was published in French, the tables had been turned: *Treasure Island* was now being used to promote a novel by

---

[27] From Stevenson's notes on the Roux illustrations, Yale GEN MSS 664, Box 44, Folder 992, Beinecke 7062. See also Kevin Carpenter, 'R.L. Stevenson on the *Treasure Island* Illustrations', *Notes and Queries*, 29.4 (August 1982), 322–5.
[28] [? 20 October 1887], *Letters*, VI, p. 40.
[29] *La Charente*, 26 December 1886, p. 3. ('As artistic as in Stevenson and Laurie's *Treasure Island*.')

its translator whereas initially (and unusually) the translator's name had been used to promote the foreign author's book.

Periodical Publications and Serials

Unsurprisingly, *Treasure Island* and *Strange Case of Dr. Jekyll and Mr. Hyde* (1886) reached foreign readers soon after their release in English: both were serialised in French within a year of their initial publication in English, although only one of these serialisations was destined for a Continental audience. Serialisation could offer distinct advantages for authors, as they could be paid for the serial and again for the book. For Stevenson, the primary benefit of serialisation in France was one of exposure, something that was particularly important for foreign authors who were operating outside of Parisian (and, in his case, London) literary circles. Other British authors were aware of this, also: Mary Elizabeth Braddon, for instance, serialised her novel *Le Pasteur de Marston* (1881) in *Le Figaro* before it was published in English.[30]

Treasure Island was Stevenson's French calling card, but some of his other works were also serialised while he was alive: *The Suicide Club*, *The Master of Ballantrae* and *The Dynamiter*, for instance, all appeared in newspapers. The *Journal des débats* serialised 'The Story of the Young Man with the Cream Tarts' from *New Arabian Nights* as *Le Club des suicidés* in 1888. *The Master of Ballantrae* was serialised in an abridged version in *Le Temps* in 1893, four years after it was published in English.[31] Like *Treasure Island*, *The Master of Ballantrae* appeared in other incarnations, as well: it was reserialised by *L'Action française* in the 1920s, when it was also released as a book in a translation by Théo Varlet; it was once again reserialised in the socialist newspaper, *L'Humanité*, in 1931. Meanwhile, *The Dynamiter* appeared in the *Revue hebdomadaire* in June 1894. By the interwar years, Stevenson's stories were reaching a wide reading public via serialisation in mainstream left- and right-leaning broadsheets.

As the above examples indicate, publication in periodicals continued after Stevenson's death in 1894. The serialisation of *The Wrecker*

---

[30] Atkinson, *French Novels and the Victorians*, p. 247, n. 27.
[31] The translator of the serial is not specified. Giroud ('Cocteau and Stevenson', p. 191) writes that *The Master of Ballantrae* was not available in French before 1914. Strictly speaking, this is true, since the serialised translation does not seem to have been published as a book.

(1892) began in July 1895.³² 'The Beach of Falesá', 'Markheim' and 'Will o' the Mill' all appeared in periodicals between 1899 and 1902. This cluster of publications is likely a response to Stevenson's death, but it also reflects realistic timeframes for translations to appear. *Kidnapped* (1886) was serialised in the *Journal des débats politiques et littéraires* in 1899 in a translation by Marie Dronsart, and again in the *Le Journal de la jeunesse* in 1905.³³ *Catriona* (1893), on the other hand, was not serialised, nor was it translated into French immediately, despite its success in the English-language market. The French translation of *Catriona* appeared in 1907, fourteen years after it was published in English.

Of particular literary-historical interest are the two novels that Stevenson was working on when he died, *Weir of Hermiston* (1896) and *St. Ives* (1897). *St. Ives* was closer to completion than *Weir of Hermiston*; because it was expected to have more popular appeal, arrangements were made to have the final six chapters written by Arthur Quiller-Couch so that the book could be published whole. As *St. Ives* was deemed the more commercially promising of the two novels, it was serialised in both Britain and the United States, where it was also syndicated.³⁴ The book was then published by Heinemann, a company described by Glenda Norquay as an 'avant-garde firm, outward-looking in their grasp of European and American markets' and 'adept at using popular fiction to subsidise more highbrow publications'.³⁵ *St. Ives* was also serialised in France, in the same newspaper that had serialised *Treasure Island* and *The Master of Ballantrae*: it appeared in *Le Temps* from 23 August to 25 October 1902. The translation was done by Teodor de Wyzewa, who, as will be seen, was heavily involved in Parisian intellectual and artistic circles, and played a major role in importing European literature into France. When the French *St. Ives* appeared in book form, it was published by Hachette, which even then was slowly taking over the publishing

---

³² It was serialised in the *Journal des voyages* and published as a volume in 1896.

³³ In 'In Search of the New Novel: Translations of R.L. Stevenson in Nineteenth-Century France', *Nineteenth Century Studies*, 27 (2013), 129–42 (p. 131), I state that *Kidnapped* was not serialised; let this stand as a correction.

³⁴ For more details, see Norquay, *Robert Louis Stevenson, Literary Networks and Transatlantic Publishing in the 1890s*, p. 55. Chapter 2 of that work deals with *Weir of Hermiston* and *St. Ives*, while chapter 6 deals with Arthur Quiller-Couch.

³⁵ *Robert Louis Stevenson, Literary Networks and Transatlantic Publishing in the 1890s*, p. 56.

world. Although the translation itself was done by someone who was decidedly cultivated, it was being sold by a company with one of the widest train station distribution networks in France.

Weir of Hermiston was considered a more highbrow text, a would-be masterpiece, so its serialisation was approached very differently. Rather than arranging for another author to finish it, it was published in its unfinished form. In January 1896, it was the opening text in the first issue of the international magazine *Cosmopolis*. The British edition was published by Fisher Unwin; the French edition by Armand Colin, which was responsible for distribution in French colonies, Alsace-Lorraine, Belgium, Switzerland, southern Europe and Spanish- and Portuguese-speaking countries. The presentation of *Weir* in the French *Cosmopolis* appears to largely coincide with the British version: it contains editorial notes by Sidney Colvin and English running heads, advertisements, and so on, but French subscription information and title and contents pages.[36]

Cosmopolis targeted a learned, multilingual readership and published foreign works in the original language, as it did *Weir of Hermiston* for French readers.[37] As a promotional insert in *Le Gaulois* explained: '*Cosmopolis* s'adresse d'une manière *spéciale* à deux sortes de lecteurs: d'une part, à ceux qui lisent les langues étrangères; d'autre part, à tous ceux qui s'intéressent au mouvement littéraire, politique, artistique et scientifique des pays voisins.'[38] *Cosmopolis* appealed to a learned, literate readership and by publishing English, French and German texts side by side it fulfilled its cosmopolitan mandate. One gets the sense that Stevenson not only would have read the magazine but would have appreciated being serialised in its pages alongside writers like Paul Bourget and Anatole France. Given its multilingualism, it necessarily served a niche market, notwithstanding its reassurance to monolingual French readers that each issue

---

[36] See Gillian Hughes's discussion of 'British serialization in *Cosmopolis*' in 'Essay on the Text', in *Weir of Hermiston*, ed. by Gillian Hughes, New Edinburgh Edition of the Works of Robert Louis Stevenson (Edinburgh: Edinburgh University Press, 2017), pp. 117–72 (pp. 148–52).
[37] Norquay discusses the American edition of *Cosmopolis* in *Robert Louis Stevenson, Literary Networks and Transatlantic Publishing in the 1890s*, p. 71.
[38] *Cosmopolis* promotional insert, *Le Gaulois*, 9 April 1896, p. 1. ('*Cosmopolis* caters *specifically* to two types of readers: on the one hand, to those who read foreign languages; on the other, to all those who are interested in the literary, political, artistic and scientific movements of neighbouring countries.')

would contain over 200 pages for them to read.[39] Even though the journal did better than expected – its first issue of 24,000 copies sold out – it was aimed at the few.[40] Other French publishers and publications made Stevenson's work available to the many in translation.

Julia Reid notes that *Cosmopolis* 'aimed to transcend national cultures, promoting cultural, and particularly linguistic and literary, exchange'.[41] It is not entirely clear how successful it was in doing so, at least in France. One French review saluted Paris for having been the birthplace of such a magazine. Writing in *Le Gaulois*, Stanislas Rzewuski touted the magazine's distinctly French nature, seemingly ignoring its international origins – only in Paris could a groundbreaking cosmopolitan publication like this have seen the light of day. The cosmopolitan for him is rooted to a very precise locale. Since Paris was the centre of the European literary world, it was only natural that *Cosmopolis* should issue from the city:

> C'est bien dans notre cher pays de France, dont l'admirable, pure et limpide langue, de tradition latine et de souplesse toute moderne est devenue et demeurée la langue universelle de la civilisation occidentale; c'est bien à Paris que devait paraître pour la première fois une publication, d'originalité tellement significative, d'importance sociale et philosophique si profonde, d'intérêt si vivace et si varié à la fois.[42]

Weir of Hermiston started its life in France in English, in an international magazine whose cosmopolitanism was perceived in France as being distinctly French in outlook, if not in language. The novel was not translated into French until 1912. This can be accounted for by the fact that it was unfinished and therefore not likely to fly

---

[39] This is stated on p. 2 of the Armand Colin informational pages that appear after the extensive 'Cosmopolis Literary Advertiser' section and immediately before the paginated pages of the actual magazine begin.
[40] See 'Librairie', *Journal des débats politiques et littéraires*, 22 February 1896, p. 3.
[41] 'The *Academy* and *Cosmopolis*: Evolution and Culture in Robert Louis Stevenson's Periodical Encounters', in *Culture and Science in the Nineteenth-Century Media*, ed. by Louise Henson and others (London: Routledge, 2016), pp. 263–73 (p. 267).
[42] 'Cosmopolis', *Le Gaulois*, 8 April 1896, p. 2. ('The fact is that it's in our beloved France, whose admirable, pure and clear language – Latin in origin and very modern in its flexibility – has become and has remained the universal language of Western civilisation; it's in Paris that this publication – so significant in its originality, so profound in its social and philosophical importance, so lively and varied in its interests – appeared.')

off the shelves: just as *Cosmopolis* was aimed at a niche multinational and multilingual audience, there was (and is) also a niche market for unfinished works. In the end, *Hermiston: le juge-pendeur* was released by Fontemoing, which also ran the highbrow journal *Minerva* where Stevenson's correspondence and 'The Beach of Falesá' had been published in 1902–3. A similar cultured readership was targeted by the journal *Vers et prose*, which published extracts of *À la pagaie* (*An Inland Voyage*) in 1906–7. Channelling Joachim du Bellay's *Défense et illustration de la langue française* (1549), *Vers et prose* bore the inscription '"Défense et illustration" de la haute littérature et du lyrisme en prose et en poésie' on its title page.[43]

It is more difficult to trace the periodical and serialisation history of Stevenson's short stories and essays. French readers were able to read translations of the stories contained in the first volume of *New Arabian Nights* as early as 1885, and their complicated publishing history has been comprehensively traced by Vincent Giroud.[44] The *New Arabian Nights* stories and *The Dynamiter* were popular in France – *Le Dynamiteur* was even a recommended book of the day in *La Justice* in 1894.[45] In other cases, individual stories appeared in their entirety in periodicals as one-off publications rather than as serials: a complete translation of 'Will o' the Mill', for example, was published in *La Vogue* ('une revue fort bohème') in March 1899.[46] The sheer number and variety of translations being published is cause for confusion, as is the fact that stories were published as stand-alone texts when they were in fact originally part of collections or novels with a genre-defying structure. Because of this, it is hard to keep track of the who, what and where of Stevenson's books in French.

Stevenson entered the literary world in English through his essays in the 1870s. If George Saintsbury is to be believed, this is a genre in which 'certain critical friends of his strongly urged him to continue'.[47] Stevenson's essays appeared only sporadically in French, sometimes published in conjunction with a novel. Generic issues are likely at play in the different translation history of the novels,

---

[43] According to David Steel ('Alain-Fournier's *Le Grand Meaulnes*', p. 125), this text was not appreciated by Alain-Fournier.
[44] 'Cocteau and Stevenson', p. 188.
[45] G.G. [? Georges Grappe], 'Le livre du jour', *La Justice*, 18 October 1894, p. 2.
[46] 'Will du Moulin', trans. by Marcel Schwob, *La Vogue*, March 1899, pp. 145–69; Gustave Kahn, 'La Vogue', *La Vogue*, January 1899, pp. 5–8 (p. 7).
[47] *The English Novel* (London: J.M. Dent, 1913), on gutenberg.org, chapter 'The Fiction of Yesterday – Conclusion'.

short stories and essays. The novel was the dominant literary genre in terms of sales and reach, and the printed book was not only valued more highly than periodicals, it also lasted longer. Stevenson's essays were originally published in assorted English and American reviews before being collected in *Virginibus Puerisque* (1881), *Familiar Studies of Men and Books* (1882), *Memories and Portraits* (1887) and *Across the Plains* (1892). English-language periodicals might have been read by the French intelligentsia, but few publishers (French or otherwise) would risk publishing collections of essays in translation if the author was not already a known quantity. As far as fiction is concerned, serials and periodicals undoubtedly have the potential to reach a wide audience when they are printed, but they do not have the longevity and visibility of a book. Nor is there any guarantee that a reader who buys a newspaper for the news is going to read the serialised fiction, although a successful serial could bolster sales. For these reasons, two explanations help clarify why Stevenson and his supporters thought that his reputation in France was not what it ought to have been: his essays were not translated, and there was the impression that Stevenson's fiction was not readily available to readers. These are legitimate concerns, especially as regards the essays, but Stevenson's French fans may not have realised how many of his stories had in fact been translated in periodicals. In one sense, the publication of Stevenson's stories in periodicals and serials obscures how much of his work was available in French translation, since few of his works were published in the same place, thereby complicating attempts to assess his impact.

French *Jekyll and Hydes*

The one glaring omission from the above overview of serialisation is *Strange Case of Dr. Jekyll and Mr. Hyde*, not because the novel was not translated, but because its early French history is itself a story of transnational convolution. *Strange Case of Dr. Jekyll and Mr. Hyde* was originally published in January 1886, and it was an immediate success in the English-speaking world: according to its publisher, Charles Longman, 40,000 copies were sold in six months in Britain, and sales took off after a review in *The Times* on 25 January 1885.[48] The novel was serialised in French, but not in France. In 1887, the

---

[48] Balfour, *The Life of Robert Louis Stevenson*, II, p. 14.

Québec newspaper *La Vérité* serialised *Le Cas extraordinaire du Dr. Jekyll et M. Hyde*; the same translation appeared as a book in Québec the following year.[49] *Le Cas étrange du docteur Jekyll* first appeared as a book in France in 1890, in a new translation.[50] It is unusual to find two translations of the same text into the same language when it is protected by copyright, yet this happened to *Strange Case of Dr. Jekyll and Mr. Hyde* during Stevenson's lifetime, apparently without Stevenson's knowledge. The existence of two French-language versions can be explained by the cultural and legal history of the nineteenth century more than by linguistic differences between metropolitan and Canadian French, which is to say that the French translation was not a reaction to perceived deficiencies in the Canadian version or concerns that the Canadian version would not be suitable for a French audience.

Under the provisions of the Berne Convention, which also dates from 1886, authors enjoyed 'the exclusive right of making or authorizing the translation of their works until the expiration of ten years from the publication of the original work in one of the countries of the Union'.[51] France and the United Kingdom both ratified the Convention, which guaranteed the reciprocal rights of authors and artists in signatory countries by protecting them against piracy and copyright infringement. As a British dominion, Canada was bound to the Convention, but it failed to embrace it wholeheartedly; indeed, Canada attempted to withdraw from the Convention in 1888, which implies that even in the face of copyright violations, it would have been unlikely to strictly enforce the Convention. The evidence points to the French-Canadian translation being in a legally doubtful position. This is significant because, as Stevenson explained to Edward L. Burlingame, he 'omitted to reserve the American rights in *Jekyll*',[52] and also because by Graham Balfour's account 250,000 copies of *Strange Case of Dr. Jekyll and Mr. Hyde* were in circulation in the United States.[53] It is highly likely that the translator of the French-Canadian edition, Jules-Paul Tardivel, used an American edition of the novel for

---

[49] Charles Buet, *Le Treizième fils*; [Robert Louis Stevenson], *Le Cas extraordinaire du Dr. Jekyll et de M. Hyde*, trans. by Jules-Paul Tardivel (Québec: Drouin, 1888).
[50] *Le Cas étrange du docteur Jekyll*, trans. by Mme B.-J. Lowe (Paris: Plon, Nourrit, 1890).
[51] Article 5 of the *Berne Convention* (1886), available at <http://global.oup.com/booksites/content/9780198259466/15550015> and <https://wipolex.wipo.int/en/treaties/textdetails/12807>.
[52] [Postmark 6 December 1887], *Letters*, VI, p. 75.
[53] *The Life of Robert Louis Stevenson*, II, p. 14.

his translation: Tardivel was an American citizen by birth, Québec is closer to the United States than to Britain, there was not yet any copyright agreement between the United States and the United Kingdom, and there are similarities between Tardivel's translation of the penultimate chapter and the American version of the text.[54]

Stevenson knew his French translator personally, but there is no evidence that he was aware of the French-Canadian translation of *Strange Case of Dr. Jekyll and Mr. Hyde*, even though, according to the National Library of Scotland's Bibliography of Scottish Literature in Translation, this was the first translation of the novel to appear in any language.[55] *Le Cas extraordinaire du Dr. Jekyll et M. Hyde* was serialised from January to April 1887 and published in 1888; Stevenson was in Saranac Lake, New York, from September 1887 to April 1888, and could possibly have seen the translation while there, given his proximity to Québec. His wife Fanny could also have become aware of the translation when she visited Montréal in October 1887.[56] But this is no more than speculation: the only thing that is certain is that Stevenson left no comments on Tardivel's translation.

Jules-Paul Tardivel was an ultramontane polemicist whose unalterable mission was to defend Catholicism in Québec and elsewhere.[57] The fact that *Le Cas extraordinaire du Dr. Jekyll et M. Hyde*

---

[54] On copyright arrangements between the United States and the United Kingdom, see Simon Eliot, 'The Business of Victorian Publishing', in *The Cambridge Companion to the Victorian Novel*, ed. by David, pp. 37–60 (p. 52). My thanks to Richard Dury for highlighting the parallels between the phrases of the penultimate chapter of Tardivel's translation and the American edition of the novel: UK edition: 'There was never a day when [. . .] I would not have sacrificed my fortune or my left hand to help you'; US edition: 'There was never a day when [. . .] I would not have sacrificed my left hand to help you'; Tardivel: '[. . .] je n'aurais pas sacrifié ma main gauche pour vous aider'.

[55] Bibliography of Scottish Literature in Translation, available at <https://data.nls.uk/data/metadata-collections/boslit/>. This is confirmed by Appendix 2 'Early Translations', in *Strange Case of Dr. Jekyll and Mr. Hyde*, ed. by Richard Dury (Edinburgh: Edinburgh University Press, 2004), pp. 164–5.

[56] Letter to his Wife, [c. 24 October 1887], *Letters*, VI, p. 45.

[57] Tardivel's politico-religious thinking is formulated in *Pour la patrie* (1895), his highly eccentric speculative novel that presents a vision of mid-twentieth-century Quebec and opens on a black mass during which Satan orders his disciple, a French Freemason, to go and carry out his orders on the other side of the Atlantic: 'Traverse les mers, rends-toi sur les bords du Saint-Laurent où tes ancêtres ont jadis planté l'Étendard de mon éternel Ennemi. C'est là que ton œuvre t'attend. La Croix est encore debout sur ce coin du globe. Abats-la. Compte sur mes inspirations.' *Pour la Patrie: roman du XXe siècle*, ed. by John Hare (Montréal: Hurtubise, 1995), p. 56. ('Cross the seas, go to the banks of the Saint-Lawrence where long ago your ancestors planted the flag of my eternal Enemy. Your work awaits you there. The Cross still stands on that corner of the earth. Strike it down. Count on my inspiration').

was Tardivel's only translation and was included in a volume with a moralistic Catholic story (which had preceded it as a feuilleton in *La Vérité*) shows that it was interpreted as relevant to the moral struggle in which Tardivel, owner and editor of *La Vérité*, was engaged. Tardivel advocated for a 'roman qui fortifie la volonté, qui élève et assainit le cœur, qui fait aimer davantage la vertu et haïr le vice, qui inspire de nobles sentiments, qui est, en un mot, la contre-partie du roman infâme'.[58] This is precisely the type of novel found in his newspaper, *La Vérité*, a pro-independence Catholic weekly. Although *La Vérité* always contained a serial within its eight pages, they were customarily representative of Catholic literature. Consequently, when announcing the publication of *Le Cas extraordinaire du Dr. Jekyll et M. Hyde* in the newspaper, Tardivel considered it necessary to explain to readers that the novel was an 'espèce d'allégorie qui nous montre la réalité des deux hommes placés au dedans de chacun de nous, et dont parle saint Paul'.[59] In this respect, Tom Hubbard is absolutely correct to assert that

> we can reasonably infer that Tardivel considered Stevenson's work to be a straightforward tract on good versus evil, and he would have been alert to the likening of Hyde to Satan; it is unlikely that he would have perceived the novella's moral and artistic subtleties.[60]

---

[58] *Pour la patrie*, p. 50. ('A novel that fortifies the will, lifts up and cleanses the heart, that makes one love virtue and hate vice even more, that inspires noble sentiments and is, in a word, the opposite of the novel of infamy.')

[59] 'Nouveau feuilleton', *La Vérité*, 8 January 1887, p. 6. ('A sort of allegory that shows us the reality of the two men living within each of us, and of which Saint Paul speaks.') He was not the first person to interpret it in this way: *Strange Case of Dr. Jekyll and Mr. Hyde* was the subject of a sermon preached at St Paul's Cathedral in London. See Bryan Bevan, *Robert Louis Stevenson: Poet and Teller of Tales* (New York: St. Martin's Press, 1993), p. 120. Another sermon, published in *The Rock*, a journal from the Unified Church of England and Ireland, discusses it in the same terms. It mentions Saint Paul in its first paragraph, and while specifying that *Strange Case of Dr. Jekyll and Mr. Hyde* is not a religious text, states that 'the book is calculated to do a great deal of good, not only to those who profess and call themselves Christians, but to those who are, in every sense of the word, true believers. Though there is nothing distinctively Christian about it, we hope none will suppose that we mean to imply that there is anything antagonistic to Christianity. The truth taught to us by the Apostle, to which we have referred above, is one recognised by those outside Christian Churches.' 'Secret Sin', *The Rock*, 2 April 1886, p. 3, in *Robert Louis Stevenson: The Critical Heritage*, ed. by Maixner, pp. 224–7 (pp. 224–5).

[60] 'Dva Brata', p. 20.

The inclusion of *Le Cas extraordinaire du Dr. Jekyll et M. Hyde* in *La Vérité* can therefore be explained by the fact that the story was perceived as having a moral that corresponded with the religious values of its translator, even if those values were not necessarily shared by Stevenson. From Tardivel's point of view, 'quoique l'auteur soit un protestant, le récit ne manque pas d'une saine morale' because 'elle nous fait voir la nécessité de dompter l'homme animal qui cherche sans cesse à dominer l'homme spirituel'.[61]

The context in which *Strange Case of Dr. Jekyll and Mr. Hyde* was published in France is very different and allows us to see once again the diversity of Stevenson's audience. The full translation did not appear until 1890, but in 1888 Thérèse Bentzon included a partial translation of the novel in a lengthy article on Stevenson published in the *Revue des deux mondes*, for which she had been a literary critic since 1872. Bentzon's article contains a detailed summary of the text interspersed with translated passages, including 'Henry Jekyll's Full Statement of the Case'.[62] The prestigious *Revue des deux mondes* was read by French cultural and political elites, and the authors and books it discussed, translated and published benefited from high cultural visibility.[63] In view of this, Bentzon starts her article with an apology of sorts, situating Stevenson – especially *L'Île au trésor*, his best-known novel at that point – in relation to children's literature. This tactic, which mirrors Hetzel's preface to *Treasure Island* even though it is not motivated by marketing, allows her to overcome any potential prejudices on the part of her readers. She then skilfully moves from the topic of children's literature to the notion of art for art's sake:

---

[61] 'Nouveau feuilleton', p. 6. ('Even though the author is a Protestant, the tale isn't lacking a sound moral' because 'it makes us see the necessity of taming the animal side of man that is constantly trying to dominate the spiritual side'.)

[62] This type of presentation was not uncommon. For example, Marie Anne de Bovet's article on Oscar Wilde's 'The Decay of Lying' contains 'a detailed summary of Wilde's critical dialogue and a full translation of the work'. Rebecca N. Mitchell, 'Oscar Wilde and the French Press, 1880–1981', *Victorian Periodicals Review*, 49.1 (2016), 123–48 (p. 132). 'Thérèse Bentzon' was a pseudonym of Marie-Thérèse Blanc, 1840–1907.

[63] Blaise Wilfert, 'Literary Import into France and Britain around 1900: A Comparative Study', in *Anglo-French Attitudes: Comparisons and Transfers Between English and French Intellectuals Since the Eighteenth Century*, ed. by Christophe Charle, Julien Vincent and Jay Winter (Manchester: Manchester University Press, 2007), pp. 173–93 (p. 177).

Quiconque écrit pour la jeunesse doit s'en tenir à l'observation superficielle, construire des caractères tout d'une pièce et s'imposer de tirer des déductions morales claires et saisissantes de chaque incident; ce qui est le contraire des règles de l'art, qui n'est astreint à rien prouver, pourvu que l'œuvre soit belle.[64]

On the one hand, this is a simple statement that fiction written expressly for children usually needs to be morally clear and simplified in terms of characterisation. On the other, her definition of art as having nothing to prove or teach, so long as it is beautiful, does not correspond to typical notions of children's literature. It does, however, point to the ways in which Stevenson through his artistry may have innovated in the genres in which he worked. Insofar as this is the case, her comments can also be read as a response to the Hetzel translation of *Treasure Island*, in which Laurie corrects some of the moral ambiguity of the original text by appending an epilogue that ties up loose ends (this would have established the 'visée educative' – the educational aims – of the novel and better fitted in with Hetzel's series).[65]

By presenting *Strange Case of Dr. Jekyll and Mr. Hyde* and Stevenson to readers in this way, Bentzon succeeds in negotiating the space between children's literature and Serious Literature. Because of her audience, she also succeeds in negotiating the space between conservative, academic literature (with which the *Revue des deux mondes* was associated) and modernising, foreign literature (the *Revue des deux mondes* was also one of the major importers of foreign literature). It was a publication that Matthew Arnold admired for its disinterestedness, and he described it as 'having for its main function to understand and utter the best that is known and thought in the world, existing, it may be said, as just an organ for a free play of the mind'.[66] Being published in the *Revue des deux mondes*, a veritable cultural institution, assured official recognition from the Paris literary centre – it was a laissez-passer of sorts.

---

[64] 'Le Roman étrange en Angleterre', *Revue des deux mondes*, April 1888, pp. 550–81 (p. 550). ('Whoever writes for youth must limit themselves to superficial observation, construct straightforward characters and make it a rule to draw clear and striking moral deductions from every incident; which is in opposition to the rules of art, which is not compelled to prove anything, so long as the work is beautiful.')

[65] Isabelle Nières-Chevrel, 'Littérature d'enfance et de jeunesse', in *Histoire des traductions en langue française. XIXe siècle: 1815–1914*, ed. by Yves Chevrel, Lieven d'Hulst and Christine Lombez (Paris: Verdier, 2012), pp. 665–726 (p. 704).

[66] 'The Function of Criticism at the Present Time', *The National Review*, 19 (November 1864), pp. 230–51 (p. 240).

Thanks in part to Bentzon's article and translation, Stevenson would no longer be perceived simply (and negatively) as a writer for young people; he would over time become a model artist for young French writers. Bentzon's essay and partial translation allowed his reputation to gradually transform, helped spread his work in France, and as such helped contribute to his eventual consecration. It was an advertisement for a hitherto unknown version of Stevenson. Its importance for Stevenson's reputation in France is underscored by the fact that Michel Raimond refers to the article in his foundational book, *La Crise du roman: des lendemains du naturalisme aux années vingt*.[67] Her essay was subsequently republished as a preface to the 1890 edition of *Nouvelles mille et une nuits*, published by Hetzel. This was the second book of Stevenson's that Hetzel published, and it resulted in Stevenson being simultaneously included in the 'Bibliothèque d'éducation et de récréation' (*L'Île au trésor*) and the 'Bibliothèque franco-étrangère' (*Nouvelles mille et une nuits*). This is a useful indication of how he was being marketed to different reading publics. Ironically, this decision to include Stevenson in two different collections serves to reinforce the notion that *Treasure Island* would primarily appeal to young readers, even though that was clearly neither the case nor the intention.

The first full authorised translation of *Strange Case of Dr. Jekyll and Mr. Hyde* was done by Berthe Low, wife of Stevenson's close friend, American artist Will H. Low.[68] Berthe Julienne was born in Caen, Normandy, in 1853, and in 1875 she married Low, with whom Stevenson became close friends during his time in Fontainebleau. The Lows led a bohemian and cosmopolitan life, with summers spent at artist colonies in France – in Barbizon, Montigny-sur-Loing, Grez – and frequent trips between Europe and the United States, where they finally settled. Rather like Fanny Van de Grift Stevenson, who wrote 'cookbook articles', Berthe Low became a cultural mediator (on a small scale) between France and the United States. Like a Julia Child *avant la lettre*, she was the author of *French Home Cooking Adapted to the Use of American Households*.[69] She was also the translator, with her husband, of *The 1895 Paris Salon: A Comprehensive Selection of the Contemporary Art of All Schools as Represented by Notable*

---

[67] (Paris: José Corti, 1966), p. 310.
[68] The translation was published under the name Lowe, which is a feminisation of her husband's last name.
[69] Thérèse Bentzon also acted as a cultural intermediary: she wrote a study on the situation of women in the United States for *La Revue des deux mondes*.

Works of the Great Exhibitions of Eighteen Hundred and Ninety-Five. As previously mentioned, in August 1886, Stevenson gave her a signed edition of the French translation of *Treasure Island*. This is ample proof of his regard for her but was also perhaps a means of assisting her as she transformed his English into French. Stevenson kept up with Mme Low's progress, enquiring, 'How does *Jekyll* go on?'[70] As he made comically, calque-ingly clear to the Lows when he refused to profit financially from the translation, he was primarily interested in his reputation:

> Glory is what I am traduced for; sir and talented madam, glory [. . .]. And now, *quel chic, mes enfants*! *Quelle bonne farce*! *Quel* Howling Sport! As *droit d'auteur*, I demand that a copy shall go to Rodin. I burn to see the traduction.[71]

Mme Low's translation appeared in 1890 with Plon, Nourrit et Cie, a publishing house with an innovative catalogue that was aimed at an educated audience.[72] From 1873 on, Plon had been publishing writers who were gaining recognition in French and European literary circles. Some were on their way to becoming celebrated figures in the 'new' French literature, the movement that sought to move away from the so-called excesses of Naturalism and to renew the language, form and themes of the French novel. Plon's catalogue included works by two close friends of Gustave Flaubert, Gustave Toudouze and Charles Edmond, the latter of whom also happened to be co-director of *Le Temps*.[73] Plon published novels by three signatories of the *Manifeste des cinq* (1887) against Zolian Naturalism: Paul Margueritte, Victor Margueritte and J.H. Rosny, who were also among the first members of the Académie Goncourt.[74] The *Manifeste des cinq* is a case of disciples turning against the master. It was published in *Le Figaro* on 18 August 1887 where Stevenson would

---

[70] Letter to Will H. Low, [Late September/early October 1886], *Letters*, V, p. 326.
[71] [? Mid-October 1887], *Letters*, VI, p. 33.
[72] Wilfert describes it as 'scholarly'. 'Literary Import into France and Britain', p. 182.
[73] Charles Edmond, *Le neveu du Comte Sérédine, scènes de la vie russe* (1898). Gustave Toudouze, *La Vie familiale et sociale. La Bête à bon Dieu* (1889).
[74] Paul Margueritte, *Simple histoire* (Plon, 1895). Paul et Victor Margueritte, *Femmes nouvelles* (Plon, 1899). Paul et Victor Margueritte, *Une époque: le désastre* (Plon, 1904). J.-H. Rosny, *L'Impérieuse bonté* (1894), *Renouveau* (1894), *Résurrection* (1895), *Les Profondeurs de Kyamo* (1896), *Une rupture* (1897), *Un autre monde* (1898), *Roman d'un cycliste* (1899), *Le Docteur Harambour* (1904).

likely have read it. Plon also published books by Paul Bourget and the occultist Joséphin Peladan, two men who were intimately linked to the emerging theories of Decadence, Symbolism and the new novel in the late nineteenth century: Bourget as a theoretician, essayist and author of psychological novels; Peladan as a practitioner known for his decadent eccentricity.[75] Plon's catalogue was not limited to so-called quality literature: it also included popular and genre fiction and books by Fortuné du Boisgobey, a protégé of Émile Gaboriau, the 'inventor' of the detective novel, as well as books by Sir Arthur Conan Doyle (but not the Sherlock Holmes series). In fact, it was primarily through the publication of foreign novels in translation that Plon made a name for itself at the end of the century. Following the publication of an article by Eugène Melchior de Vogüé on the Russian novel in the *Revue des deux mondes*, Plon published Dostoevsky's works in French, as well as novels by Tolstoy.[76]

The first Continental French translation of *Strange Case of Dr. Jekyll and Mr. Hyde* effectively targeted the same reading public that the translation of Dostoevsky targeted. Both began their French life in the *Revue des deux mondes* before being published by Plon – a trajectory that could very well have surprised readers who thought of Stevenson simply as the author of an adventure tale for children. The importance of Plon's role in disseminating the works of foreign authors in France (and beyond) is highlighted by the fact that Stevenson himself read Dostoevsky's *Crime and Punishment* (1866–7) and *The Insulted and the Injured* (1861; also known as *Humiliated and Insulted*) in the 1884 Plon translation by Victor Derely, rather than the 1885 English translation published by Vizetelly. In early March 1886, Stevenson told John Addington Symonds that '*Raskolnikoff* is the greatest book I have read easily in ten years.'[77] He went into more detail in a letter to W.E. Henley in November 1885, where, despite his humorous deliberate misspellings, he is in earnest:

---

[75] Amongst other books by Bourget, Plon published editions of *Mensonges* (1901), *Le Disciple* (1901), *L'Eau profonde* (1903) and *Études et portraits: études anglaises* (1905); between 1899 and 1911, Plon published Bourget's complete works. Peladan's *Les Drames de la conscience* was published in 1906.

[76] See Élisabeth Parinet, 'L'Édition littéraire, 1890–1914', in *Histoire de l'édition française, vol. 4, Le Livre concurrencé, 1900–1950*, ed. by Roger Chartier and Henri-Jean Martin (Paris: Fayard, 1990), pp. 161–209 (p. 166), and Christophe Charle, *Paris fin de siècle: culture et politique*, L'Univers historique (Paris: Seuil, 1998), p. 179.

[77] *Letters*, V, p. 220.

Dostoieffsky is of course simply immense: it is not reading a book, it is having a brain fever, to read it. The Judge is to me the greatest stroke of genius of all; I adore the Judge. Would you like to read another of his: *Humiliated and Offendended* it is not as good as *The Cream and the Shattiment*, but has great merit, too, has *Humiliated and Offendended* and the author Dustimuffsky is not only a man of genius, but a dam good fellow and a credit to the race, and in these days of Zolaism he shines like a star.[78]

After reading Dostoevsky, Stevenson went on to write 'Markheim' (1885), a story with obvious connections to *Crime and Punishment*.[79] This criss-crossing and refraction of ideas through a Parisian publisher reinforces the centrality of Stevenson's French reading to his creative process, but it also does two other things: it draws attention to the central importance of French publishing in the dissemination of European literature in translation, and it reveals how Stevenson's publication in France relates to this renewed French openness to European literature.

Berthe Low's *Le Cas étrange du docteur Jekyll* was published devoid of any critical apparatus – there was neither introduction, nor preface, nor notes. It is as if Bentzon's article had served as an introduction to Low's translation, which appeared two years later. The translation was well received – no small feat for a woman working under her own name. Unless there is some hidden story yet to be unearthed, it is difficult to account for Fanny Van de Grift Stevenson's description of Berthe Low as a woman who 'spoke *patois* and never thoroughly mastered proper French',[80] especially since Stevenson himself allegedly thought little of his wife's mastery of the language.[81] According to Judith Gautier, daughter of Théophile Gautier and future member of the jury for the Prix Fémina and the Prix Goncourt, Low's translation was elegant and faithful and reflected the nuance of the original well.[82] Others thought that all French translations of Stevenson's work were too literal, a discussion to which we will return.

---

[78] *Letters*, V, p. 151.
[79] These connections are analysed by Michela Vanon Alliata in '"Markheim" and the Shadow of the Other', in *Robert Louis Stevenson: Writer of Boundaries*, ed. by Ambrosini and Dury, pp. 299–311 (pp. 306 and 308).
[80] *Letters*, IV, p. 210, n. 4.
[81] As reported to Balfour and quoted in *Selected Letters of Robert Louis Stevenson*, ed. by Ernest Mehew (New Haven: Yale University Press, 2001), p. 219, n. 7.
[82] 'Les Livres nouveaux', *Le Rappel*, 2 September 1890, p. 2.

French Publishers and Translators

Over the next few years, Stevenson's works appeared with just about every publishing house imaginable: publishers with large print runs and small print runs, with money-making ambitions and artistic ambitions. He was perpetually drawn between two poles: on the one hand, the intellectual and the artistic; on the other, the popular mass market. It is worth remembering, however, that in both Britain and France the two camps – the mass of readers and the cultural elite – were never as distinct as the elite would have liked to believe and there was always a fair amount of crossover.[83] Stevenson's own reading habits testify to this. All of this contributes to confusion about Stevenson's French publication history. Without one dedicated translator and publisher, it was hard to follow where his books and stories were appearing, which perhaps gave the impression that they were not appearing in France.

Some of Stevenson's books reached French readers in unusual ways that accentuate his appeal both commercial and artistic, but also the emerging international collaboration between publishers. The translation of *Le Roman du prince Othon* in 1896, for instance, was a joint publication between Perrin (another of Tolstoy's French publishers) and John Lane, an English publisher, but not the one that had originally published *Prince Otto* in English in 1885 (Chatto & Windus). John Lane was closely aligned with Decadence in Britain and, together with Elkin Mathews, was behind the Bodley Head publishing firm and its *Yellow Book* magazine. While known as a promoter of Decadence, he was also commercially savvy, able, in the words of Kirsten MacLeod, to 'balance the claims of the literary marketplace with the aims of [. . .] idealistic writers'.[84] Insofar as this is the case, it was a fitting venue for *Prince Otto* to appear. This unusual joint Franco-British project seems even more unusual when its translator figures in the mix. Egerton Castle was an Englishman who dedicated his French translation to Sir Frederick Pollock, a Professor of Law at Oxford University. The translation itself is preceded by a long preface that quotes Thérèse Bentzon. Surprisingly, the translation was well received in France, with the *Journal des débats* commenting: 'une fort agréable curiosité littéraire nous arrive de Londres, sous la forme d'un

---

[83] On this phenomenon, see John Carey, *The Intellectuals and the Masses: Pride and Prejudice Among the Literary Intelligentsia, 1880–1939* (Chicago: Academy Chicago Publishers, 2002).

[84] *Fictions of British Decadence*, p. 54.

élégant volume intitulé: *Le Roman du prince Othon*. C'est la traduction en français par un érudit anglais, Egerton Castle.'[85]

The French version of *The Black Arrow* appeared in 1901 and is also indicative of the strange, market-defying translational journeys made by some of Stevenson's books. In England, *The Black Arrow* first appeared in serialised form in *Young Folks*; in France, by contrast, the translation targeted a very different audience: *La Flèche noire* was first published by Mercure de France, in a translation by E. La Chesnais, a French aristocrat. It was subsequently 'adapté de l'anglais' ('adapted from the English') by Nelson for a younger audience.[86] Nelson was an innovative Scottish publishing house that printed French books in Scotland in order to sell them in France at a lower cost than French publishers could (in 1911, the company pushed the envelope even further by opening a shop in Paris).[87] Nelson was an overtly commercial enterprise. By comparison, the Société du Mercure de France, under the direction of novelist Rachilde's husband, Alfred Vallette, rejected the commercial, 'affiche des idées totalement à contre-courant', 'refuse toute publicité' and 'se définit rapidement par un esprit fait d'exigence, d'indépendance vis-à-vis des autorités établies et d'attachement à l'esthétique symboliste'.[88] As Élisabeth Parinet notes, '"l'esprit" du Mercure de France ne devait pas être entamé par des

---

[85] 'Lettres, sciences et arts', *Journal des débats politiques et littéraires*, 8 July 1896, p. 3. ('A highly *agréable* literary curiosity has arrived from London in the form of an elegant volume called *Prince Otto*. It is a French translation done by Egerton Castle, an erudite Englishman.') Marcel Schwob was given permission by Stevenson to translate *Prince Otto* (Letter to Marcel Schwob, 19 August 1890, *Letters*, VI, p. 400), but this came to naught.

[86] With thanks to Georges Gottlieb, Département Littérature et art, Bibliothèque nationale de France, for checking.

[87] Diana Cooper-Richet, 'Les Imprimés en langue anglaise en France au XIXe siècle: rayonnement intellectuel, circulation et modes de pénétration', in *Les Mutations du livre et de l'édition dans le monde du XVIIIe siècle à l'an 2000: actes du colloque international Sherbrooke* 2000, ed. by Jacques Michon et Jean-Yves Mollier (Presses de l'université Laval/L'Harmattan, 2001), pp. 122–40 (p. 139); Diana Cooper-Richet, 'La Librairie étrangère à Paris au XIXe siècle: un milieu perméable aux innovations et aux transferts', *Actes de la recherche en sciences sociales*, 126–7 (1999), 60–9 (p. 69). For more on Nelson's collection, see chapter 7, 'An "Entente Cordiale" in Publishing, or a Scottish Victory? Nelson's French Collection', in Reynolds, *Paris-Edinburgh: Cultural Connections in the Belle Époque*.

[88] Parinet, 'L'Édition littéraire, 1890–1914', pp. 196–7. ('Displayed ideas that were totally against the current', 'refused all advertising' and 'defined itself by a spirit of exigency, independence from established authorities and attachment to the symbolist aesthetic.')

considérations commerciales'.⁸⁹ *La Flèche noire* was part of Mercure de France's 'Collection d'auteurs étrangers' ('Foreign Writers' collection), which was created in 1899 and included authors like Thomas Carlyle, Lafcadio Hearn, John Ruskin, Maxim Gorky and Friedrich Nietzsche. As this eclectic list suggests, the Mercure de France publishing agenda was guided more by a search for refined literature that was novel than by any consistent intellectual or aesthetic theory, although there is an overwhelming emphasis on anti-commercial and anti-popular forms. Matthew Potolsky's description of Decadent canons is relevant here, for Mercure de France was without doubt the quintessential 'community united by taste rather than by origins or geography'.⁹⁰ A critic from the *Revue blanche*, a Symbolist journal that shared the same objectives as Mercure de France, praised the translation of *La Flèche noire* and observed that, as far as Stevenson was concerned, he was an artist who delighted in adventure – 'c'est l'artiste surtout qui se plaît aux aventures'.⁹¹

This high culture/mass market tension continued into the early twentieth century and the interwar years. While beyond the immediate scope of this book, it is worth pointing out that when Stevenson's complete works were translated in the 1920s by Théo Varlet, they were published by Paul Laffitte's highbrow Éditions de la Sirène. Jules Romains vouched for the quality of Varlet's work as a translator precisely by underlining the fact that Varlet was not in it for the money.⁹² In the luxury Sirène edition, Stevenson's books shared the shelves with the works of Guillaume Apollinaire, Blaise Cendrars, Jean Cocteau and Raymond Radiguet, but were unlikely to reach a mass readership, by virtue of their cost. There is a prestige factor at play here: book as *objet d'art*, a collector's item, owning it a sign of refined tastes. Luxury editions are prepared as collectors' items, but when a book becomes an *objet d'art*, its value is both economic and symbolic, meaning that it participates in the very market system it ostensibly undermines. Varlet's translation of *L'Île au trésor* was published with Sirène in 1920. In 1926, Varlet, who clearly either loved the novel or had time on

---

⁸⁹ 'L'Édition littéraire, 1890–1914', p. 198. ('The 'spirit' of Mercure de France was not to be undermined by commercial considerations.')
⁹⁰ *The Decadent Republic of Letters: Taste, Politics, and Cosmopolitanism from Baudelaire to Beardsley* (Philadelphia: University of Pennsylvania Press, 2013), p. 71.
⁹¹ Marcel Drouin, 'Les Livres', *La Revue blanche*, August 1901, pp. 627–8 (p. 628).
⁹² Romains states: 'Théo Varlet n'est pas un de ces traducteurs à gages qui expédient sans amour une besogne mal payée.' 'Stevenson et l'aventure', p. 2.

his hands (and money on his mind), published *L'Île au trésor* with Nelson using the pseudonym Déodat Serval. This is a translator's dream scenario: translating an author whose works both generate revenue and enjoy considerable artistic prestige. By the interwar years, therefore, Stevenson's works were continuing to appear with commercially motivated publishing houses that had large print runs and more or less guaranteed commercial success, while Stevenson's artistic and intellectual credentials continued to be simultaneously upheld by smaller publishers guided by aesthetic rather than financial considerations.

In 1905, Stock published *Kidnapped* (*Enlevé!*) in its 'Bibliothèque cosmopolite' series, in a translation by Albert Savine. Savine devoted his life to translation and publishing. He began his career translating Catalan texts, then created his own publishing house that specialised in foreign literature, as well as Naturalist and Decadent books, until it went under. Savine published Henrik Ibsen, August Strindberg, Algernon Swinburne and Oscar Wilde, and was described by poet Camille Mauclair in 1901 as a man who was too literary to ever make any money as a publisher.[93] One of Savine's main business competitors was Stock; when Savine's business collapsed, he sold some of his catalogue of 600 books to Stock. Stock's 'Bibliothèque cosmopolite' series included books that had been bought over from Savine's catalogue, as well as new translations by Savine himself, including *Enlevé!*.[94] Stock has been described by Jean-Yves Mollier as the 'principale entreprise d'édition générale ouverte sur la traduction d'écrivains étrangers au début du XXe siècle'.[95] This

---

[93] Savine 'fît faillite par dévouement à cette cause ingrate, et [. . .] eut le tort d'être beaucoup trop lettré pour faire fortune'. Camille Mauclair, 'Le Roman historique français devant les étrangers', *La Nouvelle revue*, July 1901, pp. 431–45 (p. 433).
[94] See Parinet, 'L'Édition littéraire, 1890–1914', p. 167. Savine translated Oscar Wilde, Thomas de Quincey, Algernon Swinburne, Elizabeth Barrett Browning and Percy Bysshe Shelley, among many others. See also Blaise Wilfert-Portal, 'Traduction littéraire: approche bibliométrique', in *Histoire des traductions en langue française. XIXe siècle: 1815–1914*, ed. by Chevrel, d'Hulst and Lombez, pp. 255–344 (p. 312).
[95] 'L'histoire de l'édition, une histoire à vocation', *Revue d'histoire moderne et contemporaine*, 43.2 (1996), 329–48 (p. 332). ('The leading general publisher open to the translation of foreign writers at the beginning of the twentieth century.') Articles also appeared announcing Stock's publication of 'les pages consacrées à la France' ('Les lettres', *L'Homme libre*, 23 September 1924, p. 2) and Savine's translation of *Les Squatters de Silverado* (Méritan, 'Franck Norris, Albert Savine et le roman d'aventures', p. 2). I can find no evidence that Savine did end up translating *The Silverado Squatters*.

open-minded attitude to foreign literature on the part of a general publisher was not to everyone's taste. An article in *La Presse* in 1905 described Stock's 'Bibliothèque cosmopolite' – the first collection to explicitly tout its cosmopolitanism as a selling point – as a collection 'dont la puissance d'ennui atteint des proportions exagérées'. *Enlevé!*, however, was deemed an exception to this rule because it was 'un excellent roman populaire, mais un roman populaire composé par un écrivain, par un artiste'.[96] Stevenson would no doubt have appreciated this assessment.

One year later, in 1906, *Kidnapped* (*Les Aventures de David Balfour*) was published once again, this time in Hachette's 'nouvelle collection pour la jeunesse' ('new collection for young people'), and it was advertised widely.[97] Its sequel, *Catriona*, was published in Hachette's 'Bibliothèque des meilleurs romans étrangers à 1 fr. le volume' in 1907.[98] The fact that *Kidnapped* was published in two different translations, with two different titles – *Enlevé! Mémoire relatant les aventures de David Balfour en l'an 1751* and *Les Aventures de David Balfour* – can perhaps be accounted for by the fact that at the time copyright expired after ten years, although the Stevenson estate would presumably have to be consulted. Be that as it may, a later article in *L'Intransigeant* rightly conjectured that the existence of two translations could lead to confusion and misunderstanding of Stevenson's body of work: 'la mise en vente sous des noms différents d'un même ouvrage de Stevenson (combien d'exemples pourrait-on citer, déjà!) risque de provoquer des confusions regrettables'.[99]

Just as Stevenson's books appeared with publishers of all kinds, his translators came from across the social spectrum. Doubtless, some were the 'browsing, moonlit, penny-a-lining sheep' that Stevenson derided (and perhaps pitied).[100] There is no denying that some of Stevenson's

---

[96] 'Les Livres', *La Presse*, 17 June 1905, p. 4. ('Whose power to inflict boredom reaches exaggerated heights'; 'an excellent popular novel, but a popular novel composed by an author, an artist.')

[97] See, for example, the advertisement in *Le Grand Écho du Nord de la France*, 18 December 1906, p. 5.

[98] Hachette also published *The Wrecker* and *St. Ives*.

[99] Les Treize, 'Les Lettres', *L'Intransigeant*, 9 March 1921, p. 2. ('Selling the same book by Stevenson under different titles (how many examples of this could we already cite!) risks causing unfortunate confusion.')

[100] 2 February 1886, *Letters*, V, p. 193–4. He was puzzled by 'the dainty stomachs of the English supporting M. Zola with a fortitude hardly to be distinguished from gratification, and that in a translation from which the redeeming merits of the original have fled'. Letter to the Editor of *The Times*, [Early September 1886], *Letters*, V, p. 311.

translators (e.g. E. Gellion-d'Anglar, Jacques Delebecque) were relatively little known at the time. Others, like Louise Zeys, received a certain amount of recognition later in their careers.[101] This situation is in marked contrast to arrangements like those in place between Walter Scott and Defauconpret, or Dickens and his French publisher Hachette. Generally, unless translators are associated with one author's body of work, they tend to be forgotten by literary history. What is curious in Stevenson's case is that while some of his translators have been forgotten, the books they translated were often accompanied by prefaces, introductions and forewords by recognised figures, including some who are very much remembered today. This is especially the case as the twentieth century advances, and it points to Stevenson's impact on French letters. Novelist Pierre Mac Orlan, whose pseudonym alone suggests Scottish leanings, wrote a foreword to *Island Nights' Entertainment* (*Les Nuits des Îles*, 1919). In 1921, Academician Edmond Jaloux provided a preface and an essay for a 'nouvelle traduction par Mme Fanny Laparra' of *Strange Case of Dr. Jekyll and Mr. Hyde*. Academics were also in on the paratextual game: Gaston Bonet-Maury, a professor and member of the Academy of Moral and Political Sciences, wrote a foreword to *Catriona*.

There were also serious literary professionals involved in the translation and dissemination of Stevenson's work. The Colvin correspondence was translated by Madeleine Rolland, a professional translator who brought Rabindranath Tagore's oeuvre to France and also translated Thomas Hardy's *Tess of the d'Urbervilles*.[102] The translator of *Le Dynamiteur* and 'La Bouteille diabolique' also had a professional pedigree: Georges Art, who was a professor and scholar of style at the Conservatoire de Nantes, not only wrote textbooks such as *Du bon usage oral et écrit* (1932), but also translated Tolstoy, Georg Brandes, George Gissing and, with Teodor de Wyzewa, Friedrich Nietzsche. We are thus a long way from subscribers to *Young Folks* and readers of Hetzel's 'Bibliothèque d'éducation et de récréation'. Even with the benefit of historical hindsight, it is difficult to reconcile Nietzsche's ravings against mass culture, or the way that Gissing portrays his repulsion at the artistic tastes of the masses, with Stevenson's taste for and occasional appropriation of popular

---

[101] Despite her relative obscurity, in the years following her translation of *The Wrecker* (*Le Naufrageur*, 1906), Zeys received several bursaries and two prizes from the Académie française.

[102] She was also the sister of Nobel Prize-winning novelist Romain Rolland.

forms. The fact that translators, critics and intellectuals could import Stevenson alongside these other authors shows that one of the central issues facing the literary world of the time was the need to legitimise storytelling as a pleasurable activity hardwired into readers, while simultaneously fulfilling a desire for artistic beauty – to say nothing of a desire for superiority that would distinguish one from the newly emerged mass of readers.

Susan Pickford has argued that those translators 'qui bénéficient d'une certaine visibilité historique sont principalement ceux pour qui la traduction ne fut qu'une activité annexe'.[103] This certainly seems to be the case of many of Stevenson's translators. The translators whose names are still known to twenty-first-century scholars are principally those who were authors in their own right or who also played another role in spreading Stevenson's works. Alfred Jarry is a prime example of the former: renowned as the author of *Ubu roi* (1896), he translated Stevenson's *Olalla* five years *after* writing his famous play – the translation is a footnote in his literary career, but nonetheless one that illuminates the way that 'both writers envision territories at odds with the contours of their contemporary institutionalized realities of nation, language and laws of all kinds'.[104] Foremost among the early translators who are still known to literary scholars and historians of the fin de siècle are Teodor de Wyzewa and Marcel Schwob (to whom, incidentally, *Ubu roi* was dedicated). While they both translated Stevenson, they are better known for their critical works. In addition to translating *St. Ives*, *The Ebb-Tide* and *The Wrong Box*, Wyzewa wrote a preface to Albert Bordeaux's translation of *Weir of Hermiston* (1912), and was one of the most visible cultural mediators, or *passeurs de culture*, of the turn of the century – he was involved with the *Revue de deux mondes*, *Cosmopolis* and the *Revue Wagnérienne*. Meanwhile, Schwob's only translation of Stevenson was 'Will O' the Mill' in 1899, but he wrote a series of articles on Stevenson. Schwob was a prolific translator of English literature, and his output included French versions of Defoe's *Moll Flanders* and de Quincey's *The Last Days of Immanuel Kant*, as well as the translation of *Hamlet* that was performed by Sarah Bernhardt

---

[103] 'Traducteurs', in *Histoire des traductions en langue française. XIXe siècle: 1815–1914*, ed. by Chevrel, d'Hulst and Lombez, pp. 144–87 (p. 185). ('Who benefit from a certain historical visibility are mainly those for whom translation was only a secondary activity.')

[104] Michael G. Kelly, 'Jarry, Stevenson and Cosmopolitan Ambivalence', *Comparative Critical Studies*, 10.2 (2013), 199–218 (p. 199).

in 1899 and published in 1900 (the latter was done in collaboration with Paul Morand's father, Eugène Morand). He also helped prepare the French for Oscar Wilde's *Salomé*. He defended Stevenson in salons and essays, wrote the preface to Georges Art's translation of *Le Dynamiteur* (1894), dedicated his own most successful collection of short stories, *Cœur double* (1891), to Stevenson, and used a quotation from Stevenson as the epigraph to his *Le Livre de Monelle* (1894). As will be discussed in Chapter 4, Schwob's role in promoting Stevenson contributed to his own status in the French literary world.

Problems with Translations

I would like to leave aside until Chapter 4 the role that Schwob, Wyzewa and others played in interpreting Stevenson for French audiences and focus here on their critiques of translation practices and how they perceived these practices to relate to Stevenson's supposed invisibility in France. In an 1888 article in *Le Phare de la Loire*, a widely circulated provincial newspaper run by his family, Schwob argues that 'la seule œuvre que l'on connaisse de [Stevenson] en France par une traduction complète, *L'Île au Trésor*, n'est pas son coup d'essai. Il n'avait pas publié moins de six ouvrages avant celui qui a sanctionné sa réputation.'[105] This is an attempt by Schwob to reposition Stevenson as something other than a writer of boys' tales, which, of course, recalls Thérèse Bentzon's comments in her article published that same year. It is as though excuses had to be made for *Treasure Island*'s appeal and success. Part of the issue may be related to the novel itself. As Jules Romains suggested in 1920, translators could get so caught up in the story of *Treasure Island* that they could forget to adequately render its style.[106]

Schwob's complaint overlooks the fact that despite Stevenson's prior publications, *Treasure Island*, which had only been published five years earlier, was the book that consolidated Stevenson's

---

[105] 'Robert L. Stevenson', *Le Phare de la Loire*, 27 August 1888, pp. 2–3, in Robert Louis Stevenson, *Will du Moulin suivi de M. Schwob/R.L. Stevenson Correspondances*, ed. by François Escaig (Paris: Éditions Allia, 1992), pp. 57–63 (p. 59). ('The only work of his that is known through a complete translation, *Treasure Island*, is not his best effort. He published at least six books before the one that made his reputation.')

[106] 'Stevenson et l'aventure', p. 2.

reputation in English, too, so the positive French reception could hardly be qualified as anomalous. What was missing in France were translations of the books Stevenson published before *Treasure Island*. In 1890, Schwob returned to the issue of Stevenson's supposed invisibility in France, writing in the same newspaper that 'presque chaque année, un nouveau chef-d'œuvre: *Docteur Jekyll, Kidnapped, The Black Arrow, The Master of Ballantrae*. Tout cela est resté lettre-morte pour nous.'[107] This lack of familiarity with – and lack of translations of – Stevenson's other novels may have been true in 1890 when Schwob was writing. That said, it is really no surprise that in 1890 the French were not familiar with *The Black Arrow* or *The Master of Ballantrae*, given that they were only published as books in English in 1888 and 1889.[108] As we have seen, however, the situation was evolving quickly.

Translation practices were deemed to be part of the problem in terms of Stevenson's reception in France, and it stands to reason that reviewers would perceive there to be problems when the novels were being targeted at such diverse audiences. Generally, when reviewers did mention the issue of translation, they tended to limit their remarks to vague notions of fidelity and elegance (although, in fairness, a review is not the place for detailed textual analysis).[109] However, some reviewers approached the topic more thoughtfully. Thérèse Bentzon, for example, considered the issue of translation at length and argued that French readers would be right to think that English literature in general was in decline if their opinion was based primarily on available translations.[110] Teodor de Wyzewa also dealt with the issue head-on, and he explicitly linked Stevenson's alleged poor standing to the issue of translation:

---

[107] 'Robert-Louis Stevenson', *L'Événement*, 11 October 1890, p. 1. ('Almost every year a new masterpiece: *Dr. Jekyll, Kidnapped, The Black Arrow, The Master of Ballantrae*. All of this has gone unheeded by us.')

[108] *The Black Arrow* was serialised in *Young Folks* in 1883.

[109] Representative examples of this can be found in 'Librairie', *La Justice*, 30 June 1890, pp. 3–4 [review of Berthe Low's translation of *Strange Case Dr. Jekyll and Mr. Hyde*]; 'Lettres, sciences et arts', *Journal des débats politiques et littéraires*, 8 July 1896, p. 3 [review of *Le Roman du prince Othon*]; 'Les Livres', *La Justice*, 15 November 1904, p. 1 [review of Wyzewa's translation of *St. Ives*].

[110] 'Les Nouveaux romans anglais', *Revue des deux mondes*, July–August 1888, pp. 91–120 (p. 92).

Tout ce que je puis en dire est que les ouvrages les plus intéressants de Stevenson ont déjà été traduits, que leur traduction a passé à peu près inaperçue, et qu'ainsi il n'y a guère de chance qu'une traduction nouvelle soit mieux accueillie.[111]

Needless to say, this was not the most effective marketing strategy from someone on the verge of translating three of Stevenson's novels. Nevertheless, Wyzewa contends that Stevenson's lack of standing as a serious author can be blamed on the type of translations that were available to French readers at the time. Given the number of translations that were published, it seems fair to question whether there was, in fact, a lack of standing, or indeed whether all the translations suffered from the same shortcomings. To be sure, there were different audiences: the general reader and the artistic and educated classes. But, as we have seen, and as other scholars have pointed out, Stevenson figures among those authors who were 'multi-edited' – had several books simultaneously on the French market.[112] Indeed, he was not only 'multi-edited', but multi-translated: in the early years of the twentieth century, 'The Beach of Falesá', *Kidnapped*, 'The Isle of Voices', 'Markheim', 'The Merry Men', *Strange Case of Dr. Jekyll and Mr. Hyde* and *The Wrecker* were all available in more than one translation – and this reckoning does not take account of Varlet's translations that began in the 1920s.

Undeterred by this, Wyzewa maintains that the reason Stevenson did not occupy a more prominent position in France was because of the inadequacy of translations of his work, which rather than assimilating him into the French literary tradition, only highlighted his otherness. In other words, by making Stevenson's difference obvious, universality was lost, 'universal' in this instance being synonymous with 'French'. In the late nineteenth century, Paris was the capital of what Pascale Casanova calls the 'world republic of letters' – it set literary norms – and from a French perspective, imported literature was by its very nature intended to assimilate foreign authors into the Parisian centre and universalise them by making them French.[113] The

---

[111] *Écrivains étrangers. 3e série. Le Roman contemporain à l'étranger* (Paris: Perrin, 1900), pp. 203–4. ('All I can say is that Stevenson's most interesting works have already been translated, that these translations went largely unnoticed, and as such there is hardly a chance that a new translation will be better received.')

[112] Blaise Wilfert-Portal, 'La place de la littérature étrangère dans le champ littéraire français autour de 1900', *Histoire & mesure*, 23.2 (2008), 69–101 (p. 96).

[113] *La République mondiale des Lettres* (Paris: Seuil, 2008).

Dostoevsky *Crime and Punishment* translation is an example of this: the novel was translated from Russian into French, and educated English speakers like Stevenson read it in French before it was made available in English. In keeping with this strategy, despite his cosmopolitanism and multilingualism, Wyzewa clearly favours 'domesticating' over 'foreignising' translations, at least as far as their ability to engender change in the French literary field is concerned. This is because domesticating translations, with their more familiar idiom, are more likely to appeal to a wider reading public, whereas 'foreignising' translations that attempt to make linguistic and cultural difference perceptible can be more challenging for readers to navigate. The best example of a 'foreignising' translation of Stevenson at the time is probably *Le Roman du prince Othon*, since it was translated into French by a native English speaker. As translator and co-founder of the Anglo-French Society, Henry-D. Davray, remarked in the *Mercure de France*:

> c'est un travail fort bien fait, suivant de près le texte, un peu parfois au prix de bizarreries grammaticales et de souffrances syntactiques, mais qui a le grand mérite de laisser à l'original, plus qu'une autre méthode de traduction, son caractère particulier et national.[114]

The highly cultured and multilingual Wyzewa therefore appears to be using an anti-intellectual argument to promote a foreign author. While this might initially appear disingenuous, it could be argued that it in fact attests to Wyzewa's understanding of the importance of readability to Stevenson himself. Alternatively, it can be interpreted as proof of the centralising tendencies of the Parisian literary centre.

---

[114] 'Lettres anglaises', *Mercure de France*, August 1897, pp. 369–72 (p. 370). ('The work is very well done, following the text closely, sometimes at the cost of grammatical oddities and tortured syntax, but it has the great merit, more than other methods of translation, of retaining the distinctive, national hallmarks of the original.') He goes on to say that it conveys 'parfois très exactement les délicatesses, les recherches, les trouvailles de style et [. . . conserve] les couleurs et les nuances, la force et la finesse d'expression qu'a voulues l'auteur' (it 'occasionally very accurately conveys the stylistic subtleties, refinements, and coinages, and conserves the colour and the nuances, the expressive force and finesse that the author wanted'). The *Mercure de France* review was edited by Rémy de Gourmont from 1891. It had approximately 3,000 readers by 1905. See Wilfert-Portal, 'Traduction littéraire: approche bibliométrique', p. 317.

On nous a tant habitués à considérer l'exactitude littérale comme la première vertu d'une traduction, que toute traduction qui n'aurait pas l'air d'une traduction, qui ressemblerait à un livre français, expressément écrit pour notre usage, aussitôt nous deviendrait suspecte et nous déplairait. Nous reprocherions au traducteur d'avoir défiguré l'œuvre originale, de l'avoir dépouillée de sa couleur locale. A cette traduction lisible et agréable nous en préférerions une autre plus machinalement calquée sur l'original, et trop ennuyeuse avec solennité. Ce sont des traductions de ce genre qu'on nous a offertes depuis trente ans: ce sont elles qui ont empêché Tolstoï et Stevenson et maints autres écrivains étrangers de prendre pied chez nous, de devenir vraiment [les] nôtres, comme jadis l'étaient devenus les Richardson et les Daniel de Foe.[115]

To Wyzewa, then, loss of local colour is of little importance, and he is concerned neither with Stevenson's Scottishness nor with his English-language stylistic traits, at least in terms of reading Stevenson in translation. In his view, the only way for foreign authors to reach a French reading public and to effect literary change in France was for them to be naturalised through translation, in other words, to become 'les nôtres', ours. The value of importing foreign works in translation is thus directly proportional to their effect on the French literary field, and on the way in which foreign authors contribute to the evolution of French literature. Had Stevenson's texts been 'francisés' – 'Frenchified', adapted – and not treated as foreign literature at all, Wyzewa contends, they would have had more impact in France and on the development of the French novel. Wyzewa was writing this in 1900, though, and there was still ample time for Stevenson to become integrated into the French literary tradition. Indeed, Wyzewa's own work contributed to Stevenson's standing.

While this domesticating instinct is generally consistent with translation practices at the time, in which stylistic mastery of the target

---

[115] *Écrivains étrangers*, pp. 209–10. ('We have become so accustomed to considering literal exactitude as the primary virtue of translation that any translation that doesn't seem like a translation, that seems like a French book, would immediately be considered suspect and displease us. We would reproach the translator with having disfigured the original work, with having stripped it of its local colour. To this readable and agreeable translation we prefer another more mechanically calqued on the original and too dull in its formality. This is the type of translation to which we've been subjected for the past thirty years: these are what have prevented Tolstoy and Stevenson and many other foreign writers from taking root here in France, from becoming ours, as formerly the Richardsons and the Defoes were able to become.')

language was deemed more important than knowledge of the source language, it is misleading of the polyglot Wyzewa to suggest that the translations being published were literal, because this was almost never the case in the nineteenth century. Indeed, Michel Raimond has observed that translations were often very imperfect, and other critics have outlined the process by which translators hired native speakers in order to compensate for their partial or complete lack of knowledge of the source language (there is no evidence that this was happening in Stevenson's case, however).[116] Furthermore, as has been mentioned, in some cases multiple different translations were available by the early 1900s, which means that different versions of Stevenson were available to readers.

Bentzon shared Wyzewa's anti-foreignising views, since she too lamented a perceived tendency to translate books literally. In her case, it was not that literal translation prevented English literature from influencing French literature, but that literal translation was at the expense of the artistry of the original. As such, she would not have agreed with Wyzewa's proposed solution, which was to adapt translated stories to French audiences. Even though Wyzewa was surely not oblivious to the fact that some of the translations that were available were far from literal, he maintains that for Stevenson's stories to have an impact on the development of French literature, they needed to be translated differently:

> Traduits ainsi, abrégés, adaptés, *francisés* à notre usage, les romans de Stevenson s'imposeraient certainement à notre curiosité. Leur beauté poétique nous échapperait, mais la fraîcheur, l'aisance, l'imprévu de leur invention ne pourraient manquer de nous ravir; et de même qu'autrefois *Clarisse Harlowe* a préparé la voie à la *Nouvelle Héloïse*, peut-être ces légères et vivantes fantaisies nous rappelleraient-elles que l'adultère n'est pas l'unique sujet digne d'être traité par les romanciers.[117]

---

[116] *La Crise du roman*, p. 96. On the issue of hiring native speakers, see, in particular, Blaise Wilfert, 'Cosmopolis et *L'Homme invisible*: les importateurs de littérature étrangère en France, 1885–1914', *Actes de la recherche en sciences sociales*, 144.2 (2002), 33–46 (p. 36).

[117] *Écrivains étrangers*, pp. 207–8. ('Translated thus, abridged, adapted, Frenchified for our use, Stevenson's novels would certainly impose themselves upon our curiosity. Their poetic beauty would escape us, but the freshness, the fluency, the unexpectedness of their stories couldn't help but delight us; and just as once upon a time *Clarissa* paved the way for *La Nouvelle Héloïse*, so these light and vibrant fantasies could remind us that adultery isn't the only subject worthy of being treated by novelists.')

The jibe against realist-Naturalist aesthetics is palpable – no more novels of adultery are necessary – and we will come back to this aspect of the argument in the next chapter. The suggestion that interests me relative to translation is that *Clarissa*'s importance can be measured principally in terms of its impact upon Rousseau, as Stevenson's impact should be measured in terms of his influence on French authors. In this sense, Stevenson is not being assessed based on his position within British (read: English) literature, nor within the Scottish literary tradition; he is being assessed in relation to a French or European tradition. We are once again in the territory of border crossings, of the novel as a transnational genre. Like Stevenson himself, Wyzewa seems interested in the notion of the 'hand upon the dial of the clock' and how authors can change the course of literary history. Accordingly, there is a clear desire on Wyzewa's part to treat French and foreign literature as one and the same, such that, as is typical in times of literary change, 'no clear-cut distinction is maintained between "original" and "translated" writings'.[118] This position can be considered both forward- and backward-looking: forward-looking if taken to mean a breaking down of national literary barriers, an internationalisation of letters, such as Stevenson himself envisages in his essays; backward-looking if taken to mean an assimilation designed to deny literary difference, tantamount to what Casanova refers to as a process of Parisianisation, 'universalisation par déni de différence'.[119] The key is finding a balance between the two poles. In his comments on translation, Wyzewa seems to be tacitly acknowledging the different markets that Stevenson was reaching – or could reach – in France.

Either way, although Stevenson's works may have been translated, according to Wyzewa, the translations themselves did nothing to demonstrate Stevenson's originality to French readers because they were too faithful to the original, not 'French enough', and thus failed to effect change within the French literary system. The first irony in this is that Stevenson's novels were in fact taken up by the French in attempts to modernise the French novel. The second irony is that some of the first of Stevenson's works to be translated were not subject to the type of literal translation that Wyzewa denounces: *The Master of*

---

[118] Itamar Even-Zohar, 'The Position of Translated Literature Within the Literary Polysystem', in *The Translation Studies Reader*, ed. by Lawrence Venuti, 2nd edn (New York/London: Routledge, 2000), pp. 199–204 (p. 200).
[119] *La République mondiale des Lettres*, p. 226. ('Universalisation through denial of difference.')

Ballantrae was abridged and the first translation of *Treasure Island* states that it was, as was customary, 'traduit et adapté'.[120] Indeed, Bentzon may have had *Treasure Island* in mind when she condemned translators who mutilated books under the pretence of adapting them.[121] As Isabelle Nières-Chevrel has noted, Laurie's translation of *L'Île au trésor* contains multiple adaptations and additions (including an epilogue that is not in the French serial).[122] The foreignising translation of *Prince Otto* only reinforces this point (interestingly, André Gide, who would have read *Le Roman du prince Othon* in French before his own English was proficient, did not appreciate the novel[123]). The observations of translator-critics like Wyzewa and Bentzon should therefore be read as interventions in a much broader literary-cultural-historical debate relative to the role of foreign literature in France and changes in the publishing environment.

At a time when the literary field was in full evolution, publishing houses were reorienting the French novel through their editorial decisions on translations. Stevenson never stopped being published by publishers with very wide circulation and large print runs (Stock, Hachette, Nelson, Hetzel), but his reputation as an artist, the one that ensured his consecration in France and elsewhere, was established by being co-opted by a network of translators and publishers working in cosmopolitan and avant-garde publishing houses and journals (Plon, Mercure de France, Éditions de la NRF, *Cosmopolis*, *Minerva*, *La Vogue*). Stevenson's books were available to a variety of different reading publics. He could be read for education or for recreation; he could be read as a 'franco-étranger' or a cosmopolitan; he could be read in luxury editions or for one franc on a train ride.

---

[120] An advertisement for Hetzel in *Gil Blas* on 31 December 1885 (p. 3), for example, refers to *L'Île au trésor* '(d'après Stevenson)'. The managing director of *La Charente* called Laurie's translation of *Treasure Island* 'une traduction très littéraire' (F. Lugeol, 'Bibliographie: *L'Île au trésor*', *La Charente*, 2 April 1885, p. 3), but when Varlet's translation of *Treasure Island* was published, *L'Intransigeant* said more or less the same thing about it, remarking that it was 'autre chose qu'un livre pour la jeunesse' ('something other than a children's book') and 'nous apporte une traduction complète d'un tout autre accent. On conçoit mieux que cette œuvre célèbre ait achevé de révéler Stevenson comme un maître du roman' ('brings us a complete translation in an entirely different accent. It is easier to conceive how this famous work managed to reveal Stevenson as a master of the novel'). Les Treize, '. . . des romans', *L'Intransigeant*, 21 January 1924, p. 5.
[121] 'Les Nouveaux romans anglais', p. 92.
[122] 'Littérature d'enfance et de jeunesse', p. 704.
[123] 'Lettre à Angèle', *L'Ermitage*, June 1899, pp. 455–62, p. 456.

In this regard, Stevenson follows in the footsteps of Walter Scott, who 'conquered, in three decades, almost all types of audiences in France',[124] but Stevenson did so in a very different way that reflects the changing literary marketplace of the Third Republic. Christophe Charle argues that at the end of the nineteenth century, 'passée la vogue, aucun courant de littérature n'a durablement imité les œuvres ou les tendances étrangères'.[125] However, Stevenson did remain in vogue, as his importance to the Modernist generation of André Gide, Paul Valéry, Pierre Mac Orlan and Marcel Proust proves. This longevity is at least partly attributable to the fact that so many translators and publishers were working to spread his oeuvre to French readers. Thanks to French translators, editors and publishing houses working at the fin de siècle and at the turn of the twentieth century, Stevenson would henceforth belong to a pantheon of European authors, including Nietzsche, Dostoevsky, Ibsen and Tolstoy. There is no doubt that the effect of these first translations on Stevenson's reputation was lasting and contributed not only to his success as a popular author, but to his recognition as an important artist in European literary history.

---

[124] Wilfert-Portal, 'Traduction littéraire: approche bibliométrique', p. 276.
[125] *Paris fin de siècle*, p. 177. ('No literary movement lastingly imitated foreign works or trends once they had fallen out of fashion.')

Chapter 4

Stevenson in French Literary History

Le livre de R.-L. Stevenson est-il un roman?[1]

À l'étranger comme en France, le roman est malade, et, à l'étranger comme en France, son mal provient de la même cause, qui n'a rien à voir avec le manque d'échange d'idées d'un pays à l'autre. Cette cause, c'est simplement que, dans toute l'Europe, les romanciers ont désormais perdu le goût de conter.[2]

No purely academic studies of Stevenson were published in France before World War I – it was too soon and there was not enough distance to gain any historical perspective. But in the many periodical articles about Stevenson and in the first biographies, a sense emerges of how French readers of various social, cultural and literary backgrounds approached and interpreted his novels – for it was his novels that were most readily available in France.[3] Some appraisals were necessarily impressionistic, but they nonetheless illuminate the literary and cultural *zeitgeist* and the generational tensions being worked out as Naturalists morphed into Decadents into Symbolists into Modernists, and as the new generation sought to make its mark on French literature. This book began with an analysis of Stevenson's perspective on French literature, how he perceived it to be evolving,

---

[1] The question is asked in relation to Marie Dronsart's translation of *Kidnapped*, the implication being that *Kidnapped* was a true story. It appears in multiple newspapers and was clearly advertising copy provided by Hachette. For examples, see: 'Bibliographie', *L'Aurore: littéraire, artistique, sociale*, 1 January 1907, p. 3; 'Livres d'étrennes', *L'Univers*, 19 December 1906, p. 3; 'Bibliographie', *Le XIXe siècle*, 30 December 1906, p. 4.
[2] Wyzewa, 'Avant-propos', *Écrivains étrangers*, pp. iii–x (p. viii).
[3] According to Jehan Durieux, Schwob discovered Stevenson through his essays, although this does not tally with what others have said. 'Marcel Schwob', *Le Figaro, supplément littéraire du dimanche*, 25 December 1926, p. 2.

and how he might fit in to its evolution, as well as how it formed part of his literary and stylistic apprenticeship. The present chapter reverses the angle and looks at the question from a French perspective. It aims to analyse Stevenson's place in the development of French literature and position his works within the debates taking place on the evolution of the novel in France. Stevenson's role in the (re)birth of the adventure novel with the generation of Alain-Fournier, André Gide, Pierre Mac Orlan and Jacques Rivière has been established. This chapter will move the historical goalposts back slightly to show that even before this, Stevenson's work was being interpreted in France in terms of how it offered a countermodel to Naturalism; it was only subsequently that the emphasis was less immediately reactionary and shifted to the elaboration of a new concept of adventure.

Over the course of the nineteenth century, there were continual comings and goings between French and British fiction. This can be seen in Balzac's homage to Walter Scott in the 'Avant-propos' to *La Comédie humaine*, in the British George Sand mania of the 1840s, in the close connection between the French *roman feuilleton* and the English sensation novel and, later, between Naturalism and Decadence in France and English Aestheticism in the Nineties. Translation played a leading role in this literary-historical drama. In the first half of the nineteenth century, translations accounted for nearly 40 per cent of the books being published in France.[4] A series of new international copyright laws in 1838, 1847, 1851, 1852 and 1854 reduced the number of translated books circulating in both Britain and France, but there was a renewal of interest in French translations into English in the 1860s,[5] and from the 1870s, the number of translations from English into French was once again on the rise after a period of relative sluggishness. During the high point of Naturalism in the 1870s and early 1880s, foreign translations into French were still relatively few, accounting for 3 per cent of the books published in France; from the mid-1880s to the turn of the century, translation into French increased, 'attaining a maximum of 5 to 6 per cent of the total number of books published in France'.[6] Interest in foreign literature was on the rise at the fin de siècle.

---

[4] Wilfert-Portal, 'La Place de la littérature étrangère', p. 78.
[5] For a discussion of the impact of the copyright legislation and the renaissance of serialised French novels in the 1860s, see Atkinson, *French Novels and the Victorians*, pp. 318–21.
[6] Wilfert, 'Literary Import into France and Britain', p. 176.

From the perspective of translation, the fin de siècle was a turning point for French literature, a period in which 'established models [we]re no longer tenable'. This enabled translated literature to 'assume a central position', not so much in terms of the number of translations being published, as in the importance of the role of foreign works within the literary system.[7] With critics and authors searching for international models that would help (re)define French literature, the fin de siècle and pre-war years witnessed a surge of interest in foreign works in France. English literature, which had traditionally rivalled French literature for cultural dominance, was the most imported. As one reviewer in Georges Clémenceau's newspaper, *L'Homme libre*, remarked, by the 1920s it was hard to open a French book without feeling the influence of English literature and encountering some unknown island, a boat, a crew, a femme fatale, a 'bon nègre' and a storm.[8] Yet, the English-language authors who were most prominent in France during the Third Republic might come as a surprise to twenty-first-century readers, and would certainly have surprised Stevenson. By 1909, Stevenson was being described in *Le Figaro* as a 'grand artiste'.[9] In the years leading up to World War I (1908–14), the five most cited English-language authors in the influential *Nouvelle Revue française* were Shakespeare, H.G. Wells, Charles Dickens, Rudyard Kipling and Robert Louis Stevenson.[10] Stevenson was an important reference for those who were seeking to renew the novel in France.

Many factors, both personal and literary, contributed to the championing of Stevenson's writing during the Third Republic. At the most obvious level, there was his temperament, which was undoubtedly very attractive: Stevenson the man appealed just as much as Stevenson the man of letters. In a review of *Prince Otto* (1885), Stanislas

---

[7] This is part of a wider process of change that has been theorised by Itamar Even-Zohar: 'The dynamics within the polysystem create turning points, that is to say, historical moments where established models are no longer tenable for a younger generation. At such moments, even in central literatures, translated literature may assume a central position. This is all the more true when at a turning point no item in the indigenous stock is taken to be acceptable, as a result of which a literary "vacuum" occurs.' 'The Position of Translated Literature Within the Literary Polysystem', p. 201.

[8] L. Méritan, 'Les Lettres', *L'Homme libre*, 24 October 1920, p. 2.

[9] Fœmina, 'L'Âme des Anglais (hypothèses impertinentes)', *Le Figaro, supplément littéraire*, 4 December 1909, pp. 2–3 (p. 3).

[10] Maaike Koffeman, *Entre classicisme et modernité: la 'Nouvelle Revue Française' dans le champ littéraire de la Belle Époque* (Amsterdam: Rodopi, 2003), pp. 268–9.

Rzewuski describes Stevenson as 'un écrivain séduisant, personnel et puissant'.[11] For Henry-D. Davray, Stevenson was 'Écossais de nationalité, Parisien et boulevardier, Londonien et Américain du Far West, Provençal, cosmopolite'.[12] Thérèse Bentzon also approvingly evokes his cosmopolitanism, describing him as 'cet Écossais greffé de Yankee et de Parisien agréablement bohème'. His lifestyle was just as much a model of modernity as his books were, with his self-imposed exile perceived as a rejection of the values of the European cultural centre. Bentzon explains that Stevenson's wandering lifestyle 'a formé une personnalité très curieuse, très moderne et franchement très excentrique'.[13] He was a person to be admired and emulated, a writer who lived outside of circumscribed middle-class, bourgeois society, and who had distanced himself from it in order to live a life of apparent adventure in Samoa.

Stevenson's constant illnesses and his nomadic lifestyle made him a near-perfect model of the fin-de-siècle bohemian artist, and it was believed that his eccentricities were not a product of affectation. Note the emphasis on sincerity and spontaneity in the following passage, where a distinction is made between authentic and inauthentic artists. Stevenson might write with the style of an aesthete, but he was no poseur:

> La personnalité de l'auteur, on le voit, n'est pas moins romanesque que son œuvre même; si celle-ci apparaît parfois d'une fantaisie bizarre, il y a lieu de penser au moins que cette bizarrerie est bien spontanée et sincère, et ne résulte pas d'une originalité artificielle, péniblement cultivée.[14]

For many, it was as if Stevenson himself could be read as a modern adventure novel. Comment was made on his 'personnalité [. . .]

---

[11] 'Le Dernier roman de Stevenson', p. 2. ('A seductive, personal and powerful writer.')
[12] 'Lettres anglaises', *Mercure de France*, November 1897, pp. 628–9 (p. 628).
[13] 'Le Roman étrange en Angleterre', pp. 556 and 552. ('This Scotsman in whom are joined the Yankee and the pleasantly Bohemian Parisian'; 'has shaped a very curious, very modern, and frankly very eccentric personality.')
[14] M.S., '*Le Dynamiteur* de Robert-Louis Stevenson', p. 1. ('We can see that the author's personality is no less romantic than his works; if the latter sometimes seem bizarrely fanciful, there is reason at least to believe that the peculiarities are spontaneous and sincere, and do not stem from an originality that is artificial and laboriously cultivated.') Compare this with Saintsbury's description of Stevenson's 'effective but also rather affected and decidedly laboured style'. *The English Novel*, chapter 'The Fiction of Yesterday – Conclusion'.

romanesque' as early as 1894.[15] Looking back on Stevenson's life upon publication of Jean-Marie Carré's *La Vie de Robert Louis Stevenson*, an article in *L'Intransigeant* concluded that 'si Stevenson n'avait pas écrit tant de chefs-d'œuvre, on pourrait dire que sa vie est son meilleur roman. Quel mouvement dans cette existence d'un révolté contre une famille puritaine, d'un vagabond de nature, d'un sentimental.'[16] His nomadic lifestyle also corresponded with the alleged rootlessness of contemporary civilised Europeans, for whom exile and alienation were perceived as natural, inexorable states. When bibliophile Octave Uzanne imagined the literary evolution that had culminated in the typical modern artist, whom he names 'Néorphe' (New Orpheus), he included Stevenson's name in the list of literary influences on the new generation of cosmopolitan artists.[17]

Stevenson was also perceived to be a man divided, which made him a living example of a theme he so successfully depicted in his fiction. When *Le Dynamiteur* was published in French, Marcel Schwob remarked on the different versions of Stevenson that existed, comparing him to his most celebrated character(s), Dr. Jekyll and Mr. Hyde, and drawing attention to his preoccupation with both morality and adventure. Schwob writes: 'on peut distinguer une double personnalité qui le fait pencher tantôt vers John Knox le prédicateur, tantôt vers Barbe-Noire le flibustier'. He also states that 'on pourrait appliquer métaphoriquement à Stevenson lui-même la dualité qu'il a donnée au docteur Jekyll; il a une âme de pirate et une âme de sermonnaire raffiné'.[18] For Teodor de Wyzewa, the appeal of the double personality was more personal still. Wyzewa placed Stevenson beside Charles Dickens, Walter Pater and H.G. Wells in his pantheon of

---

[15] M.S., '*Le Dynamiteur* de Robert-Louis Stevenson', p. 1.
[16] Les Treize, 'Les Lettres', *L'Intransigeant*, 24 May 1929, p. 2. ('If Stevenson had not written so many masterpieces, his life would have been considered his best novel. What movement in the life of this rebel from a puritanical family, this vagabond by nature, this romantic.')
[17] 'Les Jeunes écrivains et leurs origines littéraires', *La Dépêche*, 22 October 1899, pp. 1–2. Uzanne is discussing Barrès's cosmopolitan 'déracinés'.
[18] 'Robert-Louis Stevenson', *Revue hebdomadaire*, 2 June 1894, pp. 5–10 (pp. 8 and 9). ('His divided personality makes him lean sometimes towards John Knox, the preacher, and sometimes towards Blackbeard, the pirate'; 'we could metaphorically apply to Stevenson himself the duality that he gave to Dr. Jekyll: he has the soul of a pirate and the soul of a refined preacher.') Schwob's article is printed immediately before Georges Art's translation of *Le Dynamiteur* and was also published in *Le Phare de la Loire*, 5 June 1894, pp. 1–2.

English-language writers and recorded his love for Stevenson in his journal in 1903, where it is clear he sees something of himself in Stevenson:

> Ce Stevenson [. . .] est décidément un des hommes dont l'esprit me plaît le plus parfaitement. Il y a chez lui un mélange d'enfantillage et d'ironie, de poésie sentimentale et de scepticisme, qui, peut-être, se serait aussi trouvé dans mes contes et mes romans, si j'avais eu le courage d'en écrire [. . .][19]

As these examples make clear, for many intellectuals and artists Stevenson was a model in terms of lifestyle, but also in terms of literary aspirations.

Generational Differences

The fin de siècle was a period of profound anxiety in the literary world, and responses to Stevenson's books in France illustrate the tensions being worked out as a new generation sought to formulate and assert its own literary values. Chapter 3 established that Stevenson was reaching difference audiences in France thanks to the specific emphases of the publishers translating his work. Similarly, critical reception of his books differed according to generational differences and literary affiliations, with the younger generation in particular sharing an appreciation for his work.

Among the names mentioned above are some of the earliest supporters of Stevenson's work in France and they are representative of different generations of critics and readers. Thérèse Bentzon, for example, was an established critic of the older generation who nonetheless followed new literary developments closely because of her role with the respected *Revue des deux mondes* – being cultured meant being familiar with foreign literature. As already mentioned, her essay 'Le Roman étrange en Angleterre', written in 1888, garnered

---

[19] Quoted in Paul Delsemme, *Teodor de Wyzewa et le cosmopolitisme littéraire en France à l'époque du symbolisme* (Brussels: Presses universitaires de Bruxelles, 1967), p. 111. ('Stevenson [. . .] is decidedly one of the men whose mind fits me most perfectly. There is in him a mixture of childishness and irony, of sentimental poetry and scepticism, which, possibly, could also have been found in my stories and novels if I had had the courage to write any [. . .].')

much attention when it appeared in the *Nouvelles mille et une nuits* (1890) volume.[20] On the other hand, critics like Marcel Schwob and Teodor de Wyzewa belonged to a transitional generation between Naturalism and Modernism. They also straddled two literary worlds in terms of the venues for which they wrote. Sjef Houppermans has already alluded to this in relation to Marcel Schwob, whom he describes as 'occup[ying] a peculiar position in the literary world of post-1870 France'.[21] Schwob and Wyzewa were not quite of the generation of authors like Émile Zola (1840–1902), Alphonse Daudet (1840–97) and Edmond de Goncourt (1822–96) or of critics like Bentzon (1840–1907) and Albert Wolff (1825–91). Nor were they entirely of the generation of Stevenson's twentieth-century Modernist supporters like novelists André Gide (1869–1951), Marcel Proust (1871–1922) and Alain-Fournier (1886–1914) or critics like Jacques Rivière (1886–1925) and Albert Thibaudet (1874–1936): Wyzewa was born too early (1862–1917) and Schwob died too young (1867–1905). They both knew the older generation of authors (Schwob dined with Goncourt on several occasions), but they had no vested interest in maintaining its literary norms. Critics belonging to this transitional generation contributed to recognised establishment publications, and in this they were aligned with the generation that preceded them; but, they were also concerned with the rebirth of French fiction and participated in the spread of new literary ideas by contributing to new and emerging publications. The difference is, in the terminology of Pierre Bourdieu, a difference in the 'degree of consecration'. As Bourdieu explains, 'differences in the *degree of consecration* in fact separate artistic generations defined by the interval (often very short, sometimes barely a few years) between styles and

---

[20] The *Journal des débats* commented that 'la partie la moins intéressante de ce volume n'est pas, on s'en doute bien, la remarquable préface (*Le Roman étrange en Angleterre*), dans laquelle Mme Th. Bentzon a pris soin d'analyser l'œuvre considérable et si originale de Stevenson'. F.D., 'Les Livres nouveaux', *Journal des débats politiques et littéraires*, 17 June 1890. ('The remarkable preface (*Le Roman étrange en Angleterre*) in which Mme Th. Bentzon has taken care to analyse Stevenson's considerable and very original oeuvre is not the least interesting part of the volume.') Her essay is also mentioned in 'Lettres, sciences et arts', *Journal des débats politiques et littéraires*, 8 July 1896, p. 3.

[21] 'Robert, Alexandre, Marcel, Henri, Jean et les autres: R.L. Stevenson and his "French Connections"', in *Beauty and the Beast: Christina Rossetti, Walter Pater, R.L. Stevenson and their Contemporaries*, ed. by Peter Liebregts and Wim Tigges (Amsterdam/Atlanta: Rodopi, 1996), pp. 187–207 (p. 189).

lifestyles that are opposed to each other'.[22] Taken as a whole, though, critics of this transitional generation, who were often associated with Symbolism, and critics of the emerging generation of Modernists, can be characterised as sharing the following traits insofar as they contributed to similar small publications at the fin de siècle:

> La jeunesse et le statut d'entrant dans le champ, le souci de se distinguer du naturalisme, le niveau scolaire élevé, le regroupement, à Paris, d'auteurs venus de province et de pays étrangers, enfin et surtout une organisation autour de petites revues et maisons d'édition indépendantes fondées pour l'essentiel sur le déni de l'économique.[23]

As this makes clear, these critics of the late nineteenth and early twentieth centuries were associated with precisely the types of small journals and independent publishers who brought out translations of some of Stevenson's works. Foreign literature played a central role in their quest to renew the French novel. As Wilfert explains, they associated 'leur importation de littérature étrangère à un projet global de subversion des normes littéraires et de libération de la langue'.[24]

Wyzewa emigrated to France from Poland as a child in 1870 and is linked to both avant-garde and conservative artistic circles. Able over the course of time to negotiate very different cultural spaces, he was a director of the highbrow *Revue Wagnérienne* and a contributor to other eminent periodicals, including the multilingual *Cosmopolis* and the avant-garde *Mercure de France*.[25] At the same time, he was a regular contributor to and later section editor of the conservative *Revue des deux mondes*, a veritable cultural institution

---

[22] *The Rules of Art: Genesis and Structure of the Literary Field*, trans. by Susan Emanuel (Cambridge: Polity Press, 1996), p. 122.
[23] This is Wilfert's description of Symbolist critics. '*Cosmopolis* et *L'Homme invisible*', p. 42. ('Youth and the status of newcomer to the literary field, the desire to be distinct from Naturalism, a high level of education, the grouping together, in Paris, of authors who had come from the provinces and foreign countries, finally, and above all, an organisation structured around small journals and publishing houses founded for the most part on the denial of the commercial.')
[24] '*Cosmopolis* et *L'Homme invisible*', p. 42. ('Associated their importing of foreign literature with an overall project of subverting literary norms and liberating language.') Wilfert distinguishes between the 'symbolist' (avant-garde) and 'academic' groups.
[25] On his role, see Delsemme, *Teodor de Wyzewa et le cosmopolitisme littéraire en France*, p. 210.

in nineteenth-century Paris. Francis Lacoste, for instance, qualifies the entire French literary establishment of the time as consisting of the Académie française plus the *Revue des deux mondes* and a few notable salons.[26] As a polyglot who was comfortable in half a dozen languages, Wyzewa wrote extensively about foreign authors and collected his writings in three series of essays called *Écrivains étrangers*. We have already seen in Chapter 3 that Wyzewa translated three of Stevenson's last novels.[27] According to Henry-D. Davray, by 1905 Wyzewa had done more than any other critic to make Stevenson's works known in France.[28] Rightly or wrongly, today that role is more often ascribed to Marcel Schwob.

In the Pléiade edition of Stevenson's works, Marc Porée argues that without Schwob, Stevenson's fate in France would have been very different:

> Le succès jamais démenti rencontré par *L'Île au trésor* auprès de la jeunesse fit longtemps obstacle à toute prise en compte sérieuse de l'œuvre. Il fallut attendre [. . .] Marcel Schwob en France pour voir le roman commencer à lentement sortir du purgatoire des romans pour enfants dans lequel il était tombé.[29]

This is a mostly accurate, if well-worn, assessment of Schwob's role in promoting not only *Treasure Island* (1883), but Stevenson's work more generally. Indeed, these kinds of things were already being said in the interwar years. Pierre Champion, a renowned historian, described Schwob as an 'écrivain d'une immense culture, qui a révélé à sa génération Stevenson et Meredith'.[30] Furthermore, in 1920,

---

[26] 'De Zola à Loti: l'institution face au naturalisme', in *Champ littéraire fin de siècle autour de Zola*, ed. by Béatrice Lacoste (Bordeaux: Presses universitaires de Bordeaux, 2004), pp. 93–103 (p. 93).
[27] *The Wrong Box* (1889; translated as *Le Mort vivant* in 1905); *The Ebb-Tide* (1894; translated as *Le Reflux: roman* in 1905); and *St. Ives* (1897, posthumous; translated as *Saint-Yves: aventures d'un prisonnier français en Angleterre* in 1904).
[28] 'Lettres anglaises', *Mercure de France*, September 1905, pp. 303–5 (p. 303).
[29] '*L'Île au trésor*: notice', in Robert Louis Stevenson, *Œuvres, I*, ed. by Charles Ballarin, Bibliothèque de la Pléiade (Paris: Gallimard, 2001), pp. 1180–98 (p. 1195). ('The continuing success of *Treasure Island* with young people was for a long time an obstacle to any serious consideration of his œuvre. It took Schwob in France for the novel to slowly escape from the purgatory of children's literature into which it had fallen.')
[30] 'Marcel Schwob', *Le Gaulois*, 22 January 1927, p. 5. ('An immensely cultivated writer who revealed Stevenson and Meredith to his generation.') Champion wrote a book on Schwob (*Marcel Schwob et son temps*, 1927). His father was the Honoré Champion of the celebrated publishing house.

Edmond Pilon wrote an article in which he claimed that 'si, pour nous, Français, le nom de Stevenson chanta sur nos lèvres, c'est à Marcel Schwob que nous le devons'.[31] Léon Daudet likewise evokes Schwob – and himself – among Stevenson's first French fans: 'Nous n'étions alors que quelques-uns, dont Marcel Schwob, à proclaimer son extraordinaire génie.'[32] It is probably fair to say that the younger generation of writers and critics who were trying to make a name for themselves in the literary world were pleased with their own discovery of Stevenson. There was a certain pleasure to be had in belonging to the (allegedly) small circle who appreciated Stevenson as a writer of artistic merit, and it was a mark of discernment that undoubtedly contributed to a sense of group identity for this community.

These types of comments memorialise both Schwob and Stevenson at the same time since, like Stevenson, Schwob died at a very young age (thirty-seven, in his case), not long after going on a Stevensonian pilgrimage to Samoa. Schwob also shared many of Stevenson's enthusiasms: he wrote a 'vie imaginaire' of Burke and Hare, the models for Stevenson's 'The Body-Snatcher' (1884), and, like Stevenson, was fascinated by Late Medieval poet François Villon (as was Pierre Mac Orlan).[33] What has resulted is a sort of Schwob–Stevenson mythology, in which Schwob's proselytising, his role as the curator of Stevenson's work in France, has in some respects overshadowed the importance of his own fiction in French literary history. Schwob is regarded as a minor Symbolist writer, but as a major critic of the fin de siècle, and virtually every mention of the short story collection *Cœur double* includes reference to its dedication to Stevenson.[34] Indeed, Schwob's own literary career was only just beginning when he started to write

---

[31] 'Quelques mots sur Marcel Schwob et Stevenson', *L'Intransigeant*, 31 July 1920, p. 2. ('If, for we French, Stevenson's name sang on our lips, we owe it to Marcel Schwob.')
[32] 'À propos du *Maître de Ballantrae*', *L'Action française*, 4 January 1921, p. 1. ('There were but a few of us then, including Marcel Schwob, proclaiming his extraordinary genius.') It should be noted that Schwob's first article on Stevenson appeared four years after *Treasure Island* was serialised and was printed in a provincial newspaper, which would surely have mitigated its effect: 'Robert L. Stevenson', *Le Phare de la Loire*, 27 August 1888.
[33] Schwob wrote a critical study of Villon, which was published in 1912. See Marcel Schwob, *François Villon: rédactions et notes* (Geneva: Slatkine Reprints, 1974).
[34] By way of example take this first sentence of a review of *Cœur double*: 'C'est, je crois, par ce recueil de nouvelles, dédié à Stevenson, que Marcel Schwob fit ses débuts dans les lettres, en 1891' ('I believe that Marcel Schwob made his literary début in 1891 with this collection of stories dedicated to Stevenson'). Jean-Jacques Brousson, 'Les Livres', *Excelsior*, 25 April 1921, p. 4.

about Stevenson. Appropriately, an 1894 article on *Le Dynamiteur*, for which Schwob wrote a preface, is at pains to explain who Schwob is before moving on to a discussion of Stevenson's book.[35] Similarly, an editor's note preceding an 1894 article in *Le Phare de la Loire* – whose then editor-in-chief was Schwob's older brother – states that Schwob-the-younger was in contact with Stevenson 'depuis longtemps' and was better qualified than anyone else to write about Stevenson.[36] Nonetheless, according to Octave Uzanne, by 1905 Schwob's efforts had not resulted in the public reading more Stevenson: 'de belles études que donna jadis M. Marcel Schwob n'incitèrent pas suffisamment le public à lire les œuvres émouvantes de ce parfait écrivain'.[37] There is some suggestion, however, that he may have encouraged at least one translation of Stevenson by enabling Alfred Jarry's translation of *Olalla*.[38]

Whatever the exact circumstances behind the Schwob–Stevenson mythology, Schwob has still been credited with making Stevenson known to a wider, more sophisticated, less juvenile, French audience. The fact that he corresponded with both Stevenson and Sidney Colvin added a level of authority to his reputation as a Stevenson critic.[39] While the view of him as the most important figure in spreading the gospel of Stevenson is largely accurate given the number of articles he wrote, it does something of a disservice to Bentzon and Wyzewa, as well as other critics like Georges Grappe (1879–1947). Grappe was a prolific writer whose biography of Stevenson was published in 1904. He wrote extensively on art and artists, particularly those with links to Impressionism (Fragonard, Monet, Van Gogh, Degas, Velazquez), and he later became conservator of the Musée Rodin. He also wrote on European authors (Keats, Cardinal Newman, Sainte-Beuve, Goethe, Ronsard); on contemporary French literature (Bourget, the Goncourt

---

[35] Paul Perret [P.P.], 'À travers champs', *La Liberté*, 16 October 1894, p. 2.
[36] Marcel Schwob, 'R.-L. Stevenson', *Le Phare de la Loire*, 5 June 1894, pp. 1–2. The same article was published in the *Revue hebdomadaire* on 2 June 1894, pp. 5–10.
[37] 'La Quinzaine des livres', *La Dépêche*, 18 January 1905, p. 5. ('The excellent studies formerly undertaken by Mr Marcel Schwob were not enough to incite the public to read the stirring works of this consummate writer.')
[38] Kelly, 'Jarry, Stevenson and Cosmopolitan Ambivalence', pp. 201–2.
[39] See Letter from Marcel Schwob to Sidney Colvin, 16 November 1899: 'I shall try and have articles written on the "Letters" in various places.' Manuscript Collection MS-4035, MSS_StevensonRL_2_1_036, Harry Ransom Center, The University of Texas at Austin, available at <https://hrc.contentdm.oclc.org/digital/collection/p15878coll48/id/1590/rec/11>.

brothers, Maeterlinck); and on literary relations between France and England (*Dramaturges français devant la critique anglaise*). It is fascinating to think how Stevenson fitted into this catalogue of interests. Stanislas Rzewuski also needs to be mentioned in this context: his review of *Prince Otto* goes beyond simple regurgitation of publicity materials and critical commonplaces. Many other journalists and critics, like Philippe Gille and the dandy, salonnier and poet, Gabriel de Lautrec, cousin of Henri de Toulouse-Lautrec, also need to be acknowledged, for just as there were a lot of people translating and publishing Stevenson, there were a lot of people writing about him.

Not all assessments of Stevenson were positive, of course. An obituary in *Le Petit Parisien*, for example, stated that Stevenson 's'adonna à un genre un peu gros, et il valait mieux que ce qu'il écrivait' – in other words, the unrefined genre in which he wrote was beneath him.[40] One of the earliest critics of Stevenson's work was Paul Ginisty (1855–1932), a friend of Maupassant's who became the director of the Théâtre de l'Odéon in 1896. Ginisty was also an author: he wrote regular reviews for *Gil Blas*, as well as several novels, and, towards the end of his life, a study of Eugène Sue. While Ginisty was quite harsh in his opinion of Stevenson, many of the comments he makes seem to apply to the translation itself rather than to Stevenson's own talents. In an 1885 review of Louis Despréaux's *Suicide-Club*, for instance, he concludes that the premise of the book is interesting, that the literary aspects are mediocre, but that the novel has the merit of being representative of the pessimism of contemporary literature.[41] His critique of Berthe Low's *Strange Case of Dr. Jekyll and Mr. Hyde* is in the same vein. In his 'Causerie littéraire' of 1 August 1890, Ginisty praises the 'psychologie fantastique' of the novel, but cautions that there needed to be more concern for composition and greater care for artistry, and that some of Stevenson's techniques were clumsy and showed a disdain for literary gracefulness.[42] This is echoed by another critic in *La Justice* in 1885,

---

[40] Pontarmé, 'Un romancier nomade', *Le Petit Parisien*, 22 December 1894, p. 2.
[41] 'Les Livres', *Gil Blas*, 28 October 1885, p. 3. 'La tenue littéraire en étant médiocre'; 'l'idée première est curieuse. C'est pour le coup, en tous cas, qu'on peut crier au "pessimisme" de la littérature actuelle!' Edmond de Goncourt's historical study *La Saint-Huberty* is reviewed in the same article, which is another sign of how the two literatures were intertwined. This shared space shows how foreign and French books were being treated as equal.
[42] *Gil Blas*, 1 August 1890, p. 3. (More 'pondération dans la composition, un plus complet souci d'art'; 'procédés un peu gros, joints à un certain dédain de toute grâce littéraire.') He reviews Paul Bourget's *Un cœur de femme* in the same article.

where it is written that Stevenson's style 'n'est pas tout à fait "ça"' – not altogether 'it'.[43]

Ginisty belonged to the same generation as Stevenson, but as Proust's well-known pastiche of Edmond de Goncourt makes clear, older, more established writers often failed to see the merit in this so-called writer of adventure tales for children. Curiously, in this they were aligned with certain British critics of the early twentieth century, for whom Stevenson was 'a writer of the second class'.[44] In a famous and oft-quoted passage from *À la recherche du temps perdu*, Swann defends Stevenson's work during an imaginary conversation with Edmond de Goncourt, which must be based on Proust's personal experience of Goncourt or on typical salon conversations of the time, since there is no mention of Stevenson in the Goncourt *Journal* or correspondence. Proust was friends with Lucien and Léon Daudet, and their father, Alphonse Daudet, was Edmond de Goncourt's closest friend. Alphonse Daudet's admiration for Stevenson is a matter of record: Mallarmé mentions it in his letter to the committee to erect a monument to Stevenson in Edinburgh.[45] Goncourt and Stevenson had at least one indisputable common interest – *japonisme* – which in other circumstances would suggest a shared artistic vision. Stevenson owned several volumes of Japanese woodcut prints by 'Divine Hokusai!',[46] which he bought with his earnings from *Treasure Island*; Goncourt was a prominent collector of Japanese art and his last books were *Outamaro: le peintre des maisons vertes* (1891) and *Hokusai: l'art japonais au XVIIIe siècle* (1896).[47] Despite these common points, Goncourt apparently misunderstood Stevenson's role in the evolution of the novel, presumably because of the genre with which he associated Stevenson. Swann corrects him, however: 'Mais c'est tout à fait un

---

[43] Sutter Laumann, 'Revue littéraire', *La Justice*, 13 April 1885, p. 2
[44] Frank Swinnerton, *R.L. Stevenson: A Critical Study* (London: Martin Secker, 1914), p. 189.
[45] 'Robert-Louis Stevenson', in *Œuvres complètes*, ed. by Bertrand Marchal, Bibliothèque de la Pléiade, 2 vols (Paris: Gallimard, 2003), II, pp. 689–90 (p. 689).
[46] Letter to W.E. Henley, [Early May 1883], *Letters*, IV, p. 122.
[47] Alan Sandison has identified shared literary preoccupations between Stevenson and Proust, notably the role of memory, childhood and notions of selfhood in artistic creation. He uses Stevenson's essay 'Roads' as illustrative of the similarities. 'Proust and Stevenson: Natives of an Unknown Country', in *European Stevenson*, ed. by Richard Ambrosini and Richard Dury, pp. 147–70.

grand écrivain, Stevenson, je vous assure M. de Goncourt, un très grand, l'égal des plus grands.'[48]

We learn here what some members of the older generation thought of Stevenson, but Proust also expresses a feeling shared by several young intellectuals and artists, that Stevenson was an author whose importance and influence surpassed his role in the wave of nineteenth-century boys' tales. The pastiche also reveals that Proust was not entirely dismissive of Edmond de Goncourt; it is, as Annick Bouillaguet has shown, 'laudative en somme'.[49] The laudatory nature of the pastiche emerges through the complex layering of voices, which is not unlike something one would find in a Stevenson novel: Proust is writing as 'Marcel', who is adopting Goncourt's style to write about (and quote) a conversation Swann had with Goncourt about something Mme Cottard said about Stevenson. All this in a novel in which it turns out that the person who is narrating ('Marcel') has much in common with the person who is writing (Proust) and that its seven volumes constitute a lengthy literary apprenticeship. It is not by chance that the pastiche occurs in the *Le Temps retrouvé*, the last volume of *À la recherche du temps perdu*, in which the process of artistic discovery comes to the fore. The Stevenson comment can be read as a textual working-out of aspects of the evolution of the novel at the turn of the century, a comment on how we get from generically unstable Stevensonian novels to Proust *en passant par* Goncourt. In other words, both Stevenson and Goncourt are necessary to the (artistic) creation of Proust – they are his literary heritage. When Edmond Jaloux reflected on the history of fin-de-siècle French literature, he maintained that authors born around 1880 developed in one of two directions: either they followed the path of Stevenson, like Alain-Fournier and Pierre Mac Orlan, or they followed the path of Paul Bourget and the psychological novel, like Marcel Proust.[50] Proust's pastiche of Goncourt suggests that the paths might not have been quite so divergent, since Stevenson's presence can be felt in both

---

[48] *Le Temps retrouvé*, in *À la recherche du temps perdu*, ed. by Pierre Clarac and André Ferré, Bibliothèque de la Pléiade, 3 vols (Paris: Gallimard, 1954), III, p. 716. ('I assure you, Mr de Goncourt, Stevenson is absolutely a great writer, very great, on a par with the greatest.')
[49] 'Proust, lecteur des Goncourt: du pastiche satirique à l'imitation sérieuse', in *Les Frères Goncourt: art et écriture*, ed. by Jean-Louis Cabanès (Bordeaux: Presses universitaires de Bordeaux, 1997), pp. 339–48 (p. 343). ('Is all in all laudatory.')
[50] 'Le Prix Balzac', *Le Gaulois*, 14 January 1922, p. 1.

conceptions of the novel – and as we have already seen, Stevenson himself admired Bourget.

Chapter 3 suggested how Stevenson's publishing history in France may have obscured how much of his work was available in French, thereby affecting his reception. Another reason Stevenson's merits might not have been immediately apparent to the older generation of French writers is that in France, as in Britain for that matter, there was a more or less clear socio-economic demarcation separating authors for whom writing was a profession on which they relied (e.g. Zola and Maupassant) and, on the other hand, those who were, according to Christophe Charle, financially self-sufficient (e.g. Flaubert and the Goncourts).[51] The latter did not necessarily need to consider commercial pressures (sales, marketing, reviews) when writing – which, however, is not the same as saying that they were not interested in these things privately. As Arthur Symons observes in 'A Note on Zola's Method', 'in *Germinie Lacerteux* you never forget that Goncourt is an aristocrat; in *L'Assommoir* you never forget that Zola is a bourgeois'.[52] Freedom from financial constraint meant that once Naturalism had achieved its literary aims, monied authors like Goncourt could turn their backs on it and seek to innovate by prioritising style above all else. More broadly, the financially independent could afford to distance themselves from commercially successful fiction and its bourgeois associations and turn to rarefied literary forms that embraced art for art's sake. They could afford to scorn the reading public as a way of rejecting the distasteful business aspects of the publishing world.[53]

For the younger generation of the 1880s and 1890s, this choice seemed stark. This is reflected in Camille Mauclair's essay, 'Le Roman de demain', in which Mauclair imagines a writer of the future looking back at the fin de siècle and ascertaining that books could be written either for entertainment or for artistic reasons, but not both:

> La surproduction commençait de diviser l'art d'écrire en deux orientations distinctes: le livre pour amuser, et l'œuvre d'art. La commodité de vivre conseillait la première route, le respect des beautés intellectuelles

---

[51] See Part 2, chapters 2 and 3, and Part 3, chapter 1 of *La Crise littéraire à l'époque du naturalisme: roman, théâtre et politique. Essai d'histoire sociale des groupes et genres littéraires* (Paris: Presses de l'école normale supérieure, 1979).
[52] *Studies in Two Literatures*, p. 205.
[53] Bourdieu notes in *The Rules of Art* that the 'hierarchy among genres (and authors) according to specific criteria of peer judgement is almost exactly the inverse of the hierarchy according to commercial success' (p. 114).

commandait l'autre [. . .]. Beaucoup d'entre vous ont cherché à suivre les deux chemins tout ensemble, et n'ont réussi qu'à mécontenter les artistes sans satisfaire pleinement la banalité des foules.[54]

The difficulty was in transcending this opposition. This is where Stevenson served as a point of reference in debates about the evolution of the novel. While a consummate stylist from an upper-middle-class background, Stevenson wanted financial independence from his family. Because of this, as Glenda Norquay has demonstrated, he overwhelmingly 'engages with the idea of writing as a trade'.[55] For Stevenson, it was never a binary choice. If '"pure" art and "commercial" art [. . .] are linked by their very opposition' as Bourdieu suggests,[56] Stevenson occupied the space in the middle where both coexisted. This was immensely appealing to fin-de-siècle authors and critics and suggested a way forward for the novel.

Beyond Naturalism

Several factors contributed to the importance of translated literature in late-nineteenth-century French literary debates. Foremost among these is that the novel, particularly the Naturalist novel, was perceived to be in a state of crisis. Michel Raimond, for example, states that at the turn of the twentieth century, 'on parlait beaucoup de la décadence et de la mort prochaine du roman'.[57] Writers of the time were seen to be wallowing in a 'situation stagnante, trouble, pleine d'obscurité périlleuse et de lassitude', from which they were trying to escape.[58] Naturalism was the dominant literary movement of the 1870s and 1880s, but

---

[54] *La Revue du palais*, January 1898, pp. 156–77 (p. 159). ('Because of overproduction, the art of writing started to divide along two distinct lines: books as entertainment and as works of art. The necessity of living counselled the former; respect for the intellectually beautiful called for the latter. Many among you tried to follow the two paths at the same time, and only managed to annoy artists without wholly satisfying the taste for banality of the masses.')
[55] 'Trading Texts: Negotiations of the Professional and the Popular in the Case of *Treasure Island*', in *Robert Louis Stevenson: Writer of Boundaries*, ed. by Ambrosini and Dury, pp. 60–9 (p. 60).
[56] *The Rules of Art*, p. 166.
[57] *La Crise du roman*, p. 88. ('There was a lot of talk of the decadence and impending death of the novel.')
[58] Mauclair, 'Le Roman de demain', p. 165. ('A stagnant, muddled situation, full of perilous obscurity and weariness.')

it began to implode at the very moment it began to achieve popular success; indeed, David Baguley has qualified Naturalism as inherently entropic.[59] As a result, there was sustained critical reflection on what the novel was capable of doing and what it was supposed to achieve. There was also a crisis in publishing and bookselling that lasted from 1890 to 1914, due in part to an economic recession.[60] To these circumstances can be added the fact that new audiences were emerging as a result of changes in public education, and new laws on publishing, copyright and official censorship were coming into force.

Faced with these pressures, some commentators were anxiously preoccupied with the notion of cultural decline. Other artists and critics sought to renew literature by changing the internal structures of the French literary field, either by freeing authors from commercial pressures to sell books – this was the primary objective of the creation of the Académie and Prix Goncourt, for example – or by trying to make Naturalism accepted within official hierarchies (Émile Zola's repeated attempts to enter the Académie française are the most obvious instance of this). Others still sought to identify foreign literary models in the hope of renewing the French novel from the outside, with the unstated assumption that renewing the French novel was tantamount to renewing the novel *tout court*. This left open the door for foreign authors to be naturalised into a French literary tradition. In Gilles Philippe's view, the growing cosmopolitanism of French literature in the 1890s resulted in uncoupling literature from the nation – in other words, it contributed to the disruption of the concept of a 'national' or home-grown literature.[61]

Thus, while Stevenson's writing was championed for its intrinsic worth, his supporters also believed that it had the potential to alter the path of French literature. Critics clearly appreciated Stevenson in his own right, but he was also co-opted in the mutiny against Naturalism and held up as a model of generic and stylistic innovation. His themes were also timely from the standpoint of fin-de-siècle French literature because he offered an alternative to the thematic focus typically found in Naturalist fiction, which, in broad strokes, tends to deal with how the downtrodden cope with inexorable

---

[59] *Naturalist Fiction: The Entropic Vision* (Cambridge: Cambridge University Press, 1990). Pierre Bourdieu paints the crisis in Naturalism in broad strokes in *The Rules of Art* (p. 125), while Christophe Charle analyses the dynamic of disruption in more detail in *La Crise littéraire à l'époque du naturalisme*.
[60] Parinet, 'L'Édition littéraire, 1890–1914', p. 161.
[61] *French Style*, p. 175.

social, environmental and biological forces. In Chapter 3, I briefly drew attention to a jibe against Naturalism contained in a discussion of translation practices, and I would now like to come back to those aspects of Stevenson's reception in France that relate to debates about the Naturalist conception of the novel. In the example already cited, Wyzewa comments that adultery is not the only subject worthy of being depicted in novels,[62] which is a clear reference to novels like *Madame Bovary*, *Nana*, *L'Assommoir* and *La Curée*, as well as to Naturalism more generally. There was a decided sense that Naturalism – once itself perceived as a threat – had gone mainstream and run its course. Five years after making this comment, Wyzewa wrote in the *Revue des deux mondes*:

> De même que le grand romancier russe [Dostoïevsky], l'Écossais s'abstient soigneusement de toute argumentation, de toute théorie directement exprimée: tous deux ne précèdent que par une série de petits tableaux, mais dont chacun comporte une signification typique qui se découvre aussitôt à nous. De même que Dostoïevsky, Stevenson n'admet pas que le bonheur des hommes dépende sérieusement des lois qui les régissent, des endroits qu'ils habitent, ni des conditions de leur vie; tout cela n'a, suivant lui, qu'une importance très secondaire et l'unique réforme efficace serait celle qui réussirait à modifier le dedans de l'homme, en le délivrant de ses vices et ses faiblesses.[63]

Russian and English literatures were two of the most widely read in fin-de-siècle France, and Wyzewa himself was a noted translator from the Russian (he translated Tolstoy's *Resurrection* (1899), *What is Art?* (1897) and complete theatrical works, for example). In the above passage, Wyzewa not only aligns Stevenson with Dostoevsky – which is

---

[62] 'La Correspondance de R.-L. Stevenson', in *Écrivains étrangers*, pp. 192–221 (pp. 207–8).
[63] 'Un livre nouveau de Robert Louis Stevenson' [review of *Essays of Travel*, London, 1905], *Revue des deux mondes*, 15 July 1905, pp. 457–68 (p. 462). ('Like the great Russian novelist [Dostoevsky], the Scot carefully abstains from all argumentation, from any directly expressed theories: both proceed by a series of small tableaux, each of which holds a meaning which is suddenly revealed to us. Like Dostoevsky, Stevenson does not allow that man's happiness seriously depends on the laws that govern him, the places he lives, or the conditions of his life; all this has, according to him, but a very secondary importance, and the sole useful reform would be the one that succeeded in modifying man's interior, by delivering him from his vices and weaknesses.')

consistent with the way *Strange Case of Dr. Jekyll and Mr. Hyde* (1886) was brought to the market in France – he also positions Stevenson in relation to contemporary French literary debates. By focusing on Stevenson's interest in 'le dedans de l'homme' (the inner life, psychology), Wyzewa uses him to dismiss some of the principal tenets of Zolian Naturalism, which is built upon a foundation of Positivist philosophy and social Darwinism. He claims that Stevenson is uninterested in man's relationship to the various laws that govern him (the 'lois qui les régissent'). He also claims that Stevenson is uninterested in the role of the environment on his characters (their happiness depends neither on the 'endroits qu'ils habitent' nor on the 'conditions de leur vie'). Finally, Wyzewa claims that for Stevenson fiction is not a means of illustrating a theoretical position (he abstains from 'toute théorie directement exprimée'). André Gide expressed a similar idea in 1899: in addition to referencing Wyzewa and Schwob, Gide praises *The Dynamiter*, *The Suicide Club* and *Treasure Island* by stating that 'l'absence de pensée est là volontaire et charmante'.[64] Stevenson's independence of approach was prized at this particular literary-historical juncture.

As the comment by Gide makes clear, Wyzewa was not the only one to view Stevenson's work in this light, situating it in terms of debates taking place in French, rather than English, literature. In an article introducing the serialisation of *The Wrecker* (1892) in the *Journal des voyages*, Edmond Neukomm calls Stevenson an enemy of methodical classification – this was a way of distancing the novel from the Naturalist school, but also had the knock-on effect of making *The Wrecker* acceptable for wide public consumption by the journal's readers.[65] Mauclair, on the other hand, criticises Zola's 'grossière erreur' ('crude error') and calls for characters who are not slaves to determinism and their environment.[66] Schwob also expresses anti-Naturalist ideas in the preface to *Cœur double* (1891), where he writes that if the novel as a form is to persist, 'les descriptions pseudo-scientifiques, l'étalage de psychologie de manuel et de biologie mal digérée en seront bannis'.[67] The ideas to which these critics object were central to Zola's concept of literature as 'experimental method', as expressed

---

[64] 'Lettre à Angèle', p. 456. ('The absence of ideas here is deliberate and charming.')
[65] 'Un roman de Louis Stevenson', p. 40.
[66] 'Le Roman de demain', p. 172.
[67] (Toulouse: Éditions ombres, 1996), pp. 9–22 (p. 21). ('Pseudo-scientific descriptions and displays of textbook psychology and ill-digested biology must be banished from it.')

in *Le Roman experimental* (1880) and *Les Romanciers naturalistes* (1881) and against which Stevenson himself was writing in 'A Note on Realism' (1883). This theory of the novel is given full weight in Zola's Rougon-Macquart series, which is tellingly subtitled *Histoire naturelle et sociale d'une famille sous le Second Empire* (*Natural and Social History of a Family under the Second Empire*), and explores how one family's genetic traits express themselves and evolve when faced with specific environmental and social pressures over a given time period.

Stevenson's focus on the inner life in moments of crisis corresponded with transformations in French literary tastes at the end of the nineteenth century and could be used as ammunition in the battle for literary change. Formal and generic innovation were just as important. Established authors thought that the French novel could be renewed by adapting Naturalist techniques to new, more refined subject matter. This is what Edmond de Goncourt attempted to do in his last novel, *Chérie* (1884). It is what Joris-Karl Huysmans did do in *À Rebours* (1884), the decadent bible published in that same transitional year in French literature (which is also the year that *Treasure Island* was serialised in France). The destabilising preface to *Chérie* is particularly revealing in terms of the discussion of literary evolution. Goncourt refers to his preface as 'une sorte de testament littéraire' because it not only contains the preface to his *Journal* but begins with a manifesto on the future of the novel.[68] The terms it uses are familiar:

> On trouvera bien certainement la fabulation de *Chérie* manquant d'incidents, de péripéties, d'intrigue. Pour mon compte, je trouve qu'il y en a encore trop. [. . .] Oui, je crois, – et ici, je parle pour moi bien tout seul, – je crois que l'aventure, la machination *livresque* a été épuisée par Soulié, par Sue, par les grands imaginateurs du commencement du siècle, et ma pensée est que la dernière évolution du roman, pour arriver à devenir tout à fait le grand livre des temps modernes, c'est de se faire un livre de pure analyse: livre pour lequel [. . .] *un jeune* trouvera quelque jour, une nouvelle dénomination, une

---

[68] *Chérie* [1884], ed. by Jean-Louis Cabanès and Philippe Hamon (Paris: Édition la Chasse au Snark, 2002), p. 47. ('A sort of literary last will and testament.') On the preface as a literary-historical document, see chapter 1 of Katherine Ashley, *Edmond de Goncourt and the Novel: Naturalism and Decadence* (Amsterdam: Rodopi, 2005).

dénomination autre que celle de roman. [. . .] Puis toujours, toujours, ce romancier écrira en vue de ceux qui ont le goût le plus précieux, le plus raffiné de la prose française.[69]

This new conception of the novel posits that 'fabulation', incidents, adventures and intrigue are to be banned – that narrative avenue had allegedly reached a dead end after Frédéric Soulié and Eugène Sue (whom Stevenson read and appreciated). Goncourt's hope is that a younger author will find a word to replace 'roman' ('novel'). As we saw in Chapter 1, Zola called for exactly the same thing. However, whereas Zola sought new terminology in order to accurately describe the Naturalist experimental novel, Goncourt, a Naturalist who is now reacting against Naturalism, wants a new label so as to describe a modernised novel that contains no plot – no experiment – at all. In both cases, though, it is the 'romance' part of the word 'roman' that offends. At the same time as he calls for story to be banned, Goncourt calls for authors to write for the few, for those who have the most refined sense of style and who can therefore truly appreciate art for art's sake. These ideas point to a wholesale rejection of the mass of readers and the demands of the literary marketplace.

The question, then, is how Stevenson fits into this dynamic. Stevenson had the requisite sense of style, but he steadfastly refused to write for the few. From very early on, Stevenson was intent on writing aesthetically pleasing page-turners. *The Dynamiter* (1884), for example, makes the importance of plot a central part of its plot, even for men of refinement: Somerset proposes to Challoner and Desborough that pursuing the 'great profession of intrigue', being a 'complete detective', is 'the only profession for a gentleman' (pp. 6–7). What is more, Stevenson's sense of incident and emphasis on storytelling were used as selling points for his books: two virtually identical announcements in French newspapers claim

---

[69] *Chérie*, pp. 41–2. ('The storytelling in *Chérie* will most certainly be found to be lacking in incidents, twists and turns, intrigues. For my part, I find that there are still too many. [. . .] Yes, I believe, – and here I speak for myself alone – I believe that adventure, *novelistic* machinations have been worn out by Soulié, by Sue, by the great imaginative creators of the beginning of the century, and my thought is that, to manage to entirely become the great book of modern times, the final evolution of the novel is to transform itself into a book of pure analysis: a book for which [. . .] *a young person* will some day find a new name, a name other than that of novel [. . .] Then always, always, that novelist will write with a view to those who have the most precious, the most refined taste for French prose.')

that the *New Arabian Nights* (1882) stories 'dans leur hardiesse toute moderne, sont dignes de rivaliser avec les romans à sensation les plus renommés'.[70] And sensation novels, of course, drew on the French *feuilletonistes*, authors like Sue and Soulié. Furthermore, notwithstanding their emphasis on plot, books like *The Dynamiter* do not fit the parameters of the sensation novel or detective fiction *stricto sensu*. This inability to categorise Stevenson, together with his fractured narration, his polished style (for those who read him in English), and the metafictional aspects of his writing, was a cause of perplexity for some and of lively curiosity for others.[71] Whereas established writers in France sought to move beyond Naturalism by turning to the psychological novel, the *roman à thèse* or more rarefied and Decadent forms, Stevenson framed his rejection of realism in terms of romance. He was a stylish storyteller who modelled another type of writing. For the fin-de-siècle generation, the prospect of a stylistically refined 'roman romanesque' was infinitely attractive.[72]

Towards a New Novel

Younger critics and writers, those whose careers were yet to be fully launched in the 1880s and 1890s, never succeeded in fulfilling Goncourt's injunction to find a new name for the novel. What they did do is seek inspiration from foreign, particularly northern European, models in order to move beyond the dominant aesthetic in France. Insofar as this is the case, Stevenson had an important role to play in the evolution of the novel in France. Wyzewa, for example, draws attention to the possibility of foreign literature, and Stevenson in particular, to inspire French authors. He muses: 'Qui sait même s'il ne nous aiderait pas à varier, à renouveler la forme, décidément bien

---

[70] 'Librairie', *La Justice*, 12 May 1890, p. 4. Judith Gautier, 'Les Livres nouveaux', *Le Rappel*, 10 June 1890, p. 3. It is unclear whether this was advertising copy or whether Gautier wrote the short review for *La Justice* anonymously and then published it again in *Le Rappel*. ('In their entirely modern audacity, are worthy of rivalling the most renowned sensation novels.')
[71] Alan Sandison refers to this aspect of Stevenson's work as proof of his 'abiding interest in indeterminacy, the deferral of closure, reflexivity (often represented in the *mise-en-abyme* tale), multiple narratives, artistic self-exposure and the rehabilitation of art as game'. *Robert Louis Stevenson and the Appearance of Modernism*, p. 85.
[72] Marcel Prévost, 'Le Roman romanesque moderne', *Le Figaro*, 12 May 1891, p. 1.

fatiguée, de notre roman, comme l'a fait jadis Dickens en Russie, en Allemagne, et un peu en France?'[73] In addition, in places Wyzewa tacitly situates Stevenson within a French literary tradition. When, in the preface to *Weir of Hermiston*, Wyzewa refers to the novel as Stevenson's 'testament littéraire',[74] on one level he is indicating that it was a book that Stevenson left unfinished upon his death, his literary last will and testament; on another level, the comment positions Stevenson within French literary history, recalling as it does Villon's *Testament* (1461), published shortly before Villon's disappearance.

There is, of course, another side to the discussion of Stevenson's place in the evolution of French prose. While French commentators and writers looked to Stevenson to reinvigorate the novel, we have already seen how Stevenson positioned himself vis-à-vis French literature, especially in terms of his rejection of realism as a genre. What is more, in his introduction to *The Complete Stories of Robert Louis Stevenson*, Barry Menikoff contends that 'Stevenson was by temperament aligned with the French in their emphasis on form and style in the short story' and that one of his preferred genres, the short story, 'had no modern equivalent in England' and was more closely related to the French *conte*.[75] George Saintsbury, who was generally pessimistic about the future of French literature when he wrote his essay 'The End of a Chapter' (1895), remarked that 'the short story, one of the earliest triumphs of French prose, appears to be the very stronghold of the literature, into which at its greatest pinches it retires, and where it holds out for better days'.[76] This inevitably raises the question of whether turn-of-the-century French critics admired Stevenson because his writing corresponded with long-standing French tastes and modes of expression. In other words, perhaps they were

---

[73] 'La Correspondance de R.-L. Stevenson', p. 193. ('Who knows whether he won't help us to vary, to renew the decidedly very tired form of our novel, as Dickens did in Russia, in Germany and to an extent in France?') Schwob, meanwhile, believes that this is precisely what *Treasure Island* does: 'Cette terrible histoire de flibustiers qui commence dans le fantastique et continue avec la précision de détails d'un journal de bord, a saisi le public et consacré une nouvelle forme du roman' ('This impressive story of pirates, which begins in the fantastic and continues with the précision of a traveller's log, has gripped the public and consecrated a new novelistic form'). 'Robert L. Stevenson' [1888], in *Will du Moulin*, ed. by Escaig, p. 59.

[74] 'Préface', in *Hermiston: le juge-pendeur*, trans. by Albert Bordeaux (Paris: Fontemoing, 1912), pp. v–xvii (p. viii).

[75] 'Introduction', pp. xx and xix.

[76] *The Collected Essays and Papers of George Saintsbury*, volume IV, pp. 250–80 (p. 275).

unwittingly looking for familiarity abroad? Given that the tide of novelistic change tended to flow from France to Britain and then back again in a continual coming and going, this is not outside the realm of the possible and would contribute directly to the emergence of a transnational genre.

One of the earliest French reviews of Stevenson's work cites the length of his books as a 'mérite fort apprécié en France, la brieveté', which seems to confirm Menikoff's contention.[77] Furthermore, in 1922 André Chaumeix, who was soon to be elected to the Académie française, explained to readers of *Le Gaulois* that there were two types of novelists in English: on the one hand, there were 'romanciers anglais qui ont toujours marqué leur préférence pour les longs ouvrages, en plusieurs volumes, évocateurs d'une société entière, comme Dickens ou Meredith'; on the other hand, there were 'des écrivains comme Stevenson et Kipling [qui] ont été chez eux des novateurs, et ils ont même reçu le reproche d'être des continentaux'.[78] This acknowledges Stevenson's novelty in terms of the short form and links it to Continental tastes. Apparently, the absence of a triple decker among Stevenson's works contributed to his positive reception in France. It is therefore evident that to some extent Stevenson's novels were appreciated precisely because they were atypical of British writing of the time. As Graham Good suggests, 'it is as if [Stevenson] spent his writing career of twenty years casting around in all directions which led *away from* the Victorian novel'[79] – it seems that this was recognised by Stevenson's French reviewers. Furthermore, as a columnist in *La Justice* remarked in 1890, 'ceux qui reprochent au roman anglais quels que soient ses mérites, d'être souvent noyé dans des détails fastidieux n'ont assurément jamais lu Stevenson'.[80] These

---

[77] 'Bibliographie', *L'Intransigeant*, 12 May 1890, p. 3. ('Brevity is a much-appreciated virtue in France.') An article in the *Journal des débats* also cites differences in length between the English and French novel, and lists Stevenson as one of the English authors who has contributed to the move towards the one-volume book in Britain. 'Au jour le jour', *Journal des débats politiques et littéraires*, 12 July 1894, p. 1.
[78] 'Contes et nouvelles', *Le Gaulois*, 22 April 1922, p. 3. ('English novelists who have always had a marked preference for long works, in several volumes, that evoke an entire society, like Dickens and Meredith'; 'writers like Stevenson and Kipling who were innovative in their homeland and have even been reproached for being Continentals.')
[79] 'Rereading Robert Louis Stevenson', p. 49.
[80] 'Librairie', *La Justice*, 12 May 1890, p. 4. ('Those who reproach the English novel, whatever its merits, with often drowning under fastidious details, have assuredly never read Stevenson.')

French commentators are picking up on what Richard Ambrosini has called the 'unresolved conflict' in Stevenson's relationship to the novel. Ambrosini writes that Stevenson was

> a master of stylistic prose whose artistic identity was not based on the dominant art form of his age, the novel. Thus it was that he could behold the breaking up of the Victorian three-volume novel, and the proliferation of popular subgenres aimed at a mass editorial market, as an interesting opportunity – and not as a writing on the wall, a warning that the barbarians were at the gate.[81]

The breaking up of the Victorian triple decker was of limited interest to the French; the breaking of the Naturalist stranglehold on the novel in terms of both its popular market appeal and its dubious aesthetic theory was, however, a growing concern at the end of the nineteenth century.

Stevenson was an important reference in the evolution of French literature at the turn of the century. This is not because of the *conte* as a genre *per se*, but because of the centrality of storytelling, generic experimentation and stylistic refinement to Stevenson's writing. Comments on Stevenson's storytelling powers recur, from the earliest French reviews to the most recent. Augustin Filon refers to Stevenson as 'le conteur inimitable' – the definite article makes Stevenson exemplary. Wyzewa calls Stevenson a 'poète et conteur' ('poet and storyteller'), and the 'plus parfait conteur de la littérature contemporaine' ('the most perfect storyteller in contemporary literature') at that.[82] Georges Grappe states it most eloquently, however, at least in the original French, when he writes that Stevenson is 'essentiellement un conteur, qui aimait conter pour le simple plaisir de conter'.[83]

Generic innovation was also a factor in the positive reception of Stevenson's books. When Berthe Low's translation of *Strange Case of Dr. Jekyll and Mr. Hyde* appeared, it drew attention because of the originality of the story itself and because of the manner in which the story was told. A review from 1890 highlights this:

---

[81] 'The Four Boundary-Crossings of R.L. Stevenson, Novelist and Anthropologist', p. 26.
[82] Filon, 'Balzac et les Anglais', p. 1. Wyzewa, 'La Correspondance de R.-L. Stevenson', pp. 206 and 194.
[83] *R.L. Stevenson: l'homme et l'œuvre*, p. 30. ('Essentially a storyteller, who liked telling stories for the simple pleasure of telling stories.')

Ce qui fait le mérite, l'originalité, la saveur toute particulière de ce roman, c'est que l'auteur raconte les événements les plus bizarres, les péripéties les plus terrifiantes, avec un flegme surprenant, un sang-froid tout britannique, une précision parfaite, un luxe de détails qui rendent vraisemblable et naturel le surnaturel.[84]

More than one article expressed curiosity about Stevenson's supernatural leanings. *Le Figaro* laments: 'Ah! qu'ils sont beaux les livres de peur anglaise: beaux et chargés d'aveux . . . Et nous, nous n'avons pas de livres de peur . . .'. According to the author, Fœmina, who overlooks Maupassant, tales of terror did not exist in France because the French had an outlet for their violent impulses in licentious literature (presumably Naturalism would fall under this heading); licentious literature was not acceptable in Britain, therefore the British needed shilling shockers and fear-inspiring books to rid their imaginations of certain images ('se débarrasser l'imagination de certaines images'). This resulted in fictional heroes whose genius and curiosity led them to madness, who 'se convulsent dans des aventures extra humaines', and for whom terror was a means of delighting in mystic danger.[85] By deploring the lack of this type of book in France, Fœmina suggests that Stevenson's books, along with those of Edgar Allan Poe, could fill a void in the French literary field. This recalls the title of Mme Bentzon's article, 'Le Roman étrange en Angleterre' – 'étrange' for 'strange', as in *Strange Case of Dr. Jekyll and Mr. Hyde*, but also for the emerging literary supernatural or weird fiction genre. This was not the way that French literature did evolve, however, and the supernatural largely remained a genre apart.

---

[84] 'Bibliographie', *L'Intransigeant*, 20 July 1890, p. 3. ('What gives this novel its merit, its originality, its very particular flavour is that the author relates the most bizarre events, the most terrifying incidents, with a very British stiff upper lip, a perfect precision, and lavish details that make the supernatural both natural and believable.') This article bears remarkable similarity to Judith Gautier's announcement for the novel in 'Les Livres nouveaux' (*Le Rappel*, 2 September 1890, p. 2), in which the reference to lavish details is omitted: 'Ce qui fait l'originalité et la saveur particulière de ce roman, c'est que l'auteur raconte les évènements les plus singuliers avec un flegme imperturbable, un sang-froid tout britannique et une précision parfaite qui font paraître vraisemblable l'invraisemblable.' Either Gautier wrote both, or Gautier and the author of the article in *L'Intransigeant* both relied heavily on Plon's advertising copy.

[85] 'L'Âme des Anglais (hypothèses impertinentes)', p. 3. ('Oh! How beautiful are these English tales of terror: beautiful and full of secrets . . . [. . .] we don't have tales of terror . . .'.) Fœmina was a pseudonym of Augustine Bulteau (1860–1922), who also wrote as Jacque Vontade. Her married name was Mme Jules Ricard.

More interesting in relation to the development of the mainstream novel, if such a thing can be said to exist, are the appraisals that consider Stevenson's books as defying generic categorisation. In this respect, it is hard to disagree with Alan Sandison's view that 'Stevenson's experiments, his ceaseless questing among forms, ensured that of all his contemporaries his works show the greatest and most radical diversity'.[86] Stevenson was far from a creature of habit, and he maintained that there was a connection between consciousness and change. As he writes in *Across the Plains* (1892), 'our consciousness, by which we live, is but itself the creature of variety'.[87] This declaration can be extended to his treatment of genre. This is not to say that French critics were always comfortable with Stevenson's generic variety. In the preface to *Hermiston: le juge-pendeur*, Wyzewa draws attention to literary hierarchies and the way that Stevenson confounds them, but also to how *Weir of Hermiston* was different from his other novels: 'au-dessus de ses romans d'aventure, où il ne cessait point de s'employer entre temps, il avait formé le projet d'une œuvre plus littéraire et plus haute, d'une façon de grande tragédie, très réaliste tout ensemble et très pathétique'.[88] Elsewhere, Wyzewa draws attention to Stevenson's variety, noting that 'M. Stevenson n'est, à vrai dire, ni un romancier, ni un conteur, ni un humoriste, ni un poète, ou plutôt c'est un mélange de tout cela, un mélange incohérent, désordonné, souvent un peu agaçant et souvent délicieux.'[89]

As the epigraph to this chapter – is Stevenson's book a novel? – playfully intimates, it was not uncommon for Stevenson to be presented as a creator of *sui generis* works of fiction. By way of example, when volume one of *New Arabian Nights* was presented to the public, *Le Matin* announced it by stating, '*Suicide-Club* est un roman anglais tout à fait original et composé d'une série d'histoires qui s'enchevêtrent les unes dans les autres, tout en pouvant se séparer et être lues isolément.'[90] Is it a novel, indeed. Bentzon referred to

---

[86] *Robert Louis Stevenson and the Appearance of Modernism*, p. 6.
[87] In *The Amateur Emigrant*, pp. 77–123 (p. 104).
[88] 'Préface', p. viii. ('Beyond his adventure novels, which never ceased to occupy him in the meantime, he had formed a project of a more literary and more elevated order, a type of great tragedy, very realistic on the whole and very pathetic.')
[89] 'Le Nouveau roman de M. Stevenson', *Le Temps*, 19 September 1894, p. 2. ('In truth, Mr Stevenson is neither novelist, storyteller, humorist nor poet, or, rather, he is a mix of all of these things, a mix that is inconsistent, unconventional, often a bit annoying and frequently delightful.')
[90] 'Les Livres', *Le Matin*, 11 May 1885, p. 3. ('*Suicide-Club* is an entirely original English novel made up of a series of overlapping stories that can be separated and read in isolation.') This is likely the way the publisher presented the book to newspapers.

New Arabian Nights and *Strange Case of Dr. Jekyll and Mr. Hyde* as belonging to a new genre, the 'psychologico-fantastique'.[91] Rzewuski argued in *Le Gaulois* in 1897 that Stevenson had created his own genre, a mix of fantasy and the fantastic, imagination and humour, acute psychological observations and meticulous realism.[92] Meanwhile, in 1905 the Catholic newspaper *L'Univers* referenced Stevenson's ability to 'unir à sa merveilleuse fantaisie poétique les trésors d'observation humaine'.[93] Others alluded to the mix of comedy and tragedy often found in his books.[94] Virtually all of Schwob's comments praise Stevenson's ability to break generic conventions and, in so doing, potentially pave the way for the novel of the twentieth century. Furthermore, although the title *Cœur double* ('divided heart') is enough to attest to Stevenson's impact on Schwob, his significance is also apparent in the preface to the short story collection where Schwob's discussion of him hinges on a reconfiguration of the novel as genre:

> Alors le roman nouveau sera sans doute un roman d'aventures dans le sens le plus large du mot, le roman des crises du monde intérieur et du monde extérieur, l'histoire des émotions de l'individu et des masses, soit que les hommes cherchent du nouveau dans leur cœur, dans l'histoire, dans la conquête de la terre et des choses, ou dans l'évolution sociale.[95]

This deliberately broad scope is restricted by the proposed definitions of 'adventure' and 'crisis' as they relate to fiction:

> On peut appeler 'crise' ou 'aventure' le point extrême de l'émotion. Chaque fois que la double oscillation du monde extérieur et du monde intérieur amène une rencontre, il y a une 'aventure' ou une

---

[91] 'Les Gais compagnons' [preface], *Revue des deux mondes*, 15 September 1889, pp. 94–6 (p. 94).
[92] 'Le Dernier roman de Stevenson', p. 2.
[93] 'Bulletin bibiliographique', *L'Univers*, 9 August 1905, p. 3. ('Join to his marvellous poetic imagination a wealth of human observation.')
[94] 'Bibliographie', *L'Intransigeant*, 12 May 1890, p. 3; Daudet, 'À propos du *Maître de Ballantrae*', p. 1.
[95] *Cœur double*, p. 22. ('So the new novel will no doubt be the adventure novel, in the widest sense of the word: a novel about the crises of the internal and external worlds, the story of individual and shared emotions, with men seeking novelty either in their own hearts, in history, in the conquest of the world and its things, or in social evolution.')

'crise'. Puis, les deux vies reprennent leur indépendance, chacune fécondée par l'autre.[96]

The renewal of the novel was therefore synonymous with abandoning not only Naturalism but mimetic realism more generally, in favour of what Schwob and others referred to as Stevenson's 'réalisme irréel'.[97] This recalls the earlier discussion about Stevenson's own views on the error of considering realism as a genre, rather than as a technique. The new aesthetic vision foresaw a novel that no longer exclusively told realistic tales, and that freed itself from the socio-historical, would-be mimetic trappings of Naturalism. The new novel would blend reality and fantasy, the objective and the subjective, realism and romance, would adapt new genres, such as the supernatural and detective fiction and couple them with refined stylistic simplicity. It is not hard to see how Stevenson fits within this framework.

This proposed next step in the evolution of French literature was, in short, quite the opposite of the techniques espoused by Decadent and Symbolist authors. This is doubly interesting given that while the French were looking abroad to writers like Stevenson, champions of artistic change in late-Victorian Britain were drawing inspiration from French Decadents. Indeed, in a fascinating instance of literary cross-pollination, Kirsten MacLeod has demonstrated that a counter-Decadent movement in reaction to developments in France actually preceded the emergence of home-grown Decadent writing in Britain.[98] Decadent texts were becoming more and more esoteric and devoid of plot (taking to new extremes Flaubert's dictum to write a book about nothing, and Goncourt's desire for a novel of pure analysis). Decadent language was stylistically erudite and self-consciously rarefied. Stevenson had the necessary stylistic refinement for Decadent artistic creation – he is a 'poète' who 'takes care over form', he is an 'artiste moderne'[99] – but his storytelling propensity meant that

---

[96] *Cœur double*, p. 21. ('We can call a "crisis" or an "adventure" an emotional high point. Every time the twin fluctuations of the external and internal worlds lead to an encounter, there is an "adventure" or a "crisis". Then, the two regain their independence, each fertilised by the other.')

[97] 'R.L.S.', *The New Review*, February 1895, pp. 153–60 (p. 159); Mauclair, 'Le Roman de demain', p. 174: 'd'une composition à la fois réelle et imaginaire'.

[98] See chapter 4, 'Writing Against Decadence, 1890–97' (pp. 78–98) of *Fictions of British Decadence*.

[99] Neukomm, 'Un roman de Louis Stevenson', p. 40; Savine, 'Robert-Louis Stevenson, sa vie, son œuvre, 1850–1894', pp. v–lxxii (p. lxx).

his books were also pleasurable to read. Appropriately, the introduction to the serialised translation of Stevenson's letters to Colvin explains that Stevenson saw it as a duty to make books pleasurable, believing that 'l'art doit rendre les hommes heureux; un livre cynique et amer est un crime de *lèse-humanité*'.[100] This was at odds with the way French fiction had been developing, but it offered a vision of what the novel could be.

Stevenson's defenders in France were drawn to what Stephen Arata calls Stevenson's aesthetic of idleness. Paradoxically, this aesthetic of idleness is consistent with Stevenson's aesthetic of change and movement, in which the pleasure we take from reading his books disguises the effort required to develop an accomplished and seemingly easy style. In other words, one needn't be a stylist to appreciate Stevenson's books, but it certainly added a layer of pleasure for those who did appreciate his facility with words. According to Arata, 'the commitment to stylistic perfection is in his case wholly in the service of pleasure, of literature as play, of reading as idleness'. As such, it is just as much a rejection of bourgeois conceptions of time as money, as it is of the usefulness value of art. Arata suggests that 'Stevenson tries to relieve us of the burden of paying attention. [. . .] Reading ought not to be work, though writing must be.'[101] This was something Stevenson accomplished through experimentation with popular genres, through readability, not through wallowing in Decadent or Symbolist obscurantism (which require work on the part of the writer and the reader). In this, his approach managed to reconcile the demands of the literary marketplace and the need for money with the refinement and accomplishment necessary to the creation of lasting art.

As has become apparent, storytelling and genre were not the only considerations in terms of the role Stevenson's books could play in the future of the French novel. There was an equally acute and justified appreciation of his style. Just as the themes and form of the 'roman nouveau' were to evolve away from realist representation, so its style was to change. For example, notwithstanding his assertion that translations needed to be less literal even if this resulted in a loss of 'beauté poétique', Wyzewa lauds 'l'originalité du style' found

---

[100] 'Lettres à divers', *Minerva: revue des lettres et des arts*, 1 March 1903, p. 99. ('Art needs to make people happy; a cynical and bitter book is a crime of *lèse-humanity*.')
[101] 'Stevenson, Morris, and the Value of Idleness', in *Robert Louis Stevenson: Writer of Boundaries*, ed. by Ambrosini and Dury, pp. 3–12 (p. 11).

in Stevenson's novels.[102] Moreover, in his lengthy, mostly biographical preface to *Enlevé!*, Albert Savine describes Stevenson's style using language that likens it to painting, praising his visual acuity and extraordinary artistry.[103] Meanwhile, Thérèse Bentzon's review of *Strange Case of Dr. Jekyll and Mr. Hyde* discusses the 'véritable originalité de forme et de fond' of Stevenson's stories and praises 'la concision, la clarté incisive, [et la] grande simplicité' of his style.[104] The keywords here are conciseness and simplicity, for they stand in stark opposition to Decadent affectation and mannerism.

Simplicity mattered. Marcel Schwob believed that Stevenson's power stemmed at least in part from his ability to describe complicated subjects in an uncomplicated manner: 'C'est essentiellement l'application des moyens les plus simples et les plus réels aux sujets les plus compliqués et les plus inexistants.'[105] This faith in simplicity corresponds with Henry James's assessment of Stevenson's aesthetic principles: according to James, for Stevenson 'all art is simplification'.[106] He and Schwob understood Stevenson well, because in 'A Humble Remonstrance' (1884), Stevenson emphasises the importance of simplicity, and insists on the fact that the novel is not and can never be a mimetic transcription of external reality:

> And as the root of the whole matter, let him [the budding author] bear in mind that his novel is not a transcript of life, to be judged by its exactitude; but a simplification of some side or point of life, to stand or fall by its significant simplicity. For although, in great men, working upon great motives, what we observe and admire is often their complexity, yet underneath appearances the truth remains unchanged: that simplification was their method, and that simplicity is their excellence. (p. 142)

The impetus to simplify goes against the aesthetic grain of Decadent and Symbolist writers in France, and the writers of the aesthetic

---

[102] 'La Correspondance de R.-L. Stevenson', p. 193.
[103] 'Robert-Louis Stevenson, sa vie, son œuvre, 1850–1894', p. lxxii. 'Cette merveilleuse beauté plastique qui distingue tous les écrits, sans exception, de Stevenson.'
[104] 'Le Roman étrange en Angleterre', p. 552. ('True originality of form and content'; 'the conciseness, the incisive clarity, [and the] great simplicity.')
[105] 'R.L.S.', p. 156. ('It's essentially the application of the simplest and most realistic means to the most complicated and non-existent subjects.')
[106] Henry James letter to Robert Louis Stevenson on *A Humble Remonstrance*, 5 December 1884, in *Robert Louis Stevenson: The Critical Heritage*, ed. by Maixner, pp. 143–4 (p. 143).

Nineties in Britain, for whom the more rarefied the language, subject matter or characters' tastes, the more artistic and accomplished the novel. Indeed, at the very moment that some of the stylistic excesses of *écriture artiste* (or Impressionist prose) were facilitating the short-lived transition from Naturalism to Decadence, Stevenson proclaimed to James that his two aims were 'war to the adjective' and 'death to the optic nerve'.[107] This is not far removed from Walter Pater's belief that truth in literature demands that authors 'say what [they] have to say, what [they] have a will to say, in the simplest, the most direct and exact manner possible, with no surplusage'.[108] Maupassant would have concurred, for in the preface to *Pierre et Jean*, in which he sets out his theory of the novel and implicitly rejects Naturalism, he attacks the growing obscurantism of *écriture artiste* in favour of simplicity and clarity. Although Stevenson was accused of affectation by some British critics, he was praised in France for his lack of artificiality and his innate understanding of style. Wyzewa claimed in 1894 that

> nul n'a mieux su construire une phrase, une période, un chapitre, et par là nous entendons non pas l'artifice laborieux d'un pédant, mais cette harmonie native d'un artiste-né qui donne au rythme la part qui lui revient dans la symphonie des mots.[109]

The reference to a 'symphony of words' makes sense given Wyzewa's involvement in promoting Wagnerism in France, but of course it also recalls Stevenson's own reading of Baudelaire and his essay 'On Some Technical Elements of Style in Literature' (1885), where the musicality of language is underscored.

Stevenson's new – dare I say, novel – way of approaching the novel, his generic experimentation, his rejection of realist-Naturalist theories, and his stylistic refinement drew the attention of French critics at the end of the nineteenth century and at the turn of the twentieth. At about the time Naturalism started to fade from prominence as its representatives either died or moved in other directions,

---

[107] Letter to Henry James, [c. 5 December 1893], *Letters*, VIII, p. 193.
[108] 'Style', p. 32.
[109] 'Le Nouveau roman de M. Stevenson', p. 2. ('No one has been better able to construct a sentence, a full stop, a chapter, and by this I'm not talking of the laborious artifice of the pedant, but of that natural harmony of the born artist who accords to rhythm its rightful part in the symphony of words.')

the next generation of authors shifted their attention to the concept of 'adventure'. Naturalism – only really inaugurated in 1865 upon publication of the Goncourts' *Germinie Lacerteux* – was perceived as the enemy of literary progress by the late 1880s and 1890s. With Zola's death in 1902, it lost any residual impetus. By the time Jacques Rivière's essay 'Le Roman d'aventure' was published in May–July 1913, the literary field had changed considerably. As Mark Fitzpatrick writes, by this point, 'rather than *naturalisme*, it's the *symbolisme* that took its place that must be swept away by the energy of the *roman d'aventure*'.[110] When an article in *L'Intransigeant* announced a lecture by Rivière in 1913, it was with a certain amount of bravura that it stood up to Symbolist, not Naturalist, art: 'Nous allons assister, pour la première fois en France, à une floraison d'œuvres d'imagination et d'invention pures. Fini le symbolisme, nous allons montrer aux Anglais ce que nous savons faire, quand, nous aussi, nous nous mêlons de raconter.'[111]

Marcel Schwob had, of course, already referenced the concept of adventure in his articles on Stevenson, and a letter from Stevenson to Schwob was in fact mentioned in the *Nouvelle Revue française* in 1912. That article positions Stevenson in terms of a literary dawn rather than a literary sunset and speaks of the 'lumière du jour, non celle du crépuscule'.[112] That said, I am not convinced that Schwob conceived of the adventure novel in precisely the way that the generation of authors grouped around the *Nouvelle Revue française* did. The inscription on the copy of *Cœur double* that he sent to Stevenson, for example, references romance and their shared appreciation of François Villon: 'This book is dedicated in admiration of, [sic] *Treasure Island, Kidnapped, The Master of Ballantrae* in the name of new shape he has given to the romance, for the sake of our dear Francis Villon.'[113] This suggests a different point of reference

---

[110] '"Tout à fait un grand écrivain": Stevenson's Place in French Literary History', in Richard J. Hill, ed. *Robert Louis Stevenson and the Great Affair: Movement, Memory and Modernity* (London: Routledge, 2017), pp. 202–18 (p. 210).
[111] Les Treize, 'La Boîte aux lettres', *L'Intransigeant*, 16 February 1913, p. 2. ('We are going to witness, for the first time in France, a flowering of works of pure imagination and invention. Symbolism is over and done with: we are going to show the English what we can do when we too dabble in storytelling.') For the attribution, see Houppermans, 'R.L. Stevenson and his "French Connections"', p. 197, n. 20.
[112] 'Les Revues', *Nouvelle Revue française*, February 1912, pp. 314–15.
[113] EdRLS: Stevenson's Library Database.

for the adventure novel compared with the way it would come to be conceived by André Gide, Pierre Mac Orlan or Alain-Fournier, insofar as these new discussions of adventure are less concerned with the romance versus realism debate that embroiled Stevenson and his British peers in the 1870s and 1880s – and which Schwob would have been aware of – and are more concerned with modernising the French novel in reaction to Symbolism, which was linked predominantly with poetry, theatre and the fine arts.

For Rivière, 'l'aventure, c'est la forme de l'œuvre plutôt que sa matière' – a statement that foregrounds the narrative possibilities afforded by the novelistic genre.[114] This more modern conception of adventure was recognised by authors who were not exclusively associated with the type of literature propagated by the *Nouvelle Revue française*. Jules Romains, for example, embraced so-called 'Unanimism' and is now known principally for his play *Knock* and his *roman-fleuve*, *Les Hommes de bonne volonté*. Nonetheless, in 1920 he commented that Stevenson had taught readers that they had a very childish conception of adventure: 'nous avons de l'aventure une conception un peu enfantine et grossière [. . .] c'est une question de finesse de regard, un plus ou moins de perfection dans notre sensibilité'.[115] Similarly, Henri de Régnier, who was elected to the Académie française in 1911 and was a writer of both Symbolist and neo-classical poetry, saw in Stevenson's conception of adventure something of psychological beauty:

> Il appartient au genre de roman que l'on nomme le roman d'aventures, mais ce genre, avec Stevenson, se hausse à une réelle beauté psychologique et dramatique. Avec un Stevenson, il ne s'agit plus d'une combinaison plus ou moins habile de péripéties et d'événements à surprise, destinés à entretenir chez le lecteur un intérêt quelque peu factice, puisqu'il dépend moins des personnages eux-mêmes que de ce qui leur arrive. Un roman de Stevenson n'est pas un ouvrage à trucs et à chausse-trapes, c'est une œuvre d'un art merveilleusement intelligent et logiquement inventif, dont l'action se développe dans

---

[114] 'Le Roman d'aventure', *Nouvelle Revue française*, May–July 1913, in *Études* (Paris: Gallimard, 1999), pp. 307–50 (p. 342). ('Adventure is the form the work takes rather than its subject matter.')

[115] 'Stevenson et l'aventure', p. 2. ('We have a fairly inaccurate and infantile conception of adventure [. . .] it's a question of looking at things with finesse, feeling more or less perfectly.')

une atmosphère subtile et colorée, et qui inclut non seulement un puissant mouvement dramatique, mais encore une profonde analyse des caractères et une vivante peinture des milieux.[116]

This conception of adventure bears little relation to the popular fiction with which Stevenson might have previously been associated. It also seems removed from the romance adventures of Rider Haggard and other similar contemporary writers. It was an example of the 'poetry in action' so appreciated by Alain-Fournier.[117] These interpretations legitimised Stevenson in a new way, connecting him to the development of the French modernist novel of adventure. In so doing, they contributed to the drawing to a close of the debates that had rocked the French literary world at the fin de siècle.

In the late nineteenth and early twentieth centuries, the French novel was thought to be sinking into an outmoded Naturalism that had served its literary purpose. For those who turned towards foreign literature to reorient it, Stevenson's writing opened the way for a new conception of the novel wherein artistic style coexisted with page-turning intrigues whose outcome was predetermined by neither social nor scientific theory or method. The misunderstanding of Stevenson's work by the old guard is quite understandable when we keep in mind where and by whom Stevenson was translated during the Third Republic, as well as the ways in which he flouted contemporary ideas about the realist novel, and the ways in which he navigated the channel between artistic sophistication and popular success. But the new guard, those critics and authors working towards a renaissance of the French novel at the turn of the century, found in Stevenson a pioneering model on thematic, generic

---

[116] 'La vie littéraire', *Le Figaro, supplément littéraire du dimanche*, 30 January 1921, p. 1. ('He belongs to the genre of novel we call the adventure novel, but this genre, with Stevenson, is elevated to a thing of real psychological and dramatic beauty. With a Stevenson, the adventure novel is no longer a more or less skilful combination of twists and turns and eventful surprises, destined to maintain a somewhat false interest on the part of the reader, because it depends less on the characters themselves than on what happens to them. A novel of Stevenson's isn't a work full of trickery and traps, it's a wonderfully intelligent and logically inventive work of art, in which the plot develops in a subtle and picturesque atmosphere, and that includes not only a powerful dramatic interest, but a profound analysis of character and a lively painting of the milieu.')

[117] Jacques Rivière, 'Alain Fournier', in Alain Fournier, *Le Grand Meaulnes, Miracles* (Paris: Garnier, 1986), pp. 3–56 (p. 41).

and stylistic grounds because he eschewed the ideas upon which the dominant literary tendencies of the time were based and charted his own course.

Even if Stevenson's position within the English canon remains somewhat ambiguous to this day (despite the canonical status of *Strange Case of Dr. Jekyll and Mr. Hyde*), his place in the French canon was assured from a comparatively early stage. In fact, whereas Stevenson served as a counter-model to the English modernist writers of the Bloomsbury group, to their contemporaries in France, grouped around the *Mercure de France* and the *Nouvelle Revue française*, he was a beacon. There is irony in this: the writers of the Bloomsbury group believed that in France – unlike in England, as they saw it – there was a public for serious, innovative art, yet they did not share the *Nouvelle Revue française*'s appreciation for Stevenson as a serious artist. Some of this is undoubtedly generational conflict: Virginia Woolf's father, Leslie Stephen, had given Stevenson his literary start when he commissioned 'Victor Hugo's Romances' for *Cornhill* in 1874.[118] There was likely also a sense in Britain of having been saturated with Stevenson and having simply heard enough – it was time to move on. The first concerted attempt to publish Stevenson's complete works in French translation began in 1920; Stevenson's complete novels are now available in a Pléiade edition.[119] Not only is this more than can be said of many nineteenth-century French authors who were striving to renew the novel at the end of the century (e.g. Schwob, Goncourt), it is more than can be said of major nineteenth-century English novelists like George Eliot and Thomas Hardy. It is also a sure sign that Stevenson has been consecrated in France, where he is now situated within a transnational literary pantheon because of his role in the reconceptualisation of the novel.

---

[118] For more on Bloomsbury and the *NRF*, see Koffeman, *Entre classicisme et modernité*, p. 141.

[119] On the 1920s translations, see Giroud, 'Cocteau and Stevenson', p. 192.

Postscript

This book has examined literary relations between Robert Louis Stevenson and French literature and culture in the fin de siècle, specifically how Stevenson's reading and writing, and the translation and reception of his works in France, reflect contemporary literary debates about the novel. Because of my focus, I have isolated the French Stevenson from the Scottish, the British, the American and the South Pacific Stevenson as far as possible, but of course I have done so knowing that the isolation is largely artificial: Stevenson was connected to all of these cultural traditions. What makes the French connection particularly revealing from the perspective of literary history, though, is the significance accorded to French literature and culture as a reference point by Victorian *littérateurs* – Stevenson included – at the end of the nineteenth century. As we have seen, references to the French language and French literature abound in Stevenson's private and published writing, and the French novel and French style were topics of constant discussion in British literary circles.

In Britain, as Juliette Atkinson observes, the 'critics of the 1880s and 1890s trumpeted the sophistication of French fiction as an antidote to the English novel'.[1] My approach to Stevenson allows us to see that while the British were looking to France for literary and artistic inspiration, the French were looking to Britain (or, in this case, to Scotland and Samoa) to renew their own literature. This is pertinent because as Margaret Cohen and Carolyn Dever remark, 'the modern novel did not develop along two separate, nationally distinct trajectories; it developed through intersections and interactions among texts, readers, writers, and publishing and critical institutions that

---

[1] *French Novels and the Victorians*, p. 339.

linked together Britain and France'.² The nineteenth century marks the consolidation of the idea of national literary canons, but cultural exchanges and literary relations such as those between Stevenson and France underscore the inherent internationalism of the novel. Adopting a literary-historical approach that focuses on the relationship between the British and French literary worlds of the period helps us to understand how the canon itself has affected our reading of Stevenson, and also how an author who operated on the peripheries of these two literary empires nonetheless helped shape the novel at the fin de siècle.

There are many unknowns in terms of how Stevenson's relations with French reviewers, authors, translators and publishers might have evolved around the turn of the century, if he had lived a longer life. What, for example, might have happened if Marcel Schwob had made his pilgrimage to Samoa before Stevenson had died? What if Stevenson had met Paul Bourget? Could these encounters have given additional momentum to Stevenson's standing in the international literary world? What if Stevenson had made his projected trip back to Europe, making France his temporary base?³ Could new literary friendships have developed? Or what if Stevenson had developed a working relationship with Rachilde and Alfred Vallette and the Mercure de France? Would more or different translations have been published? Would one publisher or translator have become the sole purveyor of all things RLS in France? Perhaps, with the encouragement of French novelists, Stevenson might have been 'brave enough' to write and publish in French.⁴ It is intriguing to wonder how actively he might have followed developments in French literature. Would he have approved or disapproved of the direction that French literature took at the beginning of the twentieth century? Would he have engaged directly in discussions about the adventure novel with the writers of the *Nouvelle Revue française*? Might he have joined the Franco-Scottish Society or attended the Entretiens de Pontigny? How surprised would he have been to learn that Alphonse Daudet appreciated his books, that Mallarmé wrote a letter of praise for him, or that

---

² 'Introduction', in *The Literary Channel: The International Invention of the Novel*, ed. by Margaret Cohen and Carolyn Dever (Princeton: Princeton University Press, 2000), pp. 1–34 (p. 2).
³ Stevenson mentions the possibility of a spending the summer in Royat in a letter to Henry James, 7 December 1891, *Letters*, VII, p. 210.
⁴ Letter to his Father, [5 September 1886], *Letters*, V, p. 315.

Proust later admired him? Stevenson may have rightly suspected that his reputation in French literary circles was growing, given that he was aware of an article written about him in *Le Temps* in 1893,[5] but he never had it confirmed. There is no doubt that he would have been pleased to learn that for many people in the French literary world, he did in fact write with 'the pen of angels [and] of heroes'.[6] So many questions remain unanswered because of Stevenson's untimely death, but although he never knew that he was a reference point in the development of a new model for the French novel, my hope is that this book not only sheds some light on his literary relations with France at the fin de siècle, but opens the door to studies on other aspects of the ties that bind Stevenson and France.

---

[5] On 9 June 1893, he requested a copy of the article, which was published on 6 April 1893. Letter to Sidney Colvin, 27 May 1893, *Letters*, VIII, p. 93.
[6] Letter to Marcel Schwob, 19 August 1890, *Letters*, VI, p. 401.

Appendix A

Stevenson in Translation: Serials and Magazines

This appendix lists works of Stevenson's that were serialised or published in French-language periodicals up to the beginning of World War I. It is based largely on information available through the Bibliothèque nationale de France's digital library, *Gallica*, as well as its digital newspaper repository, *Rétronews: le site de presse de la BnF*. The entries are arranged chronologically according to the earliest translation.

L'Île au trésor, trans. by André Laurie, *Le Temps*, 25 September–8 November 1884.
Le Cas extraordinaire du Dr. Jekyll et M. Hyde, trans. by Jules-Paul Tardivel, *La Vérité*, 15 January–16 April 1887.
'Le Club des suicidés; L'histoire du jeune homme aux tartes à la crème', trans. by O. Kraft [Thérèse Bentzon], *Journal des débats politiques et littéraires*, 23–28 October 1888.
'Les Gais compagnons', trans. by Thérèse Bentzon, *Revue des deux mondes*, 15 September 1889, pp. 94–132.
Le Maître de Ballantrae, [unknown translator], *Le Temps*, 22 April–24 May 1893.
Le Dynamiteur (extraits), trans. by G. Art, *Revue hebdomadaire*, 2 June–28 July 1894.
'La Bouteille diabolique', trans. by G. Art, *La Revue politique et littéraire* [*La Revue bleue*], 15–20 April 1895.
Le Secret du navire, trans. by A. Chevalier, *Journal des voyages*, 7 July 1895–8 March 1896.
'L'Île des voix', [? trans. by E. Gellion-d'Anglar], *La Revue des revues*, 15 September–1 October 1895.
Les Aventures de David Balfour, trans. by Marie Dronsart, *Journal des débats politiques et littéraires*, 26 January–16 March 1899.
'Will du Moulin', trans. by Marcel Schwob, *La Vogue*, March 1899, pp. 145–69.

'Le Démon de la bouteille', [trans. by Georges Lefèvre], *La Vogue*, December 1899–January 1900.
'Markheim', [unknown translator], *La Revue des revues*, 15 May–1 June 1900.
'L'Île des voix', trans. by E. Gellion-d'Anglar, *Mercure de France*, June 1900, pp. 596–624.
'Lettre à un jeune homme qui se propose d'embrasser la carrière de l'art', trans. by G. Lefèvre, *La Vogue*, 15 June 1900, pp. 145–52.
'Pris pour espion' [extract of *À la pagaie*], trans. by Lucien Lemaire, *La Plume: revue littéraire et artistique bi-mensuelle*, 1 December 1900, pp. 682–8.
'Markheim', trans. by E. La Chesnais, *Le Revue blanche*, January 1901, pp. 81–97.
'Olalla', trans. by Alfred Jarry, *La Vogue: revue mensuelle de littérature, d'art et d'actualité*, 15 February–15 March 1901.
Saint-Yves: aventures d'un prisonnier français en Angleterre, trans. by Teodor de Wyzewa, *Le Temps*, 23 August–25 October 1902.
'La Baie de Falesá', trans. by E. La Chesnais, *Minerva: revue des lettres et des arts*, 15 September–15 October 1902.
'Lettres à divers (ses idées sur l'Art et sur la vie d'après sa correspondance)', trans. by Madeleine Rolland, *Minerva: revue des lettres et des arts*, 1–15 March 1903.
Les Aventures de David Balfour, trans. by Marie Dronsart, *Le Journal de la jeunesse*, 16 December 1905–?
À la pagaie, trans. by L. Lemaire, *Vers et prose*, June 1906–February 1907.
L'Île au trésor, trans. by André Laurie, *Le Petit Parisien*, 15 November 1908–18 April 1909.

Appendix B

Stevenson in Translation: Books

This appendix lists the first translations of works of Stevenson's that were published as books in French up to the beginning of World War I. It is based largely on information available through the Bibliothèque nationale de France's digital library, *Gallica*, the Catalogue collectif de France, as well as various printed catalogues. The entries are arranged chronologically according to the earliest translation. The Bibliography contains information on the many other translations.

Suicide-Club. Le Diamant du Rajah, trans. by Louis Despréaux (Paris: Calmann-Lévy, 1885).
L'Île au trésor, trans. by André Laurie, Bibliothèque d'éducation et de récréation (Paris: Hetzel, 1885).
Le Cas extraordinaire du Dr. Jekyll et M. Hyde, trans. by Jules-Paul Tardivel (Québec: Drouin, 1887).
Nouvelles mille et une nuits, trans. by Thérèse Bentzon, Bibliothèque franco-étrangère (Paris: Hetzel, 1890).
Le Cas étrange du docteur Jekyll, trans. by Mme B.-J. Lowe (Paris: Plon, Nourrit, 1890).
Le Dynamiteur, trans. by Georges Art (Paris: Plon, 1894).
Le Secret du navire, [? trans. by A. Chevalier] (Paris: Charavay-Martin, 1896).
Le Roman du prince Othon, trans. by Egerton Castle (London: John Lane, 1896).
Le Roman du prince Othon, trans. by Egerton Castle (Paris: Perrin, 1897).
À la pagaie sur l'Escaut, le canal de Willbrocke, la Sambre et l'Oise, trans. by Lucien Lemaire (Paris: E. Lechevalier, 1900).
Voyage à travers les Cévennes avec un âne, trans. and adapted by A. Moulharac (Paris: Club cévénol, 1901).
La Flèche noire, trans. by E. La Chesnais (Paris: Mercure de France, 1901).
La Flèche noire, trans. by E. La Chesnais (Paris: Nelson, 1901).
Saint-Yves: aventures d'un prisonnier français en Angleterre, trans. by Teodor de Wyzewa (Paris: Hachette, 1904).

Enlevé! Mémoire relatant les aventures de David Balfour en l'an 1751, trans. by Albert Savine, Bibliothèque cosmopolite (Paris: Stock, 1905).
Le Mort vivant, trans. by Teodor de Wyzewa (Paris: Perrin, 1905).
Le Reflux: roman, trans. by Teodor de Wyzewa (Paris: Perrin, 1905).
Catriona, trans. by Jean de Naÿ, Bibliothèque des meilleurs romans étrangers à 1 fr. le volume (Paris: Hachette, 1907).
Hermiston, le juge-pendeur, trans. by Albert Bordeaux (Paris: Fontemoing, 1912).

Bibliography

Archival and Online Resources

Bibliothèque nationale de France – Gallica: <https://gallica.bnf.fr>.
Bibliothèque nationale de France – Gallica – Les Principaux quotidiens: <https://gallica.bnf.fr/html/und/presse-et-revues/les-principaux-quotidiens>.
BOSLIT (Bibliography of Scottish Literature in Translation): <https://data.nls.uk/data/metadata-collections/boslit/>.
The British Newspaper Archive: <https://www.britishnewspaperarchive.co.uk/>.
EdRLS: Stevenson's Library Database: <http://bit.ly/RLSLibrary>.
Edwin J. Beinecke Collection of Robert Louis Stevenson: GEN MSS 664.
Harry Ransom Humanties Research Center, University of Texas, Sidney Colvin Collection: Manuscript Collection MS-4034.
HathiTrust Digital Library: <https://hathitrust.org>.
Houghton Library, Harvard College Library, Harvard University, Collection: Autograph File, B, Box 22a.
Internet Archive: <https://archive.org>.
Rétronews: le site de presse de la BnF: <https://www.retronews.fr/>.
The RLS Website: <http://robert-louis-stevenson.org/>.

Primary Sources – Works by Robert Louis Stevenson

À la pagaie sur l'Escaut, le canal de Willbrocke, la Sambre et l'Oise, trans. by Lucien Lemaire (Paris: E. Lechevalier, 1900).
À la pagaie, trans. by L. Lemaire, *Vers et prose*, June 1906–February 1907.
The Amateur Emigrant, ed. by Julia Reid, New Edinburgh Edition of the Works of Robert Louis Stevenson (Edinburgh: Edinburgh University Press, 2018).
Les Aventures de David Balfour, trans. by Marie Dronsart, *Journal des débats politiques et littéraires*, 26 January–16 March 1899.

Les Aventures de David Balfour, trans. by Marie Dronsart, *Le Journal de la jeunesse*, 16 December 1905–?

Les Aventures de David Balfour, trans. by Marie Dronsart, Nouvelle collection pour la jeunesse (Paris: Hachette, 1907).

'La Baie de Falesá', trans. by E. La Chesnais, *Minerva: revue des lettres et des arts*, 15 September–15 October 1902.

'La Bouteille diabolique', trans. by G. Art, *La Revue politique et littéraire* [*La Revue bleue*], 15–20 April 1895.

Le Cas étrange du docteur Jekyll, trans. by Mme B.-J. Lowe (Paris: Plon, Nourrit, 1890).

Le Cas étrange du Dr. Jekyll et de M. Hyde, trans. by Fanny Laparra (Paris: Stock, 1924).

Le Cas extraordinaire du Dr. Jekyll et M. Hyde, trans. by Jules-Paul Tardivel, *La Vérité*, 15 January–16 April 1887.

Le Cas extraordinaire du Dr. Jekyll et de M. Hyde, trans. by Jules-Paul Tardivel (Québec: Drouin, 1888).

Catriona, trans. by Jean de Naÿ, Bibliothèque des meilleurs romans étrangers à 1 fr. le volume (Paris: Hachette, 1907).

Catriona, trans. by Théo Varlet (Paris: Albin Michel, 1928).

'Le Club des suicidés; L'histoire du jeune homme aux tartes à la crème', trans. by O. Kraft [Thérèse Bentzon], *Journal des débats politiques et littéraires*, 23–28 October 1888.

The Collected Poems of Robert Louis Stevenson, ed. by Roger C. Lewis (Edinburgh: Edinburgh University Press, 2003).

The Complete Stories of Robert Louis Stevenson, ed. by Barry Menikoff (New York: Modern Library, 2002).

Dans les mers du sud, trans. by Marie-Louise des Garets (Paris: Éditions de la Nouvelle Revue française, 1920).

Dans les mers du sud, trans. by Théo Varlet (Paris: Éditions de la Sirène, 1920).

'Le Démon de la bouteille', [trans. by Georges Lefèvre], *La Vogue*, December 1899–January 1900.

'Le Diable dans l'île', trans. by Jacques Delebecque, *Revue hebdomadaire*, 20 December 1919–10 January 1920.

Le Dynamiteur (extraits), trans. by G. Art, *Revue hebdomadaire*, 2 June–28 July 1894.

Le Dynamiteur, trans. by Georges Art (Paris: Plon, 1894).

Enlevé! Mémoire relatant les aventures de David Balfour en l'an 1751, trans. by Albert Savine, Bibliothèque cosmopolite (Paris: Stock, 1905).

Essais sur l'art de la fiction, trans. by France-Marie Watkins and Michel Le Bris (Paris: Payot, 2017).

Essays I. Virginibus Puerisque and Other Papers, ed. by Robert-Louis Abrahamson, New Edinburgh Edition of the Works of Robert Louis Stevenson (Edinburgh: Edinburgh University Press, 2018).

La Flèche noire, trans. by E. La Chesnais (Paris: Mercure de France, 1901).

La Flèche noire, trans. by E. La Chesnais (Paris: Nelson, 1901).
'Les Gais compagnons', trans. by Thérèse Bentzon, *Revue des deux mondes*, 15 September 1889, pp. 94–132.
Les Gais lurons, trans. by Théo Varlet (Paris: Éditions de la Sirène, 1920).
Hermiston: le juge-pendeur, trans. by Albert Bordeaux (Paris: Fontemoing, 1912).
Les Hommes joyeux ['Will du moulin', 'Janet la maltournée', 'Le Voleur de cadavres' and 'Olalla'], trans. by Albert Savine and Michel Georges-Michel (Paris: G. Crès, 1929).
L'Île au trésor, trans. by André Laurie, *Le Temps*, 25 September–8 November 1884.
L'Île au trésor, trans. by André Laurie, illus. by Georges Roux, Bibliothèque d'éducation et de récréation (Paris: Hetzel, 1885).
L'Île au trésor, trans. by André Laurie, *Le Petit Parisien*, 15 November 1908–18 April 1909.
L'Île au trésor, trans. by André Laurie, *L'Action Française*, 25 May–6 July 1916.
L'Île au trésor, trans. by Théo Varlet (Paris: Éditions de la Sirène, 1920).
L'Île au trésor, trans. by Théo Varlet, *Le Populaire*, 8 April–25 May 1921.
L'Île au trésor, trans. by Albert Savine and Albert Lieutaud (Paris: Albin Michel, 1924).
L'Île au trésor, trans. by Déodat Serval [Théo Varlet] (Paris: Nelson, 1926).
'L'Île des voix', [? trans. by E. Gellion-d'Anglar], *La Revue des revues*, 15 September–1 October 1895.
'L'Île des voix', trans. by E. Gellion-d'Anglar, *Mercure de France*, June 1900, pp. 596–624.
'Lettre à un jeune homme qui se propose d'embrasser la carrière de l'art', trans. by G. Lefèvre, *La Vogue*, 15 June 1900, pp. 145–52.
'Lettres à divers (ses idées sur l'Art et sur la vie d'après sa correspondance)', trans. by Madeleine Rolland, *Minerva: revue des lettres et des arts*, 1–15 March 1903.
'La Maison d'antan', *L'Humanité*, 30 June–1 July 1920.
Le Maître de Ballantrae, [unknown translator], *Le Temps*, 22 April–24 May 1893.
Le Maître de Ballantrae, trans. by Théo Varlet (Paris: Éditions de la Sirène, 1920).
Le Maître de Ballantrae, trans. by Théo Varlet, *L'Action Française*, 23 May–22 July 1921.
Le Maître de Ballantrae, trans. by Théo Varlet, *L'Humanité*, 2 May–23 June 1931.
'Markheim', [unknown translator], *La Revue des revues*, 15 May–1 June 1900.
'Markheim', trans. by E. La Chesnais, *La Revue blanche*, January 1901, pp. 81–97.

Les Mésaventures de John Nicolson, trans. by Albert Savine and Michel Georges-Michel, Collection littéraire des romans d'aventures (Paris: Édition Française Illustrée, 1922).

Le Mort vivant, trans. by Teodor de Wyzewa (Paris: Perrin, 1905).

Le Naufrageur, trans. by Louise Zeys, Bibliothèque des meilleurs romans étrangers à 1 fr. le volume (Paris: Hachette, 1906).

Nouvelles mille et une nuits, trans. by Thérèse Bentzon, Bibliothèque franco-étrangère (Paris: Hetzel, 1890).

Les Nuits des îles–Uma, roman des îles Fidji, trans. by Fred Causse-Maël, Collection littéraire des romans d'aventures (Paris: Édition Française Illustrée, 1919).

Œuvres, ed. by Charles Ballarin, Bibliothèque de la Pléiade, 3 vols (Paris: Gallimard, 2001–18).

'Olalla', trans. by Alfred Jarry, *La Vogue: revue mensuelle de littérature, d'art et d'actualité*, 15 February–15 March 1901.

Prince Otto, ed. by Robert P. Irvine, New Edinburgh Edition of the Works of Robert Louis Stevenson (Edinburgh: Edinburgh University Press, 2014).

'Pris pour espion' [extract of *À la pagaie*], trans. by Lucien Lemaire, *La Plume: revue littéraire et artistique bi-mensuelle*, 1 December 1900, pp. 682–8.

Le Reflux: roman, trans. by Teodor de Wyzewa (Paris: Perrin, 1905).

Le Reflux, trans. by Théo Varlet (Paris: Albin Michel, 1925).

Romans de la jeunesse. Le Secret du navire, [unknown translator], Romans de la jeunesse no. 15 (Paris: Juven, 1910).

Le Roman du prince Othon, trans. by Egerton Castle (London: John Lane, 1896).

Le Roman du prince Othon, trans. by Egerton Castle (Paris: Perrin, 1897).

Saint-Yves: aventures d'un prisonnier français en Angleterre, trans. by Teodor de Wyzewa, *Le Temps*, 23 August–25 October 1902.

Saint-Yves: aventures d'un prisonnier français en Angleterre, trans. by Teodor de Wyzewa (Paris: Hachette, 1904).

'The Sea Fogs' [extract from *Silverado Squatters*], *Langues modernes: bulletin mensuel de la société des professeurs de langues vivantes de l'enseignement public*, 7 (1958), 15–16.

Le Secret du navire, trans. by A. Chevalier, *Journal des voyages*, 7 July 1895–8 March 1896.

Le Secret du navire, [? trans. by A. Chevalier] (Paris: Charavay-Martin, 1896).

Strange Case of Dr. Jekyll and Mr. Hyde; Le Cas étrange du Dr. Jekyll et de M. Hyde, trans. by Théo Varlet (Paris: Payot, 1931).

Strange Case of Dr. Jekyll and Mr. Hyde, ed. by Richard Dury (Edinburgh: Edinburgh University Press, 2004).

Suicide-Club. Le Diamant du Rajah, trans. by Louis Despréaux (Paris: Calmann-Lévy, 1885).

Suicide-Club, trans. by Louis Despréaux, *La Lanterne*, 12–21 March 1920.

Les Veillées des îles, trans. by Théo Varlet (Paris: Éditions de la Sirène, 1920).

Voyage à travers les Cévennes avec un âne, trans. and adapted by A. Moulharac (Paris: Club cévénol, 1901).
Voyage avec un âne dans les Cévennes; Au fil de l'Oise, trans. by Fanny W. Laparra, Bibliothèque cosmopolite (Paris: Stock, 1925).
Voyage avec un âne dans les Cévennes, trans. by Léon Bocquet, ed. by Gilles Lapouge (Paris: Garnier-Flammarion, 1991).
Weir of Hermiston, ed. by Gillian Hughes, New Edinburgh Edition of the Works of Robert Louis Stevenson (Edinburgh: Edinburgh University Press, 2017).
'Will du Moulin', trans. by Marcel Schwob, *La Vogue*, March 1899, p. 145–69.
Will du Moulin suivi de M. Schwob/R.L. Stevenson Correspondances, ed. by François Escaig (Paris: Éditions Allia, 1992).
The Works of Robert Louis Stevenson, Edinburgh Edition, 28 vols (Edinburgh: Chatto & Windus, 1894–8).
The Works of Robert Louis Stevenson, Tusitala Edition, 35 vols (London: Heinemann, 1923–4).

Primary Sources – Other Works

Alain-Fournier, *Le Grand Meaulnes* [1913], *Miracles* (Paris: Garnier, 1986).
Allen, Grant, review of *Travels with a Donkey in the Cévennes*, *Fortnightly Review*, July 1879, pp. 153–4, in *Robert Louis Stevenson: The Critical Heritage*, ed. by Paul Maixner (London: Routledge & Kegan Paul, 1981), pp. 64–6.
Archer, William, review of *The Black Arrow*, *Pall Mall Gazette*, 13 August 1888, in *Robert Louis Stevenson: The Critical Heritage*, ed. by Paul Maixner (London: Routledge & Kegan Paul, 1981), pp. 320–3.
—, review of *Memories and Portraits*, *Pall Mall Gazette*, 1 December 1887, p. 3, in *Robert Louis Stevenson: The Critical Heritage*, ed. by Paul Maixner (London: Routledge & Kegan Paul, 1981), pp. 286–8.
Arnold, Matthew, 'The Function of Criticism at the Present Time', *The National Review*, 19 (November 1864), pp. 230–51.
Art, G., 'Mouvement littéraire', *La Revue politique et littéraire [La Revue bleue]*, 24 July 1897, p. 128 [review of *Le Roman du prince Othon*].
'Au jour le jour', *Journal des débats politiques et littéraires*, 5 June 1894, p. 1 [review of *Le Dynamiteur*].
'Au jour le jour', *Journal des débats politiques et littéraires*, 12 July 1894, p. 1 [on the triple-decker novel].
Baju, Anatole, *L'Anarchie littéraire: les différentes écoles: les décadents, les symbolistes, les romans, les intrumentistes, les magiques, les magnifiques, les anarchistes, les socialistes, etc.* (Paris: Librairie Léon Vanier, 1892).
Barbey-d'Aurevilly, Jules, *Le Chevalier des Touches* [1863], ed. by Jacques Petit (Paris: Le livre de poche, 1967).

Barrie, J.M., 'Brought Back from Elysium', 1890, <http://www.jmbarriesociety. co.uk/uploads/1/8/4/7/18474692/brought_back_from_elysium.pdf>.

Basset, Serge, 'Courrier des théâtres', *Le Figaro*, 8 June 1912, p. 5 [on *L'Île au trésor* play].

Baudelaire, Charles, *Écrits sur la littérature*, ed. by Jean-Luc Steinmetz (Paris: Livre de poche, 2005).

—, *The Painter of Modern Life*, in *Art in Theory, 1815–1900: An Anthology of Changing Ideas*, ed. by Charles Harrison and Paul Wood with Jason Gaiger (Oxford: Blackwell, 1998), pp. 493–506.

—, *Le Peintre de la vie moderne* [1863], in *Œuvres complètes de Charles Baudelaire*, 7 vols (Paris: Calmann-Lévy, 1885), III.

—, *Salon de 1859*, in *Art in Theory, 1815–1900: An Anthology of Changing Ideas*, ed. by Charles Harrison and Paul Wood with Jason Gaiger (Oxford: Blackwell, 1998), pp. 490–1.

—, *Le Spleen de Paris* [1869], ed. by Aurélia Cervoni and Andrea Schellino (Paris: Garnier-Flammarion, 2017).

Bentzon, Thérèse, 'Les Gais compagnons' [preface], *Revue des deux mondes*, 15 September 1889, pp. 94–6.

—, 'Les Nouveaux romans anglais', *Revue des deux mondes*, July–August 1888, pp. 91–120.

—, 'Le Roman étrange en Angleterre', *Revue des deux mondes*, April 1888, pp. 550–81.

Berne Convention for the Protection of Literary and Artistic Works (1886), <http://global.oup.com/booksites/content/9780198259466/15550015> and <https://wipolex.wipo.int/en/treaties/textdetails/12807>.

'Bibliographie', *L'Intransigeant*, 3 May 1885, p. 3 [on *Suicide-Club*].

'Bibliographie', *L'Intransigeant*, 12 May 1890, p. 3 [on *Nouvelles mille et une nuits*].

'Bibliographie', *L'Intransigeant*, 20 July 1890, p. 3 [on *Le Cas étrange du docteur Jekyll*].

'Bibliographie', *Le Grand Écho du Nord de la France*, 18 December 1906, p. 5 [advertisement for *L'Île au trésor*].

'Bibliographie', *Le XIXe siècle*, 30 December 1906, p. 4 [announcement for *Les Aventures de David Balfour*].

'Bibliographie', *L'Aurore: littéraire, artistique, sociale*, 1 January 1907, p. 3 [announcement for *Les Aventures de David Balfour*].

Bonet-Maury, Gaston, 'R.L. Stevenson: voyageur et romancier (1850–1894)', *Revue des deux mondes*, September 1902, pp. 164–201.

Bourget, Paul, *Le Disciple* (Paris: A. Lemerre, 1889).

—, *Sensations d'Italie: Toscane, Ombrie, Grande-Grèce* (Paris: A. Lemerre, 1891).

Brousson, Jean-Jacques, 'Les Livres', *Excelsior*, 25 April 1921, p. 4 [on Marcel Schwob].

Buet, Charles, *Le Treizième fils*; [Robert Louis Stevenson], *Le Cas extraordinaire du Dr. Jekyll et de M. Hyde*, trans. by Jules-Paul Tardivel (Québec: Drouin, 1888).

'Bulletin bibiliographique', *L'Univers*, 9 August 1905, p. 3 [announcement for *Le Reflux*].
'Bulletin du jour. Aux Antipodes', *Le Temps*, 6 April 1893, p. 1.
Champion, Pierre, 'Marcel Schwob', *Le Gaulois*, 22 January 1927, p. 5.
Chateaubriand, François-René, *Atala. René* [1802] (Paris: Garnier-Flammarion, 1964).
Chaumeix, André, 'Contes et nouvelles', *Le Gaulois*, 22 April 1922, p. 3.
Clément, Charles, 'Livres d'étrennes: publications illustrées de la maison Hetzel', *Journal des débats politiques et littéraires*, 23 December 1885, pp. 2–3.
Colvin, Sidney, 'A Note on *Weir of Hermiston*', *Cosmopolis*, May 1896, pp. 323–3.
'Correspondance de Londres', *Revue britannique*, July–August 1888, pp. 388–9 [on the play *Strange Case of Dr. Jekyll and Mr. Hyde*].
Cosmopolis promotional insert, *Le Gaulois*, 9 April 1896, p. 1.
'Cours et conférences', *Grand Écho du Nord de la France*, 7 January 1931, p. 4 [announcement for the lecture 'Un dilettante de l'aventure: Robert-Louis Stevenson'].
'Curieuses prophéties', *Le Petit Parisien*, 26 April 1906, p. 2 [on San Francisco Stevenson statue].
Daudet, Léon, *Le Partage de l'enfant: roman contemporain* (Paris: Charpentier, 1905).
—, 'À propos du *Maître de Ballantrae*', *L'Action française*, 4 January 1921, p. 1.
Davray, Henry-D., 'Lettres anglaises', *Mercure de France*, August 1897, pp. 369–72 [on *Le Roman du prince Othon*].
—, 'Lettres anglaises', *Mercure de France*, November 1897, pp. 628–9 [on 'The Suicide Club' and 'The Rajah's Diamond'].
—, 'Lettres anglaises', *Mercure de France*, January 1898, pp. 329–30 [on *St. Ives*].
—, 'Lettres anglaises', *Mercure de France*, September 1905, pp. 303–5 [on *Le Reflux*].
—, 'Lettres anglaises', *Mercure de France*, October 1905, pp. 627–8 [on *Essays in the Art of Writing*].
Delebecque, Jacques [J.D.], 'Le Prochain roman de la *Revue hebdomadaire*', *Revue hebdomadaire*, 13 December 1919, pp. 260–1.
Drouin, Marcel, 'Les Livres', *La Revue blanche*, August 1901, pp. 627–8 [review of *La Flèche noire*].
Durieux, Jehan, 'Marcel Schwob', *Le Figaro, supplément littéraire du dimanche*, 25 December 1926, p. 2.
'Échos du matin', *Le Matin*, 30 May 1892, p. 3 [on Stevenson in Samoa].
Eliot, George, 'The Natural History of German Life' [1856], in *Essays of George Eliot*, ed. by Thomas Pinney (New York: Columbia University Press, 1963; London: Routledge and Kegan Paul, 1963), pp. 266–99.

Ellis, Havelock, 'A Note Upon Paul Bourget' [1889], in *Views and Reviews. First and Second Series* (Boston and New York: Houghton Mifflin, 1932).

F.D., 'Les Livres nouveaux', *Journal des débats politiques et littéraires*, 17 June 1890, p. 4 [on *Nouvelles mille et une nuits*].

F. de P. [Francis de Pressensé], 'Robert Louis Stevenson', *Le Temps*, 18 December 1894, p. 3.

Filon, Augustin, 'L'Art de traduire', *Journal des débats politiques et littéraires*, 25 January 1899, p. 1.

—, 'Balzac et les Anglais', *Journal des débats politiques et littéraires*, 27 August 1895, evening edn, pp. 1–2.

Flaubert, Gustave, *Madame Bovary* [1857], ed. by Bernard Ajac (Paris: Garnier-Flammarion, 1986).

Fleury, Maurice de, 'Le Satanisme à la Salpêtrière', *Le Figaro*, 24 April 1891, p. 1.

Flotron, André, *Le Docteur Jancourt*, *Le Temps*, 26 June–8 July 1897.

Fly, 'Le Roman romanesque – notre enquête', *Le Gaulois*, 16–22 May 1891.

Fœmina, 'L'Âme des Anglais (hypothèses impertinentes)', *Le Figaro, supplément littéraire*, 4 December 1909, pp. 2–3.

Frollo, Jean, 'Anglais et Français', *Le Petit Parisien*, 23 September 1902, p. 1.

Gaboriau, Émile, *Le Crime d'Orcival*, London, 22 September 1877–1 June 1878.

Gautier, Judith, 'Les Livres nouveaux', *Le Rappel*, 10 June 1890, p. 3.

—, 'Les Livres nouveaux', *Le Rappel*, 2 September 1890, p. 2.

Gautier, Théophile, 'Le Chevalier double' [1840], in *Romans et contes* (Paris: A. Lemerre, 1897), pp. 417–32, <https://fr.wikisource.org/wiki/Romans_et_Contes_de_Th%C3%A9ophile_Gautier/Le_Chevalier_double>.

G.G. [? Georges Grappe], 'Le livre du jour', *La Justice*, 18 October 1894, p. 2.

Gide, André, 'Lettre à Angèle', *L'Ermitage*, June 1899, pp. 455–62.

Gille, Philippe, 'Les Livres', *Le Figaro*, 13 August 1896, p. 5 [review of *Le Roman du prince Othon*].

Ginisty, Paul, *L'Année littéraire 1885* (Paris: E. Giraud, 1886).

—, 'Causerie littéraire', *Gil Blas*, 1 August 1890, p. 3 [review of *Le Cas étrange du docteur Jekyll*].

—, 'Les Livres', *Gil Blas*, 28 October 1885, p. 3 [review of *Suicide-Club*].

Gissing, George, *New Grub Street* [1891], ed. by John Goode, Oxford World's Classics (Oxford: Oxford University Press, 1993).

Goncourt, Edmond de, *Chérie* [1884], ed. by Jean-Louis Cabanès and Philippe Hamon (Paris: Édition la Chasse au Snark, 2002).

Gosse, Edmund, *French Profiles* (New York: Dodd, Mead and Company, 1905).

Grappe, Georges, *R.L. Stevenson: l'homme et l'œuvre* (Paris: Sansot, 1904).

—, 'Robert-Louis Stevenson d'après sa correspondance', *Journal des débats politiques et littéraires*, 24 November 1902, p. 3.

Hahn, Reynaldo. *Five little songs. Cinq petites chansons. Poems selected from 'A Child's Garden of Verses'* (Paris: Heugel, 1916).
Henley, W.E., 'R.L.S.', *Pall Mall Gazette*, December 1901, pp. 505–14.
Hugo, Victor, *Hernani* [1830], in *Théâtre. I*, ed. by J.-J. Thierry and Josette Mélèze, Bibliothèque de la Pléiade (Paris: Gallimard, 1963).
Huret, Jules, *Enquête sur l'évolution littéraire* (Paris: Charpentier, 1891).
Huysmans, Joris-Karl, *Against the Grain* (New York: Dover Publications, 1969).
—, *À Rebours* [1884], ed. by Pierre Waldner (Paris: Garnier-Flammarion, 1978).
—, *Là-bas* (Paris: Tresse & Stock, 1891).
—, *Là-bas*, trans. by Brendan King (Sawtry: Dedalus, 2001).
'Idealism and Realism in Literature. A Talk with Robert Louis Stevenson', *Argus*, 13 September 1890, cited in Guy de Maupassant entry, 'Other Evidence of Ownership', EdRLS: Stevenson's Library Database.
Jackson, Holbrook, *The Eighteen Nineties: A Review of Art and Ideas at the Close of the Nineteenth Century* [1913] (London: Grant Richards, 1922).
Jaloux, Edmond, 'Le Prix Balzac', *Le Gaulois*, 14 January 1922, p. 1.
—, 'Un ami de la France', *Le Gaulois*, 25 April 1922, p. 1.
James, Henry, 'The Art of Fiction', *Longman's Magazine*, 4.23, 1 September 1884, pp. 502–21.
—, *French Novelists and Poets* [1878] (London: Macmillan, 1904).
—, *Partial Portraits* (London: Macmillan, 1888).
—, 'Robert Louis Stevenson', *Century Magazine*, April 1888, pp. 869–79.
Kahn, Gustave, 'La Vogue', *La Vogue*, January 1899, pp. 5–8.
Kuhn, Alice, 'La Compagne d'un grand écrivain', *Journal des débats politiques et littéraires*, 1 March 1914, p. 6.
Lang, Andrew, 'Realism and Romance', *Contemporary Review*, 52 (1887), pp. 683–93.
—, 'Recollections of Robert Louis Stevenson', *The North American Review*, 160.459 (1985), pp. 185–94.
—, 'R.L. Stevenson d'après M. Andrew Lang', *Le Revue politique et littéraire [La Revue bleue]*, January–June 1895, pp. 499–500.
Laumann, Sutter, 'Revue littéraire', *La Justice*, 13 April 1885, p. 2 [on *L'Île au trésor*].
Lautrec, Gabriel de, 'Robert Louis Stevenson', *Mercure de France*, 16 December 1911, pp. 673–91.
Lee, Vernon [Violet Paget], 'On Literary Construction', *Contemporary Review*, September 1895, pp. 404–7, in *Robert Louis Stevenson: The Critical Heritage*, ed. by Paul Maixner (London: Routledge & Kegan Paul, 1981), pp. 444–8.
Le Gallienne, Richard, *Robert Louis Stevenson, an Elegy; and Other Poems Mainly Personal* (London: John Lane, 1895) [from the *Daily Chronicle*, 25 December 1894].
'Les Lettres', *L'Homme libre*, 23 September 1924, p. 2.

'Lettres, sciences et arts', *Journal des débats politiques et littéraires*, 8 July 1896, p. 3 [review of *Le Roman du prince Othon*].

'Lettres, sciences et arts', *Journal des débats politiques et littéraires*, 20 November 1896, p. 3 [on *Moral Emblems* in *Studio*].

'Librairie', *Journal des débats politiques et littéraires*, 22 February 1896, p. 3 [on *Cosmopolis*].

'Librairie', *La Justice*, 12 May 1890, p. 4 [on *Nouvelles mille et une nuits*].

'Librairie', *La Justice*, 30 June 1890, p. 4 [announcement for *Le Cas étrange du docteur Jekyll*].

'Les Livres', *La Justice*, 15 November 1904, p. 1 [review of *Saint-Yves*].

'Les Livres', *Le Matin*, 11 May 1885, p. 3 [on *Suicide-Club*].

'Les Livres', *La Presse*, 17 June 1905, p. 4 [review of *Enlevé!*].

'Les Livres', *Revue britannique*, September 1894, p. 454 [on *Le Dynamiteur*].

'Livres d'étrennes', *Journal des débats politiques et littéraires*, 20 December 1906, p. 3 [announcement for *Les Aventures de David Balfour*].

'Livres d'étrennes', *L'Univers*, 19 December 1906, p. 3 [announcement for *Les Aventures de David Balfour*].

L.M., 'Livres d'étrennes', *La Charente*, 29 December 1885, p. 3 [on *L'Île au trésor*].

Longnon, Jean, 'Aventures et aventuriers d'outre-mer', *Le Gaulois*, 24 September 1921, p. 3.

Low, Will H., *A Chronicle of Friendships: 1873–1900* (New York: Charles Scribner's Sons, 1908).

Lugeol, F., 'Bibliographie: *L'Île au trésor*', *La Charente*, 2 April 1885, p. 3.

Mallarmé, Stéphane, 'Robert-Louis Stevenson', in *Œuvres complètes*, ed. by Bertrand Marchal, Bibliothèque de la Pléiade, 2 vols (Paris: Gallimard, 2003), II, pp. 689–90.

Martel, Charles, 'Les Premières', *L'Aurore: littéraire, artistique, sociale*, 23 February 1908, p. 2 [review of Mouëzy-Éon's *Les Nuits du Hampton-Club*].

Martinet, Marcel, 'Le Roman anglais de notre temps. Quelques œuvres', *L'Humanité*, 20 July 1922, p. 5 [announcement for *Les Mésaventures de John Nicholson*].

Mauclair, Camille, 'Le Roman de demain', *La Revue du palais*, January 1898, pp. 156–77.

—, 'Le Roman historique français devant les étrangers', *La Nouvelle revue*, July 1901, pp. 431–45.

Maupassant, Guy de, *Boule de Suif and Other Stories*, The Works of Guy de Maupassant, ed. by Arthur Symons (New York: Bigelow, Smith & Co., 1909).

—, *Pierre et Jean* (Paris: P. Ollendorff, 1888).

Méritan, L., 'Franck Norris, Albert Savine et le roman d'aventures', *L'Homme libre*, 5 March 1921, p. 2.

—, 'Les Lettres', *L'Homme libre*, 24 October 1920, p. 2.

'Mrs. Will H. Low', *American Art News*, 7.27 (17 April 1909), p. 6.

M.S., '*Le Dynamiteur* de Robert-Louis Stevenson', *Journal des débats politiques et littéraires*, 3 November 1894, p. 1.

Neukomm, Edmond, 'Un roman de Louis Stevenson', *Journal des voyages*, 30 June 1895, pp. 39–40.

Nordau, Max, *Degeneration* [*Entartung*, 1892] (Lincoln/London: University of Nebraska Press, 1993).

Oliphant, Margaret, 'A Few French Novels', *Blackwood's Edinburgh Magazine*, 130.794 (December 1881), pp. 703–23.

Osbourne, Lloyd, 'Stevenson at Thirty-Four', in Robert Louis Stevenson, *Prince Otto: A Romance*, in *The Works of Robert Louis Stevenson*, Tusitala Edition, 35 vols (London: Heinemann, 1923–4), IV, pp. vii–xi.

Pater, Walter, 'Prosper Mérimée', *Fortnightly Review*, 48 (December 1890), pp. 852–64.

—, 'Style' [1888], in *Appreciations, with an Essay on Style* (London: Macmillan, 1889), pp. 1–36.

Patin, Jacques, 'Chez le libraire', *Le Figaro, supplément littéraire*, 1 August 1920, p. 2 [review of *Dans les mers du Sud*].

Perret, Paul, 'Revue littéraire et historique', *La Liberté*, 5 August 1897, p. 1 [review of *Le Roman du prince Othon*].

—, [P.P.], 'À travers champs', *La Liberté*, 16 October 1894, p. 2 [review of *Nouvelles mille et une nuits*].

'Petites Nouvelles', *Gil Blas*, 15 February 1885, p. 3 [announcement for *L'Île au trésor*].

Peyrin, Lucien, 'Courrier littéraire', *L'Homme libre*, 25 November 1927, p. 2 [announcement for the lecture 'Les Écrivains de la mer'].

Pilon, Edmond, 'Quelques mots sur Marcel Schwob et Stevenson', *L'Intransigeant*, 31 July 1920, p. 2.

Pontarmé, 'Un romancier nomade', *Le Petit Parisien*, 22 December 1894, p. 2.

Prévost, Marcel, 'Le Roman romanesque moderne', *Le Figaro*, 12 May 1891, p. 1.

Proust, Marcel, *Le Temps retrouvé*, in *À la recherche du temps perdu*, ed. by Pierre Clarac and André Ferré, Bibliothèque de la Pléiade, 3 vols (Paris: Gallimard, 1954), III.

Quiller-Couch, Arthur, *On the Art of Writing* (Cambridge: Cambridge University Press, 1921).

Régnier, Henri de, 'La vie littéraire', *Le Figaro, supplément littéraire du dimanche*, 30 January 1921, p. 1 [on *Le Maître de Ballantrae*].

Review of *Edinburgh: Picturesque Notes*, *Scotsman*, 21 January 1879, in *Robert Louis Stevenson: The Critical Heritage*, ed. by Paul Maixner (London: Routledge & Kegan Paul, 1981), pp. 59–61.

Review of *New Arabian Nights*, *Westminster Review*, January 1883, p. 284, in *Robert Louis Stevenson: The Critical Heritage*, ed. by Paul Maixner (London: Routledge & Kegan Paul, 1981), p. 118–19.

Review of *Treasure Island*, *Graphic*, 15 December 1883, p. 599, in *Robert Louis Stevenson: The Critical Heritage*, ed. by Paul Maixner (London: Routledge & Kegan Paul, 1981), pp. 140–1.
Review of *Virginibus Puerisque and Other Papers*, *Spectator*, 11 June 1881, pp. 775–6, in *Robert Louis Stevenson: The Critical Heritage*, ed. by Paul Maixner (London: Routledge & Kegan Paul, 1981), pp. 82–6.
'Les Revues', *Nouvelle Revue française*, February 1912, pp. 314–15.
Rivière, Jacques, 'Alain Fournier', in Alain Fournier, *Le Grand Meaulnes, Miracles* (Paris: Garnier, 1986), pp. 3–56.
—, 'Le Roman d'aventure', *Nouvelle Revue française*, May–July 1913, in *Études* (Paris: Gallimard, 1999), pp. 307–50.
R.M., 'À la pagaie dans la région du Nord', *Grand Écho du Nord de la France*, 15 March 1900, p. 3.
Romains, Jules, 'Stevenson et l'aventure', *L'Humanité*, 16 August 1920, p. 2.
'Romancier en passe de devenir roi', *Le XIXe siècle*, 27 April 1892, p. 2.
Rzewuski, Stanislas, '*Cosmopolis*', *Le Gaulois*, 8 April 1896, p. 2.
—, 'Le Dernier roman de Stevenson', *Le Gaulois*, 30 August 1897, p. 2.
Saintsbury, George, 'Charles Baudelaire' [1875], *The Collected Essays and Papers of George Saintsbury, 1875–1923, volume IV: Essays in French Literature* (Freeport, NY: Books for Libraries Press, 1924), pp. 1–29.
—, 'The Contrasts of English and French Literature' [1892], *The Collected Essays and Papers of George Saintsbury, 1875–1923, volume IV: Essays in French Literature* (Freeport, NY: Books for Libraries Press, 1924), pp. 221–49.
—, 'The End of a Chapter' [1895], *The Collected Essays and Papers of George Saintsbury, 1875–1923, volume IV: Essays in French Literature* (Freeport, NY: Books for Libraries Press, 1924), pp. 250–80.
—, *The English Novel* (London: J.M. Dent, 1913).
—, 'New Arabian Nights', *Pall Mall Gazette*, 4 August 1882, p. 4.
—, *A Short History of French Literature* (Oxford: Clarendon Press, 1882).
Sarolea, Charles, 'La Littérature nouvelle en France', *The Evergreen: A Northern Seasonal*, Spring (1895), pp. 92–7. *Evergreen Digital Edition*, ed. by Lorraine Janzen Kooistra, 2016–18. Yellow Nineties 2.0, Ryerson University Centre for Digital Humanities, 2019, <https://1890s.ca/egv1_sarolea_nouvelle/>.
Savine, Albert, 'Robert-Louis Stevenson, sa vie, son œuvre, 1850–1894: une étude', in Robert-Louis Stevenson, *Enlevé! Mémoire relatant les aventures de David Balfour en l'an 1751*, trans. by Albert Savine, Bibliothèque cosmopolite (Paris: Stock, 1905), pp. v–lxxii.
Schwob, Marcel, *Cœur double* [1891] (Toulouse: Éditions ombres, 1996).
—, *François Villon: rédactions et notes* [1912] (Geneva: Slatkine Reprints, 1974).
—, 'R.L.S.', *The New Review*, February 1895, pp. 153–60, also printed in *Spicilège* (Paris: Mercure de France, 1896).
—, 'Robert-Louis Stevenson', *L'Événement*, 11 October 1890, p. 1.

—, 'Robert-Louis Stevenson', *Revue hebdomadaire*, 2 June 1894, pp. 5–10, also printed as 'R.-L. Stevenson', *Le Phare de la Loire*, 5 June 1894, pp. 1–2.

—, 'Robert L. Stevenson', *Le Phare de la Loire*, 27 August 1888, pp. 2–3, in Robert Louis Stevenson, *Will du Moulin suivi de M. Schwob/R.L. Stevenson Correspondances*, ed. by François Escaig (Paris: Éditions Allia, 1992), pp. 57–63.

—, *Spicilège* (Paris: Mercure de France, 1896).

'Secret Sin', *The Rock*, 2 April 1886, p. 3, in *Robert Louis Stevenson: The Critical Heritage*, ed. by Paul Maixner (London: Routledge & Kegan Paul, 1981), pp. 224–7.

Symons, Arthur, *Studies in Two Literatures* (London: Leonard Smithers, 1897).

—, 'Walter Pater: Some Characteristics', *Savoy*, 8 (December 1896), pp. 33–50.

Tardivel, Jules-Paul, 'Nouveau feuilleton', *La Vérité*, 8 January 1887, p. 6 [on *Le Cas extraordinaire du Dr. Jekyll et de M. Hyde*].

—, *Pour la Patrie: roman du XXe siècle* [1895], ed. by John Hare (Montréal: Hurtubise, 1995).

Les Treize, 'La Boîte aux lettres', *L'Intransigeant*, 16 February 1913, p. 2 [on Rivière's lecture 'Le Roman que nous attendons'].

—, 'La Boîte aux lettres', *L'Intransigeant*, 28 March 1913, p. 2 [review of *Hermiston: le juge-pendeur*].

—, '. . . des romans', *L'Intransigeant*, 21 January 1924, p. 5 [review of *L'Île au trésor*].

—, 'Les Lettres', *L'Intransigeant*, 10 January 1920, p. 2 [on *Le Diable dans l'île* and *Les Nuits des îles*].

—, 'Les Lettres', *L'Intransigeant*, 29 June 1920, p. 2 [announcement for *Dans les mers du Sud*].

—, 'Les Lettres', *L'Intransigeant*, 24 October 1920, p. 2 [on *Les Hommes joyeux* and *Les Gais lurons*].

—, 'Les Lettres', *L'Intransigeant*, 9 March 1921, p. 2 [on *Les Aventures de David Balfour* and *Enlevé!*].

—, 'Les Lettres', *L'Intransigeant*, 13 March 1921, p. 2 [review of *Les Hommes joyeux*].

—, 'Les Lettres', *L'Intransigeant*, 4 April 1921, p. 2 [on *L'Île au trésor*].

—, 'Les Lettres', *L'Intransigeant*, 17 August 1924, p. 2 [on 'Les Œuvres de Stevenson en France' and Savine's *L'Île au trésor*].

—, 'Les Lettres', *L'Intransigeant*, 13 January 1929, p. 2 [on serialisation of 'Un chapitre sur les songes'].

—, 'Les Lettres', *L'Intransigeant*, 24 May 1929, p. 2 [on *La Vie de Robert Louis Stevenson*].

—, 'Les Lettres', *L'Intransigeant*, 14 September 1931, p. 2 [on *L'Émigrant amateur*].

Uzanne, Octave, 'Les Jeunes écrivains et leurs origines littéraires', *La Dépêche*, 22 October 1899, pp. 1–2.

—, 'La Quinzaine des livres', *La Dépêche*, 18 January 1905, p. 5.
Vapereau, G, ed., *Dictionnaire universel des contemporains*, 6th edn (Paris: Hachette, 1893).
Wyzewa, Teodor de, 'La Correspondance de R.-L. Stevenson', *Revue des deux mondes*, 15 December 1899, pp. 921–32.
—, *Écrivains étrangers. 3ᵉ série. Le Roman contemporain à l'étranger* (Paris: Perrin, 1900).
—, 'Le Nouveau roman de M. Stevenson', *Le Temps*, 19 September 1894, p. 2 [review of *La Marée* (sic)].
—, 'L'Œuvre posthume de Robert Louis Stevenson', *Revue des deux mondes*, 1 July 1896, pp. 216–25.
—, 'Préface', in *Hermiston: le juge-pendeur*, trans. by Albert Bordeaux (Paris: Fontemoing, 1912), pp. v–xvii.
—, 'Un livre nouveau de Robert Louis Stevenson' *Revue des deux mondes*, 15 July 1905, pp. 457–68 [review of *Essays of Travel*].
Zola, Émile, *The Attack on the Mill and Other Sketches of War* (London: Heinemann, 1892).
—, *Du roman: sur Stendhal, Flaubert et les Goncourt*, ed. by Henri Mitterrand (Brussels: Éditions Complexe, 1999).
—, 'La Formule critique appliquée au roman' [1879], in *Du roman: sur Stendhal, Flaubert et les Goncourt*, ed. by Henri Mitterrand (Brussels: Éditions Complexe, 1999), pp. 51–8.
—, 'Le Sens du réel' [1878], in *Du roman: sur Stendhal, Flaubert et les Goncourt*, ed. by Henri Mitterrand (Brussels: Éditions Complexe, 1999), pp. 33–42.
Zola, Émile, and others, *Les Soirées de Médan* (Paris: Charpentier, 1880).

Correspondence

Atkinson, Damian, ed., *The Selected Letters of W.E. Henley* (London: Routledge, 2016).
Booth, B.A., and E. Mehew, eds, *The Letters of Robert Louis Stevenson*, 8 vols (New Haven/London: Yale University Press, 1994–5).
Bourget, Paul, letter to Robert Louis Stevenson, 3 August 1893, Autograph File, B, Houghton Library, Harvard College Library, Harvard University, Collection: Autograph File, B, Box 22a.
Demoor, Marysa, ed., *Dear Stevenson: Letters from Andrew Lang to Robert Louis Stevenson with Five Letters from Stevenson to Lang* (Leuven: Uitgeverij Peeters, 1990).
Escaig, François, ed., *Will du Moulin suivi de M. Schwob/R.L. Stevenson Correspondances* (Paris: Éditions Allia, 1992).
Henley, W.E., letter to Stevenson, April 1881, in *Robert Louis Stevenson: The Critical Heritage*, ed. by Paul Maixner (London: Routledge & Kegan Paul, 1981), pp. 75–7.

Holland, Merlin, and Rupert Hart-Davis, eds, *The Complete Letters of Oscar Wilde* (New York: Henry Holt, 2000).
James, Henry, letter to Stevenson, 5 December 1884, in *Robert Louis Stevenson: The Critical Heritage*, ed. by Paul Maixner (London: Routledge & Kegan Paul, 1981), pp. 143–4.
Leclerc, Yvan, and Daniel Girard, eds, *Correspondance électronique de Flaubert*, Laboratoire Cérédi, Université Normanie Rouen, <https://flaubert.univ-rouen.fr/correspondance/>.
Mehew, Ernest, ed., *Selected Letters of Robert Louis Stevenson* (New Haven: Yale University Press, 2001).
Meredith, George, letter to Stevenson, 4 June 1878, in *Robert Louis Stevenson: The Critical Heritage*, ed. by Paul Maixner (London: Routledge & Kegan Paul, 1981), pp. 53–5.
Schwob, Marcel, letter to Sidney Colvin, 16 November 1899. Manuscript Collection MS-4035, MSS_StevensonRL_2_1_036, Harry Ransom Center, The University of Texas at Austin, <https://hrc.contentdm.oclc.org/digital/collection/p15878coll48/id/1590/rec/11>.
Steegmuller, Francis, ed., *The Letters of Gustave Flaubert* (London: Picador, 2001).

Secondary Sources

Abrahamson, R.L., 'Living in a Book: RLS as an Engaged Reader', in *Robert Louis Stevenson: Writer of Boundaries*, ed. by Richard Ambrosini and Richard Dury (Madison: University of Wisconsin Press, 2006), pp. 13–22.
Alblas, Jacques B.H., 'The Early Production and Reception of Stevenson's Work in England and the Netherlands', in *Beauty and the Beast: Christina Rossetti, Walter Pater, R.L. Stevenson and their Contemporaries*, ed. by Peter Liebregts and Wim Tiggs (Amsterdam/Atlanta: Rodopi, 1996), pp. 209–19.
Alliata, Michela Vanon, '"Markheim" and the Shadow of the Other', in *Robert Louis Stevenson: Writer of Boundaries*, ed. by Richard Ambrosini and Richard Dury (Madison: University of Wisconsin Press, 2006), pp. 299–311.
Ambrosini, Richard, 'The Four Boundary-Crossings of R.L. Stevenson, Novelist and Anthropologist', in *Robert Louis Stevenson: Writer of Boundaries*, ed. by Richard Ambrosini and Richard Dury (Madison: University of Wisconsin Press, 2006), pp. 23–35.
—, 'The Miracle: Robert Louis Stevenson in the History of European Literature', in *European Stevenson*, ed. by Richard Ambrosini and Richard Dury (Newcastle upon Tyne: Cambridge Scholars Publishing, 2009), pp. 127–45.
Ambrosini, Richard, and Richard Dury, eds, *European Stevenson* (Newcastle upon Tyne: Cambridge Scholars Publishing, 2009).

—, *Robert Louis Stevenson: Writer of Boundaries* (Madison: University of Wisconsin Press, 2006).

Anderson Galleries, *Autograph Letters, Original Manuscripts, Books, Portraits, Curios from the Library of the Late Robert Louis Stevenson* (New York, 1914).

Arata, Stephen, 'Decadent Form', *ELH*, 81 (2014), 1007–27.

—, 'Realism', in *The Cambridge Companion to the Fin de Siècle*, ed. by Gail Marshall (Cambridge: Cambridge University Press, 2007), pp. 169–87.

—, 'Stevenson, Morris, and the Value of Idleness', in *Robert Louis Stevenson: Writer of Boundaries*, ed. by Richard Ambrosini and Richard Dury (Madison: University of Wisconsin Press, 2006), pp. 3–12.

—, 'Stevenson's Careful Observances', *Romanticism and Victorianism on the Net*, 47 (2007), DOI: https://doi.org.10.7202/016704ar.

Ashley, Katherine, *Edmond de Goncourt and the Novel: Naturalism and Decadence* (Amsterdam: Rodopi, 2005).

—, 'In Search of the New Novel: Translations of R.L. Stevenson in Nineteenth-Century France', *Nineteenth Century Studies*, 27 (2013), 129–42.

Atkinson, Juliette, *French Novels and the Victorians* (Oxford: Oxford University Press, 2017).

Baguley, David, *Naturalist Fiction: The Entropic Vision* (Cambridge: Cambridge University Press, 1990).

Balfour, Graham, *The Life of Robert Louis Stevenson*, 2 vols (London: Methuen, 1901).

Barnaby, Paul, 'Restoration Politics and Sentimental Poetics in A.-J.-B. Defauconpret's Translations of Sir Walter Scott', *Translation and Literature*, 20.1 (2011), 6–28.

Beattie, Hilary J., 'The Enigma of Katharine de Mattos: Reflections on her Life and Writings', *Journal of Stevenson Studies*, 14 (2008), 47–71.

Bevan, Bryan, *Robert Louis Stevenson: Poet and Teller of Tales* (New York: St. Martin's Press, 1993).

Blanch, Josephine Mildred, *The Story of a Friendship: Robert Louis Stevenson, Jules Simoneau; a California Reminiscence of Stevenson* (New York: Charles Scribner Sons, 1921).

Bouillaguet, Annick, 'Proust, lecteur des Goncourt: du pastiche satirique à l'imitation sérieuse', in *Les Frères Goncourt: art et écriture*, ed. by Jean-Louis Cabanès (Bordeaux: Presses universitaires de Bordeaux, 1997), pp. 339–48.

Bourdieu, Pierre, 'Le Marché des biens symboliques', *L'Année sociologique*, 22 (1971), 49–126.

—, *The Rules of Art: Genesis and Structure of the Literary Field*, trans. by Susan Emanuel (Cambridge: Polity Press, 1996).

Brake, Laurel, *Print in Transition, 1850–1910: Studies in Media and Book History* (London: Palgrave Macmillan, 2001).

Bristow, Joseph, *Empire Boys: Adventures in a Man's World* (Abingdon: Routledge, 2016).

Brown, Neil Macara, 'The French Collection: RLS's Vailima Library', *Scottish Book Collector*, 5.9 (1997), 22–5.
Campos, Christophe, *The View of France from Arnold to Bloomsbury* (London: Oxford University Press, 1965).
Carey, John, *The Intellectuals and the Masses: Pride and Prejudice Among the Literary Intelligentsia, 1880–1939* (Chicago: Academy Chicago Publishers, 2002).
Carpenter, Kevin, 'R.L. Stevenson on the *Treasure Island* Illustrations', *Notes and Queries*, 29.4 (August 1982), 322–5.
Casanova, Pascale, *La République mondiale des Lettres* (Paris: Seuil, 2008).
Charle, Christophe, *La Crise littéraire à l'époque du naturalisme: roman, théâtre et politique. Essai d'histoire sociale des groupes et genres littéraires* (Paris: Presses de l'école normale supérieure, 1979).
—, *Paris fin de siècle: culture et politique*, L'Univers historique (Paris: Seuil, 1998).
Clements, Patricia, *Baudelaire and the English Tradition* (Princeton: Princeton University Press, 1986).
Cohen, Margaret, and Carolyn Dever, eds, *The Literary Channel: The International Invention of the Novel* (Princeton: Princeton University Press, 2000).
Cohen, William A., 'Why is there so much French in *Villette*?', *ELH*, 84 (2017), 171–94.
Compère, Daniel, 'Hetzel et la littérature pour la jeunesse', *Europe*, 58.619 (1980), 31–8.
Cooper-Richet, Diana, 'Les Imprimés en langue anglaise en France au XIXe siècle: rayonnement intellectuel, circulation et modes de pénétration', in *Les Mutations du livre et de l'édition dans le monde du XVIIIe siècle à l'an 2000: actes du colloque international Sherbrooke 2000*, ed. by Jacques Michon et Jean-Yves Mollier (Presses de l'université Laval/ L'Harmattan, 2001), pp. 122–40.
—, 'La Librairie étrangère à Paris au XIXe siècle: un milieu perméable aux innovations et aux transferts', *Actes de la recherche en sciences sociales*, 126–7 (1999), 60–9.
Daly, Nicholas, *Modernism, Romance, and the Fin de Siècle: Popular Fiction and British Culture, 1880–1914* (Cambridge: Cambridge University Press, 1999).
Davies, Laurence, 'The Time of His Time: *Travels with a Donkey* and *An Inland Voyage*', in *European Stevenson*, ed. by Richard Ambrosini and Richard Dury (Newcastle upon Tyne: Cambridge Scholars Publishing, 2009), pp. 73–89.
Delsemme, Paul, *Teodor de Wyzewa et le cosmopolitisme littéraire en France à l'époque du symbolisme* (Brussels: Presses universitaires de Bruxelles, 1967).
Dowling, Linda, *Language and Decadence in the Victorian Fin de Siècle* (Princeton: Princeton University Press, 1986).

Duncan, Ian, 'On the Study of Scottish Literature', *ScotLit*, 28 (2003), <http://www.gla.ac.uk/ScotLit/ASLS/Studying_Scottish_Literature.html>.
—, 'Stevenson and Fiction', in *The Edinburgh Companion to Robert Louis Stevenson*, ed. by Penny Fielding (Edinburgh: Edinburgh University Press, 2010), pp. 11–26.
Dury, Richard, 'Crossing the Bounds of a Single Identity: *Dr. Jekyll and Mr. Hyde* and a Paper in a French Scientific Journal', in *Robert Louis Stevenson: Writer of Boundaries*, ed. by Richard Ambrosini and Richard Dury (Madison: University of Wisconsin Press, 2006), pp. 237–51.
—, 'Reading "Forest Notes"', *Journal of Stevenson Studies*, 13 (2017), 5–34.
—, 'Robert Louis Stevenson's Critical Reception', *The Robert Louis Stevenson Archive*, <http://www.robert-louis-stevenson.org/richard-dury-archive/critrec.htm>.
—, 'Stevenson and Bourget: An Enigma', EdRLS blog, 3 May 2020, <https://edrls.wordpress.com/2020/05/03/stevenson-and-bourget-an-enigma/>.
—, 'Stevenson's Essays: Language and Style', *Journal of Stevenson Studies*, 9 (2012), 43–91.
—, 'Stevenson's Shifting Viewpoint', *The Bottle Imp*, 12 (2012), 1–2, <https://www.thebottleimp.org.uk/issues/page/2/>.
Eliot, Simon, 'The Business of Victorian Publishing', in *The Cambridge Companion to the Victorian Novel*, ed. by Deirdre David (Cambridge: Cambridge University Press, 2001), pp. 37–60.
Even-Zohar, Itamar, 'The Position of Translated Literature Within the Literary Polysystem', in *The Translation Studies Reader*, ed. by Lawrence Venuti, 2nd edn (New York/London: Routledge, 2000), pp. 199–204.
Farr, Liz, 'Stevenson and the (Un)familiar: The Aesthetic of Late-Nineteenth-Century Biography', in *Robert Louis Stevenson: Writer of Boundaries*, ed. by Richard Ambrosini and Richard Dury (Madison: University of Wisconsin Press, 2006), pp. 36–47.
Federico, Annette R., *Thus I Lived with Words: Robert Louis Stevenson and the Writer's Life* (Iowa City: University of Iowa Press, 2017).
Fielding, Penny, ed., *The Edinburgh Companion to Robert Louis Stevenson* (Edinburgh: Edinburgh University Press, 2010).
Fitzpatrick, Mark, 'R.L. Stevenson, Joseph Conrad and the Adventure Novel: Reception, Criticism and Translation in France, 1880–1930' (unpublished doctoral thesis, Université Sorbonne Nouvelle – Paris 3, 2015).
—, '"Tout à fait un grand écrivain": Stevenson's Place in French Literary History', in Richard J. Hill, ed. *Robert Louis Stevenson and the Great Affair: Movement, Memory and Modernity* (London: Routledge, 2017), pp. 202–18.
Flint, Kate, 'The Victorian Novel and its Readers', in *The Cambridge Companion to the Victorian Novel*, ed. by Deirdre David (Cambridge: Cambridge University Press, 2001), pp. 17–36.

Gaucheron, Jacques, 'Un éditeur, pourquoi?', *Europe*, 58.619 (1980), 3–12.
Gibbons, Luke, 'Peripheral Modernities: National and Global in a Post-Colonial Frame', *Nineteenth-Century Contexts*, 29.2–3 (2007), 271–81.
Giroud, Vincent, 'Cocteau and Stevenson', in *European Stevenson*, ed. by Richard Ambrosini and Richard Dury (Newcastle upon Tyne: Cambridge Scholars Publishing, 2009), pp. 185–98.
Good, Graham, 'Rereading Robert Louis Stevenson', *The Dalhousie Review*, 62.1 (1982), 44–59.
Graham, Lesley, 'I Have a Little Shadow: Travellers After Stevenson in the Cévennes', in *European Stevenson*, ed. by Richard Ambrosini and Richard Dury (Newcastle upon Tyne: Cambridge Scholars Publishing, 2009), pp. 91–107.
—, 'Toing and Froing in Stevenson's Construction of Personal History in Some of the Later Essays (1880–94)', *Journal of Stevenson Studies*, 14 (2018), 5–17.
Guy, Josephine, ed., *The Edinburgh Companion to Fin-de-Siècle Literature, Culture and the Arts* (Edinburgh: Edinburgh University Press, 2018).
—, 'Introduction', in *The Edinburgh Companion to Fin-de-Siècle Literature, Culture and the Arts*, ed. by Josephine Guy (Edinburgh: Edinburgh University Press, 2018), pp. 1–22.
Harman, Claire, *Robert Louis Stevenson: A Biography* (London: HarperCollins, 2005).
Harrison, Charles, and Paul Wood with Jason Gaiger, eds, *Art in Theory, 1815–1900: An Anthology of Changing Ideas* (Oxford: Blackwell, 1998).
Hext, Kate, 'Henry James's Impressionistic Satire of the Decadent Movement in the *Yellow Book*', *Henry James Review*, 38 (2017), 37–52.
Higgins, Jennifer, 'English Responses to French Poetry between Decadence and Modernism', *Franco-British Cultural Cultural Exchanges, 1880–1940: Channel Packets*, ed. by Andrew Radford and Victoria Reid (London: Palgrave Macmillan, 2012), pp. 17–33.
Holmes, Morgan, 'Donkeys, Englishmen, and Other Animals: The Precarious Distinctions of Victorian Interspecies Morality', in *European Stevenson*, ed. by Richard Ambrosini and Richard Dury (Newcastle upon Tyne: Cambridge Scholars Publishing, 2009), pp. 109–24.
Houppermans, Sjef, 'Robert, Alexandre, Marcel, Henri, Jean et les autres: R.L. Stevenson and his "French Connections"', in *Beauty and the Beast: Christina Rossetti, Walter Pater, R.L. Stevenson and their Contemporaries*, ed. by Peter Liebregts and Wim Tigges (Amsterdam/Atlanta: Rodopi, 1996), pp. 187–207.
Hubbard, Tom, 'Dva Brata: Robert Louis Stevenson in Translation Before 1900', *Scottish Studies Review*, 8.1 (Spring 2007), 17–26.
Hughes, Gillian, 'Essay on the Text', in *Weir of Hermiston*, ed. by Gillian Hughes, New Edinburgh Edition of the Works of Robert Louis Stevenson (Edinburgh: Edinburgh University Press, 2017), pp. 117–72.

Irvine, Robert P., 'Introduction', in *Prince Otto*, ed. by Robert P. Irvine, New Edinburgh Edition of the Works of Robert Louis Stevenson (Edinburgh: Edinburgh University Press, 2014), pp. xxiii–liv.

—, 'Stevenson in the Third Republic: Fiction and Liberalization', *Victorian Review*, 39.1 (2013), 125–40.

Jaëck, Nathalie, 'To Jump or Not to Jump: Stevenson's Kidnapping of Adventure', *Journal of Stevenson Studies*, 6 (2009), 23–42.

Jay, Elisabeth, *British Writers and Paris: 1830–1875* (Oxford: Oxford University Press, 2016).

Jolly, Roslyn, 'Stevenson and the European South', in *European Stevenson*, ed. by Richard Ambrosini and Richard Dury (Newcastle upon Tyne: Cambridge Scholars Publishing, 2009), pp. 19–36.

Kaiser, Matthew, 'Mapping Stevenson's Rhetorics of Play', *Journal of Stevenson Studies*, 6 (2009), 5–22.

Kelly, Michael G., 'Jarry, Stevenson and Cosmopolitan Ambivalence', *Comparative Critical Studies*, 10.2 (2013), 199–218.

Koffeman, Maaike, *Entre classicisme et modernité: la 'Nouvelle Revue Française' dans le champ littéraire de la Belle Époque* (Amsterdam: Rodopi, 2003).

Lacoste, Francis, 'De Zola à Loti: l'institution face au naturalisme', in *Champ littéraire fin de siècle autour de Zola*, ed. by Béatrice Lacoste (Bordeaux: Presses universitaires de Bordeaux, 2004), pp. 93–103.

LeBris, Michel, and Jean Rouaud, eds, *Pour une littérature-monde* (Paris: Gallimard, 2007).

—, *R.L. Stevenson: les années bohémiennes, 1850–1890* (Paris: NiL Éditions, 1994).

Luis, Raphaël, *La Carte et la fable. Stevenson modèle de la fiction latino-américaine (Bioy Casares, Borges, Cortázar)* (doctoral thesis, l'université de Lyon, Université Jean Moulin (Lyon 3), 2016), <http://www.theses.fr/2016LYSE3040>.

MacLean, Cecil, *La France dans l'œuvre de R.L. Stevenson* (Paris: Jouve, 1936).

MacLeod, Kirsten, *Fictions of British Decadence: High Art, Popular Writing, and the Fin de Siècle* (New York: Palgrave Macmillan, 2006).

MacPherson, Harriet Dorothea, *R.L. Stevenson: A Study in French Influence* (New York: Institute for French Studies, 1930).

Maixner, Paul, ed., *Robert Louis Stevenson: The Critical Heritage* (London: Routledge & Kegan Paul, 1981).

Marshall, Gail, ed., *The Cambridge Companion to the Fin de Siècle* (Cambridge: Cambridge University Press, 2007).

Mathews, Jackson, 'Baudelaire in English', *Sewanee Review*, 57.2 (Spring 1949), 292–303.

Menikoff, Barry, 'Introduction', in Robert Louis Stevenson, *The Complete Stories of Robert Louis Stevenson*, ed. by Barry Menikoff (New York: Modern Library, 2002), pp. v–liii.

—, 'Stevenson on Style', *The Bottle Imp*, 12 (2012), 1–4, <https://www.thebottleimp.org.uk/2012/11/stevenson-on-style/>.
Mitchell, Rebecca N., 'Oscar Wilde and the French Press, 1880–1981', *Victorian Periodicals Review*, 49.1 (2016), 123–48.
Mitterrand, Henri, 'Zola théoricien et critique du roman', in Émile Zola, *Du roman: sur Stendhal, Flaubert et les Goncourt*, ed. by Henri Mitterrand (Brussels: Éditions Complexe, 1999), pp. 7–29.
Moi, Toril, *Henrik Ibsen and the Birth of Modernism: Art, Theatre, Philosophy* (Oxford: Oxford University Press, 2006).
Mollier, Jean-Yves, 'L'Histoire de l'édition, une histoire à vocation', *Revue d'histoire moderne et contemporaine*, 43.2 (1996), 329–48.
Monte, Steven, *Invisible Fences: Prose Poetry as a Genre in French and American Literature* (Lincoln: University of Nebraska Press, 2000).
Mullin, Katherine, 'Pernicious Literature: Vigilance in the Age of Zola (1886–1899)', in *Prudes on the Prowl: Fiction and Obscenity in England, 1850 to the Present Day*, ed. by David Bradshaw and Rachel Potter (Oxford: Oxford University Press, 2013), pp. 30–51.
Naugrette, Jean-Pierre, *Robert Louis Stevenson: l'aventure et son double* (Paris: Presses de l'École normale supérieure, 1987).
Nières-Chevrel, Isabelle, 'Littérature d'enfance et de jeunesse', in *Histoire des traductions en langue française. XIXe siècle: 1815–1914*, ed. by Yves Chevrel, Lieven d'Hulst and Christine Lombez (Paris: Verdier, 2012), pp. 665–726.
Norquay, Glenda, *Robert Louis Stevenson and Theories of Reading* (Manchester: Manchester University Press, 2007).
—, *Robert Louis Stevenson, Literary Networks and Transatlantic Publishing in the 1890s: The Author Incorporated* (London: Anthem Press, 2020).
—, 'Trading Texts: Negotiations of the Professional and the Popular in the Case of *Treasure Island*', in *Robert Louis Stevenson: Writer of Boundaries*, ed. by Richard Ambrosini and Richard Dury (Madison: University of Wisconsin Press, 2006), pp. 60–9.
Orel, Harold, *Victorian Literary Critics* (London: Macmillan, 1984).
Pagès, Alain, and Owen Morgan, eds, *Guide Émile Zola* (Paris: Ellipses, 2016).
Parinet, Élisabeth, 'L'Édition littéraire, 1890–1914', in *Histoire de l'édition française, vol. 4, Le Livre concurrencé, 1900–1950*, ed. by Roger Chartier and Henri-Jean Martin (Paris: Fayard, 1990), pp. 161–209.
Parménie, Antoine, and C. [Catherine Hetzel] Bonnier de La Chapelle, *Histoire d'un éditeur et de ses auteurs: P.-J. Hetzel (Stahl)* [1953] (Paris: Albin Michel, 1985).
Philippe, Gilles, *French Style: l'accent français de la prose anglaise* (Brussels: Les Impressions Nouvelles, 2016).
—, 'Quelques réflexions sur les imaginaires stylistiques: le *Criterion* et la question du style français', *COnTEXTES: Revue de sociologie de la littérature*, 18 (2016), DOI: https:doi.org/10.4000/contextes.6225.

—, *Le Rêve du style parfait* (Paris: Presses universitaires de France, 2013).
Picard, Gaston, 'Histoire des Treize', *Les Nouvelles littéraires, artistiques et scientifiques*, 17 November 1934, p. 4.
Pickford, Susan, 'Traducteurs', in *Histoire des traductions en langue française. XIXe siècle: 1815–1914*, ed. by Yves Chevrel, Lieven d'Hulst and Christine Lombez (Paris: Verdier, 2012), pp. 144–87.
Porée, Marc, '*L'Île au trésor*: notice', in Robert Louis Stevenson, *Œuvres*, I, ed. by Charles Ballarin, Bibliothèque de la Pléiade (Paris: Gallimard, 2001), pp. 1180–98.
Potolsky, Matthew, *The Decadent Republic of Letters: Taste, Politics, and Cosmopolitanism from Baudelaire to Beardsley* (Philadelphia: University of Pennsylvania Press, 2013).
Rabbitt, Kara, 'Reading and Otherness: The Interpretative Triangle in Baudelaire's *Petits poèmes en prose*', *French Studies*, 33.3–4 (Spring–Summer 2005), 358–70.
Radford, Andrew, and Victoria Reid, eds, *Franco-British Cultural Exchanges, 1880–1940: Channel Packets* (London: Palgrave Macmillan, 2012).
Raimond, Michel, *La Crise du roman: des lendemains du Naturalisme aux années vingt* (Paris: José Corti, 1966).
Reid, Julia, 'The *Academy* and *Cosmopolis*: Evolution and Culture in Robert Louis Stevenson's Periodical Encounters', in *Culture and Science in the Nineteenth-Century Media*, ed. by Louise Henson and others (London: Routledge, 2016), pp. 263–73.
—, '"King Romance" in *Longman's Magazine*: Andrew Lang and Literary Populism', *Victorian Periodicals Review*, 44.4 (2011), 354–76, DOI: https:doi.org/10.1353/vpr.2011.0042.
—, 'Stevenson, Romance, and Evolutionary Psychology', *Robert Louis Stevenson: Writer of Boundaries*, ed. by Richard Ambrosini and Richard Dury (Madison: University of Wisconsin Press, 2006), pp. 215–27.
Reid, Victoria, 'Marcel Schwob and Robert Louis Stevenson', in *Franco-British Cultural Exchanges, 1880–1940: Channel Packets*, ed. by Andrew Radford and Victoria Reid (London: Palgrave Macmillan, 2012).
Reynolds, Siân, *Paris-Edinburgh: Cultural Connections in the Belle-Époque* (Farnham: Ashgate, 2007).
Riach, Alan, 'What is Scottish Literature?' (Glasgow: Association for Scottish Literary Studies, 2009).
Sandison, Alan, 'Proust and Stevenson: Natives of an Unknown Country', in *European Stevenson*, ed. Richard Ambrosini and Richard Dury (Newcastle upon Tyne: Cambridge Scholars Publishing, 2009), pp. 147–70.
—, *Robert Louis Stevenson and the Appearance of Modernism* (London: Macmillan, 1996).
Sarolea, Charles, *Robert Louis Stevenson and France* (Edinburgh: Robert Louis Stevenson Fellowship, 1924).

Saunders, Corinne, 'Introduction', in *A Companion to Romance: From Classical to Contemporary*, ed. by Corinne Saunders (Oxford: Blackwell, 2004), pp. 1–9.

Shaw, Michael, *The Fin-de-Siècle Scottish Revival: Romance, Decadence and Celtic Identity* (Edinburgh: Edinburgh University Press, 2020).

Simpson, Juliet, 'Bourget's Oxford Aesthetes: Towards Decadent Cosmopolitanism', *Comparative Critical Studies*, 10.2 (2013), 183–97.

Spehner, Norbert, *Jekyll & Hyde, Opus 600* (St. Hyacinthe: Ashem Fictions, 1997).

Starkie, Enid, *From Gautier to Eliot: The Influence of France on English Literature, 1851–1939* (London: Hutchinson/Scholarly Press, 1971).

Steel, David, 'Alain-Fournier's *Le Grand Meaulnes*, the *Nouvelle Revue Française* and the English Adventure Novel', in *Franco-British Cultural Cultural Exchanges, 1880–1940: Channel Packets*, ed. by Andrew Radford and Victoria Reid (London: Palgrave Macmillan, 2012), pp. 116–30.

Stott, Louis, *Robert Louis Stevenson & France* (Milton of Aberfoyle: Creag Darach Publications, 1994).

Swearingen, Roger G., *Prose Writings of Robert Louis Stevenson: A Guide* (London: Palgrave Macmillan, 1980).

Swinnerton, Frank, *R.L. Stevenson: A Critical Study* (London: Martin Secker, 1914).

Vanfasse, Nathalie, 'Translating the French Revolution into English in *A Tale of Two Cities*', *Cahiers victoriens et édouardiens*, 78 (2013), DOI: https://doi.org/10.4000/cve.776.

Wickman, Matthew, 'Stevenson, Benjamin, and the Decay of Experience', *International Journal of Scottish Literature*, 2 (2007), <https://www.ijsl.stir.ac.uk>.

Wilfert, Blaise, '*Cosmopolis* et *L'Homme invisible*: les importateurs de littérature étrangère en France, 1885–1914', *Actes de la recherche en sciences sociales*, 144.2 (2002), 33–46.

—, 'Literary Import into France and Britain around 1900: A Comparative Study', in *Anglo-French Attitudes: Comparisons and Transfers Between English and French Intellectuals Since the Eighteenth Century*, ed. by Christophe Charle, Julien Vincent and Jay Winter (Manchester: Manchester University Press, 2007), pp. 173–93.

Wilfert-Portal, Blaise, 'La Place de la littérature étrangère dans le champ littéraire français autour de 1900', *Histoire & Mesure*, 23.2 (2008), 69–101.

—, 'Traduction littéraire: approche bibliométrique', in *Histoire des traductions en langue française. XIXe siècle: 1815–1914*, ed. by Yves Chevrel, Lieven d'Hulst and Christine Lombez (Paris: Verdier, 2012), pp. 255–344.

Wolkenstein, Julie, 'Henry James in France', in *A Companion to Henry James*, ed. by Greg W. Zacharias (Oxford: Blackwell, 2008), pp. 416–33.

Wood, Michael, *The Magician's Doubts: Nabokov and the Risks of Fiction* (London: Pimlico, 1994).

Index

Abrahamson, R. L., 66
The Academy, 30
L'Action Française, 116, 119
adultery, 147, 167
advance in self-consciousness, 34–5
adventure, 182–4, 187
Aestheticism, 86, 87, 97, 107, 151, 180–1
Aimard, Gustave, 7
Alain-Fournier *see* Fournier, Alain-
Albin Michel, 116
Alexis, Paul, 52
Allen, Grant, 87
Ambrosini, Richard, 17, 21, 32, 174
American Art News, 111
Arata, Stephen, 179
Archer, William, 91–2, 106
Armand Colin, 121
Arnold, Matthew, 13, 15, 65, 129
art for art's sake principles, 25, 87, 108, 128–9, 170
Art, Georges, 139, 141
Athenaeum, 26, 41
Atkinson, Juliette, 77, 186

Baguley, David, 166
Baju, Anatole, 23
Balfour, Graham, 68, 125
Balzac, Honoré de, 9, 11–12, 20, 32, 51, 67, 151
Barbey d'Aurevilly, Jules, 59–61
  Le Chevalier des Touches, 60
Barrie, J. M., 62
Baudelaire, Charles, 19, 26, 29, 88, 181

influence on Stevenson, 92–4, 100–2, 103–4, 108
L'Art romantique, 7
Le Peintre de la vie moderne, 99–100
Petit Poèmes en Prose, 93, 96–9
Baxter, Charles, 67, 70, 73–5
Bentzon, Thérèse, 21, 128, 129–30, 134, 141, 142, 146, 148, 153, 160, 176–7, 180
  'Le Roman étrange en Angleterre,' 129, 155–6, 175
Béranger, Pierre-Jean de, 17, 28, 30–1, 33, 34
Berne Convention, 125
'Bibliothèque d'éducation et de récréation' collection, 113–14
Bloomsbury group, 185
Bodley Head, 134
Bonet-Maury, Gaston, 139
Booth, B. A., 74
Bouillaguet, Annick, 163
Bourdieu, Pierre, 12, 156–7, 165
Bourget, Paul, 59, 61–2, 104, 121, 132, 163–4, 187
Braddon, Mary Elizabeth, 119
Bristow, Joseph, 43
Brontë, Charlotte, 85
Brown, Neil Macara, 41–2
Bulwer-Lytton, Edward, 77
Burlingame, Edward L, 59, 125
Burns, Robert, 33
Byron, Lord George, 33

calques, 71–2, 77, 81–2
Canada, 125–6

Carré, Jean-Marie, 154
Casanova, Pascale, 143, 147
Cassell, 112, 118
Castle, Egerton, 134–5
Catholicism, 58, 126–7
Céard, Henry, 52
Champion, Pierre, 158
La Charente, 116
Charle, Christophe, 149, 164
Chateaubriand, François-René, Vicomte de, 37
　René, 6–7
Chaumeix, André, 173
children's literature, 128–9
Cohen, Margaret, 186–7
Cohen, William A., 77–8, 85
Colet, Louise, 92, 94
Colvin, Sydney, 11, 12, 28, 42, 55, 59–60, 73, 121, 139, 160, 179
compositional method, 49–51
Conan Doyle, Sir Arthur, 132
Le Constitutionnel, 114
Contemporary Review, 93
copyright, 125, 138, 151, 166
Cornhill Magazine, 5, 28, 70, 185
Cosmopolis, 121–3, 157

Daudet, Alphonse, 15, 51, 156, 162, 187
Daudet, Léon, 22, 116, 159, 162
Davies, Laurence, 4, 7
Davray, Henri-D., 144, 153, 158
Decadence, 18, 24, 26, 46, 54, 65, 86, 87, 88, 92, 97, 107, 134, 136, 151, 178, 180–1
Defauconpret, Auguste, 111, 139
degree of consecration, 156–7
Delebecque, Jacques, 139
Derely, Victor, 132
Desjardins, Paul, 22
description, 45–6
Despréaux, Louis, 161
detail, 45–6, 48
Dever, Carolyn, 186–7

Dickens, Charles, 104, 139, 152, 154, 173
Dictionnaire universel des contemporains, 20
Dostoevsky, Fyodor, 132–3, 143–4, 167–8
Dronsart, Marie, 120
du Bellay, Joachim, 123
du Boisgobey, Fortuné, 18, 57, 58, 132
du Camp, Maxime, 72
du Terrail, Ponson, 54
Dumas, Alexandre, 8, 9, 17, 28, 31, 32, 38–9, 47, 55
　Le Vicomte de Bragelonne, 38–9
Duncan, Ian, 1
Dury, Richard, 10, 17, 21, 76, 89, 103

Edmond, Charles, 131
Eliot, George, 55, 185
enfranchisement, 33–4
The Evergreen: A Northern Seasonal, 16

Farr, Liz, 36–7
Federico, Annette R., 69
Le Figaro, 3, 44, 63, 114, 119, 131–2, 152, 175
Fielding, Henry, 33, 34
Filon, Augustin, 9, 174
Fisher Unwin, 121
Fitzpatrick, Mark, 182
Flaubert, Gustave, 15, 18, 19, 26, 32, 44, 52, 57–8, 88, 89, 92, 93, 108, 131, 164, 178
　on prose and music, 94–5
Fleury, Maurice de, 63
Flint, Kate, 58
Fœmina, 175
Fontemoing, 123
Forest of Fontainebleau, 14
Fortnightly Review, 26, 52, 53, 87
Fournier, Alain-, 151, 156, 163, 183, 184
France, Anatole, 121

Franco-British literary relations, 1–2, 25, 26–7, 65, 151, 152, 186–7
Franco-Prussian War, 5–6, 42, 52
French language writing, 66–108
  Baudelaire's influence on Stevenson, 100–2, 103–4, 108
  calques, 71–2, 77, 81–2
  complaints about Frenchness, 91–2
  early French letters, 67, 68–9
  evidence of ability to write French, 73–6
  French in Stevenson's published works: (anti-) realism, 77–85
  French style and English literature, 86–99
  Gallicisms, 81–2
  mockery, 84–5
  multilingualism, 3, 67, 76–7, 121–2, 123, 144, 157
  parody, 74
  patois, 80–1
  phonetic spellings, 69–71, 72, 77
  play, theories of, 72–3
  playing with French, 69–77
  poetical prose, 95–103, 104–7
  Stevenson's French qualities, 88–9
  word play, 73
French literature and literary history, 26–65, 150–85
  beyond Naturalism, 165–71
  essays on French literature, 27–40
  evolution of the novel in France, 171–85, 186–7
  fin de siècle literature, 24, 25, 33, 40, 48, 149, 151–2, 155, 157, 159, 163–4, 166–7
  generational differences, 155–65
  realism, Naturalism and Stevenson, 40–54
  short stories, 172
  socio-economic differences among writers, 164–5
  Stevenson's love of French literature, 8–10, 18–19
  Stevenson's pleasure reading, 54–65

Gaboriau, Émile, 55, 132
Gallicisms, 81–2
Le Gaulois, 110, 121, 122, 173, 177
Gautier, Judith, 133
Gautier, Théophile, 18, 26, 33, 78, 93
  'Le Chevalier double,' 10
Geddes, Patrick, 22
Gellion-d'Anglar, E., 139
Gide, André, 148, 149, 151, 156, 168, 183
Gilder, Richard Watson, 52
Gille, Philippe, 161
Ginisty, Paul, 161–2
Giroud, Vincent, 123
Gissing, George, 12, 139
Gladstone, William, 4–5, 115
Goncourt, Edmond de, 156, 162–4, 169–70, 178
Goncourts, the, 26, 92, 93
  Germinie Lacerteux, 164
Good, Graham, 20, 28, 173
Gosse, Edmund, 15, 25, 42, 43, 52
Graphic, 89
Grappe, Georges, 87, 160–1, 174
  R. L. Stevenson: l'homme et l'œuvre, 16

Hachette, 120–1, 138, 139
Haddon, A. Trevor, 41
Hahn, Reynaldo, 22
Hardy, Thomas, 139, 185
Hawthorne, Nathaniel, 32
Heinemann, 120
Henley, W. E., 3, 9, 15, 28, 42–3, 55, 70, 73–4, 75–6, 90, 103, 132–3
Hennique, Léon, 52
Hetzel, Pierre-Jules, 112–14, 117, 118, 128, 129, 130
Hokusai, 162
L'Homme libre, 152
Houppermans, Sjef, 156
Houssaye, Arsène, 96
Hubbard, Tom, 114, 127

Hugo, Victor, 17, 26, 28, 29–30, 32, 33–4, 35–6, 39, 40, 45, 47, 48–9
 Hernani, 31
 Les Misérables, 29, 30, 34, 36, 37
 L'Homme qui rit, 49
 Notre Dame de Paris, 29, 30, 34, 36, 37
L'Humanité, 119
Huret, Jules, 23
Huysmans, Joris-Karl, 46, 52, 59, 169
 Là-bas, 63–4

identity, 2–3, 83, 84, 85
illustrations, 117–18
Impressionism, 104, 150, 160, 181
L'Intransigeant, 116, 138, 154, 182
Irvine, Robert P., 4, 13–14, 107

Jackson, Holbrook, 87–8
Jaloux, Edmond, 13, 14, 139, 163
James, Henry, 13, 15, 25, 26, 28, 41, 42–3, 52, 53, 61, 62, 65, 180, 181
 French Poets and Novelists, 18, 32
Jenkin, Fleeming, 45
japonisme, 162
Jarry, Alfred, 140, 160
Journal des débats, 2, 16, 20, 119, 120, 134–5
Journal des voyages, 110, 168
La Justice, 123, 161–2, 173

Kaiser, Matthew, 72–3
Kipling, Rudyard, 20, 86–7, 152, 173

La Chesnais, E., 135
Lachèvre, Henry, 14–15
Lacoste, Francis, 158
Laffitte, Paul, 136
Lane, John, 134
Lang, Andrew, 10, 25, 55, 58
Laparra, Fanny, 139
Laurie, André, 114–15, 116, 118, 129, 148
Lautrec, Gabriel de, 161

Le Gallienne, Richard, 86
Lee, Vernon, 107–8
Léna, Maurice, 22
La Liberté, 46
Lieutaud, Albert, 116
l'Isle-Adam, Villiers de, 59
Low, Berthe, 111, 117, 130–1, 133, 161, 174
Low, Will H., 42, 58, 67, 70, 130–1

MacLean, Cecil, 16–17
MacLeod, Kirsten, 134, 178
MacMahon, Patrice de, 5
Mac Orlan, Pierre, 139, 149, 151, 163, 183
MacPherson, Harriet Dorothea, 16, 57–8, 83, 91, 92
Magazine of Art, 41
Mahalin, Paul, 55
Mallarmé, Stéphane, 15, 162, 187
Manifeste des cinq, 131–2
Margueritte, Paul, 131
Margueritte, Victor, 131
Martin, Arthur Patchett, 3
Mathews, Elkin, 134
Le Matin, 176
Mattos, Katharine de, 96, 97–8
Mauclair, Camille, 137, 164–5, 168
Maupassant, Guy de, 52–3, 181
Mehew, E., 74
Meiklejohn, John, 57
Melchior de Vogüé, Eugène, 132
Menikoff, Barry, 89, 172, 173
Mercure de France (journal), 63, 144, 157, 185
Mercure de France (publisher), 135–6, 187
Le Messager d'Europe, 44
Meredith, George, 25, 104, 173
Minerva, 123
Modernism, 16, 17, 51, 149, 156, 157
Molière, 8, 9
Mollier, Jean-Yves, 137
Montaigne, Michel de, 8, 9, 27, 92

Montépin, Xavier de, 18, 55–7, 58
Moore, George, 54, 65, 77
  Confessions of a Young Man, 13
morality, 36, 44, 62
mot juste concept, 92
music, 94–5, 107–8
Musset, Alfred de, 2, 8, 9, 32

Nabokov, Vladimir, 90
National Vigilance Association, 43, 44
Naturalism, 1, 18, 24, 26, 40–53, 54, 58, 63–4, 88, 107, 131–2, 151, 156, 164, 174
  beyond Naturalism, 165–71, 178, 181–2
Nelson, 135, 137
Neukomm, Edmond, 168
Nières-Chevrel, Isabelle, 148
Nietzsche, Friedrich, 136, 139, 149
Nordau, Max, 61–2
Norquay, Glenda, 38, 39, 84, 120, 165
Nouvelle Revue française, 152, 182, 183, 185, 187
novel, the
  adventure novels, 182–4, 187
  evolution of, in France, 26, 166, 171–85, 186–7
  as genre, 177–8
  sensation novels, 58, 151, 171
  theory of, 18, 27, 28, 32–4, 44, 53, 91, 165–6, 168–70

Orléans, Charles d', 17, 28
Osbourne, Lloyd, 57, 68

Parinet, Élisabeth, 135–6
Paris, 11, 122, 143–4, 147
parody, 74
Pater, Walter, 13, 29, 62, 86, 97, 154, 181
patois, 80–1
Payn, James, 5
Peladan, Joséphin, 132
Perret, Paul, 46
Perrin, 134

Le Petit Parisien, 116, 161
Le Phare de la Loire, 141, 160
Philippe, Gilles, 86, 94, 166
phonetic spellings, 69–71, 72, 77
Pickford, Susan, 140
Pilon, Edmond, 158–9
Pivert de Senancour, Étienne de, 92
play, theories of, 72–3
Plon, Nourrit et Cie, 131–3
Poe, Edgar Allan, 60, 175
poetry, poetical prose, 95–103, 104–7
Le Populaire, 116
Porée, Marc, 158
positivism, 62
Potolsky, Matthew, 136
prefaces, 14, 31, 36–7, 53, 62, 115–16, 130, 134, 139, 140, 141, 169, 172, 176
La Presse, 96, 138
prose
  likened to music, 94–5
  poetical prose, 95–103, 104–7
Proust, Marcel, 23, 149, 156, 162, 162–3, 163–4, 188
  À la recherche du temps perdu, 163
  Le Temps retrouvé, 163

Quiller-Couch, Arthur, 83, 90, 120

Rabelais, François, 31
Rachilde, 62–3, 135, 187
Raimond, Michel, 130, 146, 165
realism, 24, 34–5, 37, 40–53, 54, 58, 65, 66, 76, 91, 172, 178
  (anti-) realism, 77–85
Régnier, Henri de, 183–4
Reid, Julia, 38, 122
Reid, Thomas Mayne, 114
Revue blanche, 136
Revue des deux mondes, 128, 129, 132, 155, 157–8, 167
Revue hebdomadaire, 119
Revue Wagnérienne, 157
Richepin, Jean, 8
Rider Haggard, H., 184
Rivière, Jacques, 151, 156, 182, 183
Rodin, Auguste, 15, 47, 73

Rolland, Madeleine, 139
Romains, Jules, 110, 136, 141, 183
romance, 7–8, 11, 25, 34–6, 37, 40–1, 48
Rosny, J. H., 131
Roux, Georges, 117–18
Rzewuski, Stanislas, 20, 122, 152–3, 161, 177

Sainte-Beuve, Charles Augustin, 15, 44
Saintsbury, George, 25, 32, 41, 65, 86, 88, 96, 123, 172
  A Short History of French Literature, 9, 18
Sand, George, 7–8, 26, 47, 80, 112, 151
Sandison, Alan, 10, 31, 176
Sarolea, Charles, 48, 54, 65, 92
  Robert Louis Stevenson and France, 16
Saunders, Corinne, 35
Savine, Albert, 14, 111, 116, 137–8, 180
Schérer, Edmond, 112–13, 115
Schwob, Marcel, 15, 20, 21, 109, 140–1, 141–2, 154, 156, 180, 187
  Cœur double, 141, 159, 168, 177–8, 182
  promotion of Stevenson's works, 158–60
Scotland, romance revival, 22, 25, 33
Scotsman, 101
Scott, Walter, 32, 33, 34, 111, 139, 149, 151
Scribner, Charles, 5, 59, 118
serialisation, 119–24
Sharp, William, 16
Shaw, Michael, 25
short stories, 172
Simoneau, Jules, 2, 73
simplicity, 180–1
Sitwell, Frances, 7–8, 102, 103, 105
Les Soirées de Médan, 52–3
Soulié, Frédéric, 55, 170
Starkie, Enid, 25
Stephen, Leslie, 28, 185

Stevenson, Bob, 6, 18, 39, 70, 72, 97, 99
Stevenson, Fanny Van de Grift, 11, 23, 126, 130, 133
Stevenson, Robert Louis
  comments on French education, 4
  conception of literature and generic tradition, 29
  criticism of, 161–3, 172–5
  criticism of English writers, 54
  early encounters with France, 2–3
  early essays, 17, 27–9
  emotions, 5–7
  French history, interest in, 5–6
  and the French language, 19
  generic variety, 176–7, 179
  identity, 2–3
  idleness, aesthetic of, 179
  independence of literary spirit, 15, 24
  and innovation, 30–1, 32
  internationalism, 24–5, 187
  and national cultures, 32
  personal character and lifestyle, 152–5
  political views, 4–5
  principle of growth conception, 29–30
  speaking French, 3, 67–8
  reading for pleasure, 54–65
  reputation in France, 19–24, 109–12, 124, 130, 141–4, 147, 148–9
  and romance, 7–8, 11, 34–6, 37, 40–1, 48
  and simplicity, 180–1
  storytelling powers, 174–5, 179
  studies of, 16–17
  style, 19, 24, 57–8, 65, 66
  supernatural leanings, 175
  transnational approach to literature, 18
  travel, 7, 10, 13–14, 32, 45
  wit, 3
  see also French language writing; French literature and literary history; translations and translators

Stevenson, Robert Louis, works of, 49, 134
À la pagaie, (translation, An Inland Voyage), 123
Across the Plains, 61, 124, 176
The Amateur Emigrant, 12
'An Autumn Effect,' 104
Les Aventures de David Balfour, (translation Kidnapped), 138
'The Beach of Falesá,' 120, 123, 143
'Béranger,' 28, 30–1, 33, 34
The Black Arrow, 11, 63, 104–7, 135, 142
'The Body-Snatcher,' 159
'The Bottle Imp,' 21, 139
'La Bouteille diabolique', (translation, 'The Bottle Imp'), 139
Le Cas étrange du docteur Jekyll, (translation, Strange Case of Dr. Jekyll and Mr. Hyde), 125, 133
Le Cas extraordinaire du Dr Jekyll et M. Hyde, (translation, Strange Case of Dr. Jekyll and Mr. Hyde), 125–6, 126–8
Catriona, 11, 83, 107, 108, 120, 138, 139
'Charles of Orléans,' 28
A Child's Garden of Verses, 11, 22, 91
Le Club des suicidés, (translation, The Suicide Club), 119
'A College Magazine,' 27, 92
complete works, 136
The Dynamiter, 10, 11, 38, 119, 123, 139, 168, 170–1
Le Dynamiteur, (translation, The Dynamiter), 123, 139, 141, 154, 160
The Ebb-Tide, 140
Edinburgh: Picturesque Notes, 10, 101
Enlevé!, (translation, Kidnapped), 137–8, 180
Familiar Studies of Men and Books, 36–7, 124
La Flèche noire, (translation, The Black Arrow), 135–6
'Fontainebleau,' 11, 104
'The Foreigner at Home,' 3, 32
'Forest Notes,' 104
'François Villon, Student, Poet and House-Breaker,' 28, 29, 31
'Good Content,' 99
'A Gossip on a Novel of Dumas's,' 28, 36, 38–9
'A Gossip on Romance,' 17–18, 28, 40, 46, 49
Hermiston: le juge-pendeur, (translation, Weir of Hermiston), 123, 176
'To the Hesitating Purchaser', (preface, Treasure Island), 113
'A Humble Remonstrance,' 18, 28, 40, 49, 51, 180
L'Île au trésor, (translation, Treasure Island), 113–17, 128, 130, 136–7, 141, 148
An Inland Voyage, 4, 10, 13, 14–15, 79, 104, 115
'In the Lightroom,' 99, 101–2
Island Nights' Entertainment, 139
'The Isle of Voices,' 143
'Jules Verne's Stories,' 28, 30, 37–8, 39
Kidnapped, 14, 38, 111, 120, 137, 138, 142, 143, 182
'On the Lighthouse Roof,' 99
'A Lodging for the Night,' 10, 82–3
'Markheim,' 21, 120, 133, 143
The Master of Ballantrae, 36, 119, 120, 142, 147–8, 182
'Memoirs of an Islet,' 5
Memories and Portraits, 91–2, 124
'The Merry Men,' 21, 111, 143
The Misadventures of John Nicholson, 111
More New Arabian Nights, 60
'My First Book,' 116

New Arabian Nights, 10, 38, 60, 79, 81, 83, 88, 100, 115, 119, 123, 170–1, 176–7
'A Note on Realism,' 18, 28, 40–1, 43–4, 45, 47, 48, 51, 169
Nouvelles mille et une nuits, (translation, *New Arabian Nights*), 130, 156
Les Nuits des Îles, (translation, *Island Nights' Entertainment*), 139
Olalla, 140, 160
'Ordered South,' 10, 32
'The Pavilion on the Links,' 70
Prince Otto, 10, 11, 38, 53, 78, 107, 134, 148, 152–3, 161
'Providence and the Guitar,' 98
'The Quiet Waters By,' 99, 102–3, 104, 105
Le Roman du prince Othon, (translation, *Prince Otto*), 134–5, 144, 148
'The Sinking Ship,' 93
'The Sire de Malétroit's Door,' 81–2
'On Some Technical Elements of Style in Literature,' 19, 93–4, 96–7, 107, 181
St. Ives, 11, 19, 63, 79, 83–5, 120, 140
'The Story of the Young Man with the Cream Tarts,' 119
Strange Case of Dr. Jekyll and Mr. Hyde, 10, 36, 38, 62, 109, 111, 119, 124–33, 139, 142, 143, 161, 168, 174–5, 177, 180, 185
The Suicide Club, 63, 119, 161, 168, 176
'A Summer Night,' 99, 100–1
'Sunday Thoughts,' 99
Travels with a Donkey in the Cévennes, 10, 13, 79–80, 87, 114–15
Treasure Island, 3, 11, 21, 22, 28, 36, 38, 89, 109, 111, 112–19, 120, 128, 129, 131, 141–2, 148, 158, 168, 182

'The Treasure of Franchard,' 4, 10
triolets on Montépin, 55–7
'The Two Matches,' 93
A Vendetta in the West, 72
'Victor Hugo's Romances,' 28, 29–30, 32, 33, 34, 35–6, 37, 39, 40, 45, 48–9, 185
Virginibus Puerisque, 90, 124
Weir of Hermiston, 120, 121, 122–3, 140, 172, 176
'Will o' the Mill,' 101, 120, 123, 140
The Wrecker, 6, 9, 11–12, 98, 119–20, 143, 168
The Wrong Box, 140
Stevenson, Thomas, 68
Stock, 137–8
Stoddard, Charles Warren, 53
Stott, Louis, 17
Strong, Belle, 67
style, 19, 24, 57–8, 65, 66
  definitional difficulty, 89–90
  French style and English literature, 86–99
  stylistic affectation, 91
Sue, Eugène, 10, 18, 47, 55, 161, 170
Swinburne, Algernon, 15, 29, 39, 93
Symbolism, 24, 157, 178, 180–1, 182, 183
Symonds, John Addington, 132
Symons, Arthur, 15, 32, 41, 46, 51, 65, 97, 164

Taine, Hippolyte, 5, 44
Tardivel, Jules-Paul, 125–8
Le Temps, 3, 113, 114, 116, 119, 120, 131, 188
terror literature, 175
Thackeray, W. M., 13
Thibaudet, Albert, 156
The Times, 44, 47, 124
Tolstoy, Leo, 132, 139, 145, 149
Toudouze, Gustave, 131

translations and translators, 21, 109–49, 151–2, 174–5, 187
   advertising, 114
   domesticating and foreignising translations, 144–6
   French *Jekyll and Hydes*, 124–33
   French publishers and translators, 134–41
   French *Treasure Islands*, 112–19
   literal translation, 146, 147–8
   multi-editing and translating, 143
   periodical publications and serials, 119–24
   problems with translations, 141–9
   reviews of, 142–8, 161
   of Stevenson's essays, 123–4
   and Stevenson's reputation, 141–4, 147, 148–9

L'Univers, 177
Uzanne, Octave, 154, 160

Valéry, Paul, 149
Vallette, Alfred, 63, 135, 187
Varlet, Théo, 111, 116, 119, 136–7, 143
Verne, Jules, 17, 30, 37–8, 39, 55, 58, 113, 114
La Vérité, 125, 127
Vers et prose, 123

Villon, François (poet), 17, 28, 29, 30, 31, 33, 82–3, 159, 172, 182
Vizitelly (publishers), 62, 65, 132
La Vogue, 123
Le Voltaire, 44

Wells, H. G., 152, 154–5
Westminster Review, 88
Wilde, Oscar, 54, 87, 88–9
Wilfert, Blaise, 157
Wolff, Albert, 156
Wood, Michael, 90
Wyzewa, Teodor de, 21, 120, 140, 141, 154–5, 156, 157–8, 160, 167–8, 171–2, 174, 176, 179–80, 181
   and translations, 142–7

Young Folks, 104, 112, 135, 139

Zeys, Louise, 139
Zola, Émile, 43–5, 46–8, 49–51, 54, 156, 164, 166, 168–9, 170, 181–2
   L'Assommoir, 74, 164
   La Débâcle, 42, 52
   'La Formule critique appliqué au roman', 46–7
   L'Œuvre, 41–2
   'Le Sens du reel', 47, 49–50
   Travail, 116

EU representative:
Easy Access System Europe
Mustamäe tee 50, 10621 Tallinn, Estonia
Gpsr.requests@easproject.com

www.ingramcontent.com/pod-product-compliance
Lightning Source LLC
Chambersburg PA
CBHW070350240426
43671CB00013BA/2455